Lords of Things

Lords of Things *The Fashioning of the Siamese Monarchy's Modern Image*

Maurizio Peleggi

University of Hawai'i Press

Honolulu

Library of Congress Cataloging-in-Publication Data
Peleggi, Maurizio.
   Lords of things : the fashioning of the Siamese monarchy's modern image / Maurizio Peleggi.
       p.   cm.
Includes bibliographical references and index.
   ISBN 0–8248–2448–2 (hardcover : alk. paper)—ISBN 0–8248–2558–6 (pbk. : alk. paper)
   1. Monarchy—Thailand.   2. Thailand—Politics and government.
3. Thailand—Social conditions.   I. Title: Fashioning of the Siamese monarchy's modern image.   II. Title.
JQ1746 .P4   2002
959.3—dc21   2002001546

University of Hawai'i Press books are printed on acid-free paper and meet the guidelines for permanence and durability of the Council on Library Resources.

Designed by Jeff Cosloy

Printed by The Maple-Vail Book Manufacturing Group

Contents

List of Illustrations

Acknowledgments

This book was born out of a doctoral dissertation undertaken at the Australian National University, where my stay was made possible by scholarships from ANU and the Australian government's Department of Employment, Education, and Training. The Division of Pacific and Asian History, Research School of Pacific and Asian Studies, ANU, covered all fieldwork expenses. Source materials were freely provided by Ronald Mahoney, Special Collection of the Henry Mann Library, California State University at Fresno; Amy A. Begg, Smithsonian Institution Libraries, Washington, D.C.; and Maryse Goldemberg, Bibliothèque Historique de la Ville de Paris. Chintana Sandilands helped with the translation of Thai sources. I benefited from the comments made to the draft at different stages by Benedict Anderson, John Clark, Charles Keyes, Bruce Lockhart, Thongchai Winichakul, and an anonymous reader for the University of Hawai'i Press. My greatest intellectual debt is to my teacher and friend, Craig Reynolds. A thank you also to Michael Montesano and Paola Inzolia. Dayaneetha has seen me through all of this and always kept her beautiful smile.

A Note on Romanization

The Romanization of Thai words in this book follows the Royal Institute of Thailand General System of Phonetic Transcription of Thai Characters into Roman but without diacritic marks.

The names of major historical figures and contemporary scholars are given in the Romanized form adopted by the individuals themselves (e.g., Vajiravudh; Nidhi Auesriwongse). All other names are Romanized according to the simplified form of the Royal Institute system used for words (e.g., Wachirayan).

Finally, the Romanization of Chinese words follows the Pinyin system of phonetic transcription.

Introduction

Monarchy and Modernity

In 1996 the people of Thailand rejoiced in an unprecedented celebration: the Golden Jubilee of King Bhumibol Adulyadej, ninth monarch of the Chakri dynasty and the longest-reigning in the world today. Among the events that punctuated Bhumibol's jubilee was the October visit of Elizabeth II, herself a long-serving monarch, on the throne since 1953. This exchange of royal courtesy had a notable precedent in the visit that Bhumibol's grandfather, King Chulalongkorn (Rama V), had paid to Queen Victoria, Elizabeth's great-great-grandmother, on the occasion of her Diamond Jubilee (sixtieth anniversary of reign) in 1897. Victoria's Golden Jubilee in 1887 had initiated the fashion for such royal celebrations; her Diamond Jubilee, ten years later, became a touchstone for other monarchs including Chulalongkorn, who in 1908 celebrated with great pomp his fortieth anniversary on the throne.

The unfolding of history is fraught with irony. When one considers the 1996 meeting of King Bhumibol and Queen Elizabeth, both remnants of a bygone era of crowned heads, the former would appear to enjoy today a far more comfortable position than the latter. Apart from his dynastic achievement, Rama IX is regarded by most observers—both local and foreign—as a crucial balancing factor in Thailand's often tumultuous political arena and by the majority of the population as a man of merit (*phu mi bun*) endowed with the moral virtues befitting a Buddhist monarch. True, gossip about the royal family is an entrenched feature of Bangkok's social life; but open criticism of the throne is shunned in virtue of deeply rooted taboos as well as a legal code that still envisages the anachronistic offense of lèse-majesté.[1] One could only speculate that Queen Elizabeth looked to King Bhumibol, if not with envy, at least with longing for a time past when the authority of the crown would have prevented relentless tabloid exposure of the House of Windsor's matrimonial tribulations (not to mention their fictionalization in a TV movie).

Feelings of an opposite nature must have animated the encounter

1

between King Chulalongkorn and Queen Victoria in August 1897. Arriving in England shortly after the celebration in the streets of London of Victoria's Diamond Jubilee, the king of Siam was received at Osborne House, on the Isle of Wight, in the presence of the Prince and Princess of Wales (the later Edward VII and Queen Alexandra), Prince Charles of Denmark, and the king of Belgians (and Victoria's relative), Leopold II.[2] The reception made it to the front page of the *Illustrated London News,* then Britain's leading weekly, which carried an imaginative sketch of the banquet held in Osborne House's Indian Room. Yet in announcing Rama V's imminent visit a few weeks earlier, the British Press Association had somewhat condescendingly pointed out that "the King of Siam is coming to Britain not on a ordinary state visit . . . but with a view of educating himself in the matters of British customs and resources."[3] In fact, Chulalongkorn's visit to England was but one stop in a journey that took him throughout most of Europe, Russia included.

The centennial of Rama V's first European tour, fortuitously coinciding with King Bhumibol's seventieth birthday, was commemorated by the national media in 1997 as Thailand's entry into the modern world. To mention only two examples, the widely circulated cultural magazine *Sinlapa watthanatham* ran a series of articles on the various stages of the tour; and a twenty-four-part TV series, broadcast on Thailand's Channel 5, documented the places visited during the follow-up to that first tour, ten years later.[4] Academia joined in the celebrations with a colloquium appositely held at Chulalongkorn University. Whether Rama V's visit to Europe in 1897 marked a turning point in the history of Thailand, then known as Siam, may be a matter of contention. But the direct encounter with Europe's ruling dynasties and heads of state unquestionably provided a litmus test for the endeavor examined in this book: the fashioning of the public image of the Siamese monarchy as a modern, civilized, and civilizing institution.

Because of the transformation that the Siamese economy and institutions underwent in the Fourth and especially the Fifth Reigns (1851–1868 and 1868–1910, respectively), these periods have attracted considerable scholarly attention. Existing studies, however, are concerned almost exclusively with the reform of the administrative, educational, and financial systems and with foreign relations. Historians have paid hardly any attention to the new material and symbolic attributes that came to define the monarchy despite their visibility as signifiers of both royal status and *siwilai*—the condition of being civilized as it came to be expressed by this lexical cast whose signification was distinct from *arayatham*, the Sanskrit-derived Thai word for "civilization."[5] And yet, as early as 1966 Fred Riggs proposed, in a study on the modernization of the Thai bureaucracy, that the reforms accomplished in the Fourth and Fifth Reigns "although directed primarily toward transformations in the total polity, indirectly also changed the character and the public image of the monarchy itself."[6]

This book argues that, far from being a by-product of the wider process of administrative and institutional reformation, the refashioning of the royal elite's public image was a key element in the project of asserting their "civilized" status and, consequentially, their claim to "national" leadership. An image of the monarchy conforming to contemporary European norms was fashioned and propagated in the later decades of the nineteenth century and the first decade of the twentieth, when novel forms of etiquette, dress, habitation, patronage, and pageantry made their way to the court and were manifested by its members in state visits abroad. At a time of imperialist encroachment in Southeast Asia, the demonstration of being civilized individuals and instigators of progress obviously supported the royal elite's hold onto power. But one would be mistaken to consider this endeavor mere camouflage or "rebranding,"[7] to employ the jargon of spin doctors and image consultants: a makeup operation aimed at manipulating the perception of the threatening colonial powers. I propose, instead, that the royal elite fashioned a new sense of themselves, both as individuals and as a social group, vis-à-vis their aspirations to status and authority in the late-nineteenth-century globalized arena. Self-regard was at least as important a concern as the foreign/*farang* gaze in the refashioning of the elite's image. By contemplating themselves in their new clothes, new domestic settings, and new urban spaces, the Siamese court ended up convincing themselves, above all, of being modern.

Part I of this book examines the practices of consumption and self-presentation whereby the modernizing elite fashioned a new sense of self, along with the visual representations whereby this new image was refined and projected outside of the court. Part II focuses on Bangkok's Dusit district, built at the end of the nineteenth century as the royalty's modern residential quarter and then endowed with a monumental tableau celebrating Rama V's reign. Part III discusses public spectacles that, while different in genre and intended audience, were equally important for the diffusion of the monarchy's image as a national institution under

whose leadership Siam was advancing on the path to progress: the celebrations of King Chulalongkorn's fortieth anniversary of reign, which
saw the restyling of the traditional theater of power; and international
exhibitions in Europe and the United States, which were the sites for the
fashioning of an image of Siam as one number in the family of modern
nations.

It is necessary to state beforehand that the modernization of
courtly life and the political theater in the period under review was not all
encompassing. The royal harem, to mention a Siamese institution par excellence, became obsolete only in the Sixth Reign as a result of growing
public criticism of polygamy as well as King Vajiravudh's sexual inclinations. Also, the performance of Brahmanic state rituals continued throughout 1932, when the absolute monarchy was finally overthrown;[8] indeed,
these rituals underwent a neotraditionalist refashioning in the early years
of the Fifth Reign. The scope of the present study is, however, limited to
those novel practices, spaces, and spectacles associated with the monarchy
from the late nineteenth to the early twentieth centuries that had a lasting
effect on both social constructions of modernity in Thailand and popular
ideas about the monarchy that have made possible its impressive revival
since the 1960s.

Monarchy, Modernity, and Nation-building

The view of the Fifth Reign as a period of momentous change and of
King Chulalongkorn as a Prometheus-like figure who bestowed the gift of
modernity on Thai society is deeply entrenched in both historical writings on Thailand and in the Thai collective consciousness. Such a view
owes a great deal to a number of dissertations submitted at U.S. universities in the late 1960s and early 1970s that documented the establishment
in Siam of administrative, educational, military, and ecclesiastic institutions after the Western pattern—a process that goes under the name of
Chakri Reformation.[9] The pioneering use of archival materials makes such
studies still valuable thirty years after they were written; however, their
present-day reader cannot fail noticing the extent to which their analytical
framework was informed by modernization theory—the dominant paradigm in the social sciences of the 1950s and 1960s, championed by the
likes of Walter Rostow and Shmuel Eisenstadt. From the perspective of

modernization theory, the establishment in late nineteenth-century Siam of a centralized administration, educational system, and transportation and communication infrastructures was per se an index of progress and, indeed, of nation-building. To make its accomplishments even more remarkable, the Chakri Reformation was cast against the domestic opposition of a conservative clique and the menace of Western imperialism. In the words of the foremost historian of the Fifth Reign,

> *Being firmly committed personally to reform and vitally convinced of its importance to the survival of the nation, he [Chulalongkorn] had to battle and overcome the resistance to change and modernization. This was a slow, painful, and delicate task, to which few men would have been equal. He accomplished it with great skill, consummate patience, supreme determination, and a single-minded dedication to the ultimate good of the nation.*[10]

This appraisal of King Chulalongkorn's achievements, originally sketched by David Wyatt in the early 1960s, clearly reflects the view of Asia's postcolonial governments then prevalent among scholars and policy makers as being characterized by a "blend of nationalism and earnest commitment to modernization," to quote a self-proclaimed apologist of developmentalist theory.[11] In fact, the ultimate result of the studies of Fifth Reign institutional modernization by American scholars was the historiographical institutionalizing of the Chakri dynasty's role as a nationalist elite. In this respect, Western historians of Thailand were following in the footsteps of the historical narrative outlined almost single-handedly by Prince Damrong Rajanubhap (1862–1943). One of Chulalongkorn's many half-brothers and a key figure of the Chakri Reformation as minister of the interior from 1892 to 1913, Prince Damrong is commemorated in the national pantheon as the "father of Thai history." After resigning his ministerial office in 1913, Damrong became the director of the Wachirayan City Library (predecessor of the National Library) and there devoted his energy to the editing of court chronicles and the compilation of biographies of state notables, which were published as mementos on the occasion of cremations.[12] Yet, rather surprisingly, both Damrong's chronicles of the Fifth Reign and his personal memoirs cover only the first couple of years of his brother's rule.[13] Prince Damrong's historiographic project was thus brought to completion by American historians in more than merely a chronological sense. It is also worth noting, even though this is not the place to pursue this subject, that Western scholarship's legitimation of the royalist historical narrative coincided with the renewed emphasis placed on modernization in the 1960s and early 1970s by the authoritarian governments of Thailand, which were the recipients of considerable U.S. economic aid with the aim of containing the spread of communism (the so-called domino effect) in Southeast Asia.[14]

The loosening up of Thai politics in the mid-1970s had important repercussions on historiography, allowing the articulation of dissenting views in the public arena. Exhaustive discussions of Thai radical historiography already exist,[15] so I shall limit myself to recapitulating the main objections moved to the view of the Chakri Reformation as the initial stage in the nation-building enterprise. Relying on the Marxian concept of the Asiatic mode of production, the economic historians who in the 1970s animated the Political Economy Group at Thammasat University argued, probably influenced by the *dependencia* theorists of Latin America, for the parasitic nature of economic relations in the second half of the nineteenth century and the Chakri dynasty's function as a guarantor of foreign economic interests. From this perspective, the motivation for the abolition of bondage, cornerstone of the national myth of Rama V as civilizer, appeared to be the increasing need of manpower for rice cultivation —the single export commodity providing the economic base of Siamese monarchical absolutism.[16] Other revisionist historians have considered the development of transportation, the railways system in particular, arguing that its main purpose was to facilitate territorial control and military intervention in Thailand's Northeast (Isan), a region inhabited predominantly by an ethnic Lao population where the imposition of Bangkok's central authority met with considerable opposition.[17] Even one of the most enduring nationalist myths, the dynasty's defense of national independence paid for by the territorial losses to Britain and France, has been disputed recently. Thongchai Winichakul, a historian of the generation that came of age in the student uprising of October 1973, has provocatively contended that through the imposition of national-style borders in mainland Southeast Asia, colonialism actually engendered—rather than endangered— modern Siam as a geopolitical entity.[18]

Notwithstanding the plurality of voices that has emerged within Thai historiography over the past quarter of a century, Thailand's master historical narrative remains locked in a royalist-nationalist discourse that posits the country's experience as a unique case of indigenous modernization and nation-building in the context of colonial Southeast Asia. Two factors in particular may be pinpointed to account for the enduring hegemony of this master narrative: first, the monarchy's remarkable degree of authority at present, which makes scrutiny of any subject even remotely connected to it highly sensitive; second, the multifaced, yet for this no less pervasive, Thai cultural nationalism, which nourishes a defensive attitude toward those symbols and institutions, the monarchy above all, that are regarded as the pillars of the Thai identity and heritage. In addition, one could mention the apparent obsession of Thai society with figures of founding fathers, from kings to art teachers, which makes any attempt at critical appraisal equivalent to a symbolic parricide. This insistence on Thailand's uniqueness in both historical and sociocultural terms has largely precluded the examination of its route to modernity in a comparative framework that might highlight differences as well as similarities with that constellation of phenomena characteristic of modernity in both metropolitan and colonial contexts.

In fact, the refashioning of the Siamese monarchy's public image did not take place in isolation. On the contrary, it paralleled contemporary trends in Europe and other parts of Asia, where the period 1870–1914 marked the heyday of the "invention of tradition." This felicitous oxymoron, which served as the title of a seminal collection of essays,[19] indicates the efflorescence of political spectacles along with the creation of a host of new social practices by means of which both national and class identities were forged and strengthened. While the main purpose of royal ceremonies under the ancien régime was to manifest the purportedly divine nature of kingship, the newly invented rituals of the last quarter of the nineteenth century emphasized the bond between the citizens of the modern nation-states and royal figures, whose decreasing power was to be balanced by their new public role as embodiments of the nation and even exemplars of moral and civic virtues.

This shift of emphasis had actually begun in the early nineteenth century, when the dynasties restored to power at the end of the Napoleonic wars realized the necessity for capturing popular favor in order to overcome their weakened legitimacy. The identification of reigning houses with the national destiny was promoted, especially in the last quarter of the nineteenth century (when the only two republics in Europe were France and Switzerland) by both constitutional and autocratic governments. According to Eric Hobsbawm,

> *Technically there was no significant difference between the political use of monarchy for the purpose of strengthening effective rulers . . . and building the symbolic function of crowned heads in parliamentary states. . . . Both made the ruler the focus of his people's or peoples' unity, the symbolic representative of the country's greatness and glory, of its entire past and continuity with a changing present.*[20]

Dictating this common response were, for Hobsbawm, two interrelated developments that unfolded in the four and a half decades between the Franco-Prussian War (1870) and the start of World War I and threatened the very basis of monarchical states: the progress of electoral democracy and the emergence of mass politics.[21] Hobsbawm admittedly focuses almost exclusively on Europe, reserving only a passing comment to an extra-European country: "A 'modernization' which maintained the old ordering of social subordination (possibly with some well-judged invention of tradition) was not theoretically inconceivable, but apart from Japan it is difficult to think of an example of practical success."[22]

The reinvention of the symbolic attributes of the Japanese emperor as part of the modernizing project carried out in the Meiji Restoration (1868–1910) is examined in a recent study whose author advances the following argument: "Japan's modern political leaders, not less than their counterparts in the liberal nation-states of Europe and the United States, conceived of the entire cultural apparatus of the modern state as a mechanism for enlightening the masses."[23] Drawing a parallel with the French Revolution, Takashi Fujitani argues for the Meiji Restoration as an equally revolutionary project in the specific sense of being "propelled by a faith in human plasticity and a new civilizing mission for the state."[24] Most importantly, however, the invention of new imperial traditions in Meiji Japan was accompanied by "a change in the praxis of politics," whose obvious results were the promulgation of the constitution in 1889 and the election of the Diet in 1890.[25] The formalization of novel rituals and cultural practices occurred also as part of the modernization attempted during the last hundred years of the Ottoman Empire, particularly under Sultan Abdulhamid II (1876–1909), defined as "an autocrat with no time for experiments with democracy."[26] Although the Young Turks' constitutionalist insurrection in 1908 makes it impossible to consider Abdulhamid's a politically successful instance of invention of tradition, the chronological concurrence with Europe is worthy of note.

In fact, the Eurocentric periodization of 1870–1914 as the heyday of the invention of tradition can be held valid for Siam as well. Stanley Tambiah has argued, in relation to the Fourth and Fifth Reigns, that "never before did the ceremonies surrounding kingship reach such an elaboration in Thailand as in this era; but then never before had the kings exercised so much real and effective power as in this era."[27] According to Tambiah, "Thailand is a conspicuous example of traditional features—of historical continuities that modify modernization—and also of transformations based on tradition."[28] Similar to most national and colonial projects of the later nineteenth century, the Chakri Reformation sought to impose control and discipline over society as a necessary condition for the creation of a modern state—an enterprise that is not directly addressed by this book. Unlike Western Europe and Meiji Japan, however, changes in the administrative sphere and the political theater of Fifth Reign Siam were neither a result of, nor a reaction to, increasing popular participation in politics. Apologists of the dynasty have often deemed "revolutionary" the import of the Chakri Reformation, but hardly in the same vein as the qualification of revolutionary attributed to the Meiji Restoration by Fujitani for its faith in the power of the state to enlighten the masses and make them into "knowledgeable and self-disciplined subjects."[29]

I would argue that primary goals of the Chakri Reformation were the establishment of the monarchy's authority over a newly bounded "national" territory and the uplifting of its prestige in the international arena. The overlap of dynasty and government characteristic of the latter half of the Fifth Reign (1892–1910) proves the success of the Chakri Reformation in this sense but also makes it highly problematic to talk of it in terms of nation-building. In other words, it would be hard to sustain that the aim of the reforms implemented in the Fifth Reign was to make "peasants into Siamese," to paraphrase the title of Eugene Weber's book on the nation-building project in Third Republic France.[30] When compared against the yardstick of European history, the modernizing policies of Fifth Reign Siam bear a much closer similarity to the creation of the absolutist state in the seventeenth century than to the emergence of the modern nation-state in the nineteenth.[31] At the same time Chulalongkorn, alert to the changed rhetoric of European monarchies, projected increasingly in the last decade of his reign an image of himself as the king of the Siamese rather than the king of Siam. The imposing celebrations of the final years of his reign inscribe Siam on the list of countries struck by the turn-of-the-century fever for political spectacles. Hobsbawm's contention that monarchical rhetoric "made the ruler the focus of his people's unity, the symbolic representative of the country's greatness and glory, of its entire past and continuity with a changing present,"[32] holds true for Rama V, too, by the time he celebrated his fortieth anniversary of reign in 1908. The development of the transportation system in Bangkok and the presence of that quintessentially modern phenomenon, "the growing armies of the state's employees and the growing captive public of schoolchildren,"[33] conferred a novel resonance to the Siamese theater of power and provided it with a novel audience as well.

There were, however, inherent hazards in the culturally innovative yet politically conservative project of a demotic refashioning of the monarchy that upheld the sociopolitical status quo of royal absolutism. This project might have been viable in the latter decades of the Fifth Reign, when the throne's authority was more or less undisputed and the Siamese public sphere still in its formative stage. Still, the increasing symbolic proximity of sovereigns to their subjects eventually entailed, as in Europe after 1815, a desacralization of the former to be balanced, in theory at least, by the popular legitimation conferred on them. But such a balancing act was by no means in the natural order of things, as Chulalongkorn's sons and successors, Vajiravudh (Rama VI) and Prajadhipok (Rama VII), were to discover in the long crisis of legitimacy that eventually resulted in the overthrow of the absolute monarchy, in June 1932.[34] The Western-educated commoners who replaced the royal elite at the country's head had their own vision of how to make Siam a modern nation, and their vision involved bridging social disparities and improving in particular women's condition.[35] And although in the following years, especially under the premiership of Luang Phibun Songkhram (1938–1944), a nationalist ideology complete with racialist overtones replaced the democratic ethos of the 1932 coup's promoters, national progress and civilization continued to be preeminent catchwords in the rhetoric of the successive regimes in power.

Still, if one agrees with Craig Reynolds' contention that the mastering of modernity constitutes the leitmotif of the last one and a half centuries of Thailand's history,[36] the need becomes obvious for a reappraisal of the monarchy's role as a civilizing agent in order to understand Thai modernity (*than samai*). It would be tempting to argue that the selective import and promotion of Western culture, from geography to photography and the Grand Tour, by kings such as Mongkut and Chulalongkorn made the throne a mediator of modernity intimately associating the two and endowing the Chakri dynasty with a lasting aura of authority. Besides, the intellectual ability of these monarchs to appropriate those elements of the culture of the Western "other" they saw as conducive to their political project is evidence of an agency that, independently from what judgment is passed on the nature of that project, runs counter to the Saidian idea of the East as the passive object of the West's imperial domination and ideological representation.[37]

The comparison recently advanced by some Thai academics between the modernizing thrust of the Fifth Reign and the recent fascination of the most cosmopolitan segment of Thai society with globalization should not come as a surprise. There are, indeed, significant parallels in the way in which the royal elite at the fin de siècle and the new middle class in the 1980s appropriated the perceivably global markers of civilization to assert their group identity as the country's arbiters of taste and vanguard of modernity. We shall return to this analogy in the Epilogue. In the remainder of this Introduction I intend to discuss globalization as a conceptual framework for examining the reinvention of the Siamese elite's self- and public image. According to Jonathan Friedman, a necessary precondition for globalizing processes is the existence of a global arena resulting from the interaction of central and peripheral structures—what Friedman calls in its entirety a global system.[38] Because such global systems have existed since antiquity in the form of both territorial empires and trading networks, globalization would appear a viable conceptual framework for studying phenomena of cultural diffusion and assimilation independently of the taken-for-granted linkage to modernity, the defining attributes of which remain largely grounded in the historical experience of the Euro-American world.

Globalized Identities and Localized Modernities

In the debate about globalization (translated in Thai as *lokhanuwat* or, alternatively, *lokhapiwat*) that animated the media and academia of Thailand in the early 1990s, three positions emerged: supporters and opponents at opposite poles and, in between, those who saw no reason to either worry or bother too much about globalization given Thai society's long experience in successfully reworking outside imports.[39] This perceived ability to adopt and adapt foreign cultural influences is, indeed, deeply internalized to the point of being a leitmotif in the elite's own discursive self-representation; Prince Damrong articulated it in the following terms: "The Tai knew how to pick and choose. When they saw some good feature in the culture of other peoples, if it was not in conflict with their own interests, they did not hesitate to borrow it and adapt it to their own requirements."[40] A similar viewpoint informs the concept of localization put forth by the late O. W. Wolters, a pioneer historian of early Southeast Asia. Localization, the combined process of adoption and adaptation of Indic cultural materials, is for Wolters the unifying trait of Southeast Asia's diverse cultures.[41] By shifting emphasis from the imposition of an exogenous cultural matrix, as denoted by Cœdès' concept of Indianization (or *hinduisation*, as he had it),[42] to indigenous agency, the notion of localization highlights the interactive nature of cultural exchange in early Southeast Asia as a resultant of the globalizing thrust of the Indian Ocean's trading networks, which long predated the emergence of an integrated world system around the mid-nineteenth century.[43]

The authority and prestige of early Southeast Asia's ruling elites was predicated upon a common cultural idiom of Indian origin that, through interaction with indigenous values, beliefs, and practices, resulted in an elite culture, at once distinctive and cosmopolitan, that encompassed courtly civility, self-presentation, monumental architecture, and, perhaps most notably, political theatrics. Long before the assertion of Europe's political and cultural hegemony in the region, the identity of Southeast Asian elites had resulted from the localization of what were arguably global cultural and symbolic forms—forms that, to paraphrase Friedman, were "either produced by or transformed into globally accessible objects and representations."[44] In other words, drawing from external sources to cast their social identity and public image was not unprecedented for Southeast Asian royalty, especially not for the royalty of Ayutthaya and early Bangkok. Like elites in most time and place, the Siamese aristocracy would have regarded themselves as carriers of novelty and models of sophistication, and such self-perception would have provided, in turn, a degree of self-esteem as well as "international" prestige. Wolters himself, in a gloss to his initial formulation of localization, has spoken of the "opportunist and pragmatic attitude towards the present" of Southeast Asia's precolonial elites, their "sense of being an integral part of the whole of the known 'world,' " and their "remarkable propensity for being 'modern.' "[45] The pursuit of *siwilai* can therefore be conceptualized as a later instance of earlier globalizing trends such as Indianization and (notwithstanding its narrower scope) Sinicization, in whose milieu the Siamese royalty's social and cultural identity had been forged through a creative process of selection and adaptation. Military uniforms, oil portraits, and suburban villas played, in this sense, a function similar to silk robes, Brahmanic rituals, and Indic architecture in proclaiming the Bangkok royalty's association with a foreign civilization whose potency was manifested by means of trade, diplomacy, and proselytizing, as well as military might.

Social anthropologist Carol Breckenridge has written an astute essay on the cultural flows that occurred in the globalized space of the latter half of the nineteenth century, which she terms "Victorian ecumene": "This Victorian ecumene encompassed Great Britain, the United States, and India (along with other places) in a discursive space that was global while nurturing nation-states that were culturally highly specific."[46] In pointing out what she sees as the "cultural paradoxes of imperialism," Breckenridge goes on to argue,

> *The formation of national cultures in the second half of the nineteenth century was accompanied by the development of transnational practices that recurred in the creation of a global class united by their relation to newly invented rituals, newly constructed metropoles, newly naturalized objects. Though all classes and ethnic groups, both in Britain and in India, were implicated . . . in these constructions, some benefited more than others. The greatest beneficiaries of the newly constructed colonial edifices were those members of the ruling elite of the respective nations who, through their associations, practices, and consumption patterns were also members of a global and increasingly cosmopolitan elite.*[47]

Breckenridge's argument contains *in nuce* an understanding of globalizing processes that, unlike most sociological formulations, does not posit a contraposition between globalization and national cultural identities but, rather, underscores the relationship between their formation in the late nineteenth century and the emergence of a transnational elite whose cosmopolitan identity was predicated upon shared tastes and cultural practices spanning East and West, colony and metropole. The new self-perception of the House of Chakri as members of the fraternal order of world royalty was a distinctive trait of the modernizing project pursued in the Fifth Reign.

King Mongkut's way of addressing Queen Victoria as (in his own English), "Our most respected and distinguished Friend, and by race of royalty Our very affectionate Sister,"[48] was an early intimation of the claim to equal status with European royalty pursued to much greater effect by King Chulalongkorn. Also, Breckenridge's contention that the web of interrelationships put in place by imperialism benefited not only the British but the Indian elite as well can be safely extended to Siam's ruling elite, who from the colonial pacification of Southeast Asia derived the geopolitical conditions and financial resources necessary to assert their "national" political authority.

The political theatrics of fin-de-siècle Europe, discussed above in terms of "invention of tradition," is another prime example of such transnational cultural flows. Majestic pageants performed on vast open spaces against a backdrop of imposing edifices represented a potent expression of modernity that the rulers of countries such as Japan and Siam imitated in order to claim equal status to Europe's governing elites. It was, of course, not an accident that the appearance of a globalized political theatrics followed the emergence of a global marketplace as a result of the worldwide diffusion of capitalist modes of production and exchange, which furnished imperialism's prime rationale. While the monumental expansion of capital cities and the effusion of public commemorations in Europe aimed to rekindle the ashes of the royal mystique with the rising breath of nationalist fervor, other newly invented spectacles—international exhibitions above all —revolved around (indeed celebrated) what Karl Marx famously termed "the fetishism of the commodity."[49] In his study of consumer culture in Victorian Britain, Thomas Richards incisively argues, "As political theater the spectacles of the early and mid-nineteenth century bore only a superficial resemblance to the royal progresses, public pageants, and elaborate rituals of the eighteenth. Display, extravagance, and excess survived—but less for the sake of those who staged the spectacle than for the sake of the spectacle itself."[50]

Needless to say, the association of kings and things long predated the modern period. As regalia and royal paraphernalia, clothing items whose use was restricted by sumptuary laws, and even holy relics show, the connection between conspicuous ownership and personal and political authority lay at the very root of the institute of kingship in both Europe and Asia. As Clifford Geertz and others have shown,[51] the rulers of precolonial Southeast Asia had nothing to learn from the likes of Elizabeth I and

Louis XIV on how to project a superhuman image of themselves by means of their sartorially enhanced personae, material possessions, and the physical setting of their courts.[52] In Europe, however, the industrial revolution, the rise of romantic love, and the fall of the ancien régime combined to bring about by the end of the eighteenth century a modern mode of consumption that broke away from the political regulation and the fixed notion of wants of preindustrial society to become a means of self-construction available to an ever-increasing segment of society.[53] It is also an intriguing coincidence that major political developments in Europe in the second half of the nineteenth century, such as the demotion of ruling dynasties and the rise of nationalism, were accompanied by the advent of mass consumerism.

As already argued, the political and socioeconomic institutions of Fifth Reign Siam were not analogous to Victorian and Edwardian Britain's, or even Meiji Japan's. It is important to remember that, until 1932, Siam had neither an elected house of representatives, however few the voting-rights holders, nor a written constitution of any sort. But the reconfiguration of the Siamese monarchy's public image testifies to the ruling elite's appreciation of visuality as the dominant trait of the culture of modernity,[54] as well as to their ability to make use of its globalized political theatrics. King Chulalongkorn's keen interest in photography (characteristic of the incumbent sovereign, too) bears aptly upon the elite's manifest preoccupation with the image they projected; and it is hardly surprising that even the origins of Thai cinema go back to one of Rama V's brothers, who made a series a short films documenting the king's public activities and royal ceremonies in the early 1900s.[55] Most significantly, the large number of photographs of the Fifth Reign in circulation allows for a visual memory of that period that helps explain its grip on the Thai collective imagination today.[56] Whether beheld as historical documents or as "Chulalongkorniana," these photographic images are crucial to the media representation of the Fifth Reign as the cradle of Thai modernity in accordance with the common wisdom that "a society becomes 'modern' when one of its chief activities is producing and consuming images."[57]

In conclusion, I propose to conceptualize the early formation of Thai modernity not according to a "nationalist/anticolonialist" paradigm, but as the localized product of globalizing trends occurring in the late-nineteenth-century global arena that I shall call, after Breckenridge, Victorian ecumene. If, economically and politically speaking, the most powerful of these globalizing forces were capitalism and colonialism, equally important in engendering localized modernities were globally circulating ideological constructs such as "progress," and even technological inventions such as photography. From this perspective, the fashioning of the Siamese monarchy's modern public image can be understood as the result of the localization of perceivably global markers of civilization. In examining the appropriation and localization in turn-of-the-century Siam of social and cultural practices and material culture from the West, it is important to bear in mind that the attitude to borrowing and reworking foreign imports was embedded in the elite's cultural identity. It could thus be expected that Western imports too acquired new or additional meanings or, at the very least, new nuances. Sorting out this question is the task of the following chapters.

Part I
PRACTICES

Chapter 1

Consumption Modes, Tastes, and Identity of Siam's Modernizing Elite

In February 1889, while cruising the South China Sea, the Duke of Sutherland's yacht moored in Bangkok, where the duke and his party were the guests of King Chulalongkorn. Florence Caddy, a lady of the party with a Victorian bent for matters of fashion and décor, later published a travelogue that contains a vivid description of the banquet held at the Siamese court: "Dinner was served in European style, the glass and porcelain, all from Europe, were engraved and painted with the royal arms and King Chulalongkorn's long name. . . . The king and princes all drank European wines. The dessert was the only thing presenting any great novelty to us."[1] European aristocracy was not alone on the Victorian ecumene's travel routes. A few years earlier, in 1881, the last Hawaiian king, Kalakaua, had also stopped in Bangkok en route to Europe; and, as recorded by Kalakaua's accompanying American minister, at the banquet thrown for him "the dishes and the service of them, as well as the wines, were European."[2] A glimpse "behind the scenes" at court banquets in the Fifth Reign's later years is found in the memoirs of Malcolm Smith, personal physician to Queen Saowapha (1864–1919), Chulalongkorn's first-ranking consort. According to Smith, Rama V himself arranged the banquets in consultation with his Western-educated sons: "One of them usually remained in the kitchens to see that everything was served in its right order, particularly the wines," while "the decoration of the tables and the room was supervised by the Queen."[3] Although Queen Saowapha was not in attendance at court receptions until nearly the end of the reign,[4] her grandson, litterateur Prince Chula Chakrabongse, stated, "She was a great enthusiast for European dinner services, glass, and silver, and was always buying them, so many that I do not think it is accurately known how many sets she possessed."[5]

The provision of European wines, cutlery, and dinnerware might be easily regarded as a means to please, and favorably impress, foreign guests; in fact, courtly consumption modes in the Fifth Reign show clearly an acquired taste for Western luxuries, even though the context and motivations of this phenomenon are largely unaccounted for. Things Western had randomly found their way to the Bangkok court since the early decades of the nineteenth century, but it was only in its last quarter that a definite change in courtly consumption took place as the royalty became accustomed to living in mansions built and furnished according to contemporary European fashion; enjoying themselves with the latest exotic gadgetry, from cameras to gramophones to motor cars; traveling to Europe and America for education and leisure; and entertaining in style their Western guests.

In the absence of an ad hoc analysis, the transformation in courtly modes of consumption has been subsumed more or less explicitly under either one of the two diverging interpretations of the Chakri Reformation: as a facet of the overall modernization promoted by the throne or, conversely, as the result of the royal elite's participation in the late-nineteenth-century global marketplace.[6] In both perspectives, the significance of the modernizing elite's novel lifestyle is subordinated to what are deemed to be the more fundamental transformations that concerned the political and economic realms. In the wake of the recent reconceptualization of consumption as a practice constitutive of both individual and social identity,[7] I shall put forth a different argument in this chapter: namely, that the consumer behavior of Siam's modernizing elite was central to the fashioning of their social identity as both "national" ruling class and one number of the enduring world aristocracy. As Pierre Bourdieu remarks, "The representation that individuals and groups inevitably project through their practices and properties is an integral part of social reality. A class is defined as much by its *being-perceived* as by its *being,* by its consumption . . . as much as by its position in the relations of production."[8] On the one hand, the lifestyle of Siam's modernizing elite fulfilled their aspirational self-image and desire to identify with European royalty; on the other, it mirrored, via the travelogues by the court's foreign guests and the later visits of Rama V to Europe, a recognizably "civilized" image back onto the West itself.

Changing Modes of Courtly Consumption

A historical background is necessary to best appreciate the change in the habits of consumption, and the underlying tastes, of the Siamese court in the last quarter of the nineteenth century. But since documents relating to the early Bangkok—or Rattanakosin—era (1782–1851) are scarce and even the earliest foreign reports date to the 1820s,[9] such a background has to be sketched with broad strokes and complemented by hypotheses.

The early Bangkok court obviously indulged in forms of prestige consumption, the two main foci of ostentatious display previous to the 1870s being the building of royal and religious edifices, an activity that was deemed to accrue merit, and the staging of state ceremonies, whose most magnificent expression was royal cremations. The linkage between the wealth of the royalty and the degree of patronage is illustrated by developments in the Third Reign (1824–1851), when the expansion of the royal monopolies was mirrored by a building boom in new monasteries (*wat*).[10] The Catholic bishop of Bangkok during 1828–1843, Monseigneur Jean-Baptiste Pallegoix, although familiar with France's grand cathedrals, described the city temples as being "d'un magnificence dont on ne se fait pas un idée en Europe."[11] Besides building projects and ritual performances, another major avenue of courtly expenditure in the early Bangkok period was the importation of luxury goods, mostly from India and China. In Ingram's opinion, prior to 1850, "the goods imported probably represented only a tiny fraction of total consumption, with some exceptions."[12] According to contemporary witnesses, cotton, silk, and precious metals made up the bulk of imports; local artisans then transformed these materials into objects representative of the status of king, princes, and high-ranking officials. Gold and silver were used in making regalia, embroidered ceremonial garments, jewelry for both personal and household adornment, and a wide array of ritual objects (bowls, trays, vases, etc.).[13] Specially designed textiles, particularly silks, were also produced in India according to the specifications of the Siamese court.

Although necessarily impressionistic, this picture of courtly patterns of prestige expenditure suggests a substantial continuity from the later Ayutthaya (ca. 1600–1767) to the early Bangkok periods.[14] Prestige goods such as silk, and silverware and goldware, were unrivaled for some two and a half centuries; Western luxury goods, on the other hand, apparently aroused no great interest at the Siamese court. Nor was the conservatism of royal taste due to isolation or ignorance of European fashions and lifestyle. On the contrary, a sizeable community of foreign traders had resided in Ayutthaya, and among them the French had enjoyed particular favor in the reigns of Prasat Thong (1629–1656) and especially Narai

(1656–1688), in whose reign embassies were dispatched to Louis XIV and Pope Innocent XI.[15] The apparent continuity in courtly modes of consumption from the seventeenth century to the mid-nineteenth can be explained in the light of Nidhi Auesriwongse's argument that Ayutthaya's self-conscious royalty was replaced by the more "bourgeois" Bangkok court.[16] Accordingly, continuity in the patterns of prestige consumption would have served the purpose of emphasizing sociocultural linkages between the newly established Chakri dynasty and its predecessor precisely because of their significant differences in terms of lineage, power networks, and source of legitimation.

Starting from the Third Reign, both Bangkok's Catholic diocese, whose See was the Church of Conception (on the Chao Phraya River's west bank, Thonburi), and the American Protestant missionaries, who had been coming to Siam in increasing number since the late 1820s, must have somehow publicized Western material culture. Yet the establishment of a trading station in Bangkok by the Englishman Robert Hunter in 1824, following the exploratory mission by the East India Company's envoy, John Crawfurd, in 1822, stood out as an isolated entrepreneurial initiative. A report presented by an agent of the Borneo Company to the Royal Society of Arts in 1894 stated, "One hears the name [Hunter's] nowadays as being that of the man who made a very bad venture in cheap Staffordshire cups and saucers, which were quite unable to compete with the excellent pottery imported from China."[17] The commercial treaties signed with Great Britain in 1826 and the United States in 1833 (negotiated by Henry Burney and Edmund Roberts, respectively) had a disappointing outcome, too. Notwithstanding the royal monopoly, the court's lukewarm interest in things Western must be regarded as a major reason for such an outcome; the concomitant factor was the full revival of the tributary relationship with China during the early Bangkok period, with thirty-five tribute missions sent to Beijing between 1782 and 1853 (an average of one mission every two years).[18]

Tributary missions, while taking place within the symbolic framework of submission to the authority of the Heavenly Emperor, constituted a major source of acquisition of luxury goods, a source complemented by the junk trade along China's southeastern coast and Southeast Asia (which was accompanied by selected Chinese immigration to fill in the offices of customs officials and tax farmers).[19] This pattern of commerce understandably led to a considerable Sinicization of courtly taste, particularly evident in the architecture and decorative styles of the Third Reign. Tributary missions to China were discontinued in the mid-1850s concurrently with the establishment of regular trade relations with Europe. By abolishing the system of royal monopoly and establishing a fixed rate of duty on all imported goods, the treaty negotiated in 1855 by the British diplomat John Bowring ushered in a new era for the economy of Bangkok and the nearby provinces, where monetary transactions became the norm. As a result, expenditure on imported luxury goods can be imagined to have increased. However, the absence of state expenditure figures prior to 1892 makes it difficult to assess the correlation between the coming into place of a market economy and change in elite patterns of consumption.

King Mongkut's properties, as indexed by the translators of the *Dynastic Chronicles of the Fourth Reign,* were still very much those of a traditional monarch: palaces and other residences, regalia (ceremonial weapons, tiered umbrellas, etc.), barges, jewelry and precious objects, horses and white elephants, and slaves.[20] John Bowring, taken by Mongkut on a tour of his private apartments, noticed pendulums, watches, barometers, thermometers, microscopes—"all the instruments and appliances which might be found in the study or library of an opulent philosopher in Europe"—and concluded, with obvious parochial bias, "Almost everything seemed English."[21] Even more appreciative was Bowring of the residence of Prince Chutamani (also known by his honorific name, Phra Pinklao), Mongkut's half-brother and the kingdom's *uparaja,* or "second king":

> *His own apartments are conveniently, tastefully fitted up, and, except from [sic] the suspended punkah and the great height of the rooms, the furniture and ornaments would lead you to believe you were in the house of an English gentleman. . . . He has a well-selected library of English books, a considerable museum of mechanical instruments, with models of late improvements in many of the departments of science, excellent sextants and quadrants, miniature screw-steamers, and a variety of modern weapons.*[22]

It is worthy of note that Bowring in his book, rather than stressing the "otherness" of his hosts, represented Mongkut and Chutamani to be as Anglicized as the situation allowed—perhaps because "tastefulness," in the eyes of a mid-Victorian, was by definition an English prerogative. It is significant that Bowring's impressions contrasted to the highest degree with the claim by a French publication of the mid-1860s (quoted in Henri

Mouhot's travel diary), according to which "the whole nation [Siam] has a great taste for our Parisian furniture, cotton, silk, and wollen fabrics, porcelain, chine, glass, bronzes, cutlery, ironmongery, and toys. Other articles in much esteem with them, and exported by us, are fire-arms, side-arms, saddlery, quilts, carpets, clocks, and windows."[23] As the "them" in the last sentence may hardly be taken to refer to the average Siamese, or even Bangkok inhabitant, the consumers of such a wide array of Western goods could only have been members of the royal household and the high-ranking officialdom. Curios and technological novelties (notably a daguerreotype) were also presented to King Mongkut by the envoys of both Queen Victoria and Napoleon III.[24]

The best illustration of the emergence of new modes of prestige expenditure within a few years of Chulalongkorn's coming of age in 1873 is the construction of the Chakri Throne Hall (Chakri Maha Prasat) during 1876–1880. Bangkok's grandest palace to date, the Chakri Throne Hall had a monumental marble staircase and furniture that, according to a contemporary visitor, had been imported from London at a cost of "not less than 80,000 Sterlings."[25] Replete with upholstered furniture, draperies, paintings, billiard tables, and a library with "all the leading European and American periodicals and newspapers being regularly taken in,"[26] the palace's interior provided the court with a novel living environment that served quite literally as the site for the domestication of Western material culture.

Figures of state expenditures are available for the latter half of the Fifth Reign, which saw the implementation of the administrative reforms. Between 1892 and 1910, as a result of changes in the tax system, such as the monopolization of revenue collection and the creation of land and head taxes, annual state revenues grew from 15 to 63 million baht. Over the same period, royal household expenditures increased from some 3.75 to 10.37 million baht—although, when considered as a proportion of the total state revenues and the total state expenditures, they actually decreased from 25 to 16.5 percent, and from 29 to 18 percent, respectively.[27] When Rama VI staged a fortnight extravaganza in December 1911 for the entertainment of guests from Europe, the United States of America, and Japan as part of his coronation, its cost reached the staggering figure of almost five million baht—more than double that of George V's coronation ceremonies that same year.[28] Unsurprisingly for an absolutist government, in which the court was also the central organ of administration and hence managed all revenues, the royal household's finances and state finances were not clearly distinct, at least until the establishment of the Privy Purse in 1890; separation between the crown's funds and the public treasury remained, in any case, more nominal than real until the establishment of the constitutional government in 1932.[29]

Although a considerable proportion of revenues was still destined to traditional forms of prestige consumption, such as the staging of court rituals, modes of consumption informed by Westernized tastes stand out as the novelty of the second half of the Fifth Reign. At the beginning of the twentieth century, the royalty had a new residential district built in Bangkok's rural outskirts on land bought by the Privy Purse. Increasing expenditures on the building, furnishing, and upkeep of royal and princely palaces in the last decade of the Fifth Reign contrasted with the decline in the patronage of monasteries. Compared to the five royal *wat* founded in the nineteen years of the previous reign, only two new monasteries were built in Bangkok during the Fifth Reign's forty-two years: Wat Ratcha Bophit at the beginning and Wat Benchama Bophit toward the end. The suggestion made by King Chulalongkorn to the patrons of the monkhood (*sangha*) in the nobility to have shop-houses built within the monasteries' precincts for rent, to ensure a stable source of income, is most telling in this regard.[30] This was the sharpest departure from traditional patterns of prestige expenditure along with the downsizing of royal cremations, despite the fact that Chulalongkorn's own cremation in March 1911 still cost almost 1 million baht.[31]

The other two major foci of expenditure in the latter half of the Fifth Reign were the education of princes and other young noblemen in European (mostly British) institutions and the extensive overseas travels by the king, princes, and high-ranking officials. In 1884 Prince Naret Worarit (1855–1925), at the time head of the Siamese legation in London, undertook a tour of the United States of America visiting, among other cities, Washington, D.C., New York, San Francisco, Cincinnati, St. Louis, Kansas City, and Denver. Following his return to Bangkok, Prince Naret was appointed minister first of Municipal Government, then of Public Works, and finally of the Privy Seal; he was also one of the signatories of the petition for constitutional reforms submitted to the king in 1885.[32] In 1891 Prince Damrong visited a number of European countries (Italy, France, Britain, Germany, Denmark, and Russia), as well as Turkey, for the purpose of improving diplomatic relations and visiting Chulalongkorn's sons studying in Britain.[33] At his return, instead of the foreseen position as head of the Ministry of Education, Damrong became Minister of Interior, a role he retained until 1915.

The longest and most imposing of these overseas travels were Rama V's two journeys to Europe. The first journey (7 April to 16 December 1897) was undertaken on board the *Maha Chakri,* a 2,500-ton vessel built four years earlier in Scotland and captained by a Briton. After disembarking in Venice, Chulalongkorn reached Switzerland and then went back to Italy, stopping in Florence and Rome, where he joined King Humbert I in the celebrations for Constitution Day and was received, first among non-Christian heads of state, by the pope. Chulalongkorn then proceeded to Austria-Hungary, visiting Vienna, Budapest, and Warsaw and meeting Emperor Francis Joseph I. In Russia (Peterhof, St. Petersburg, Moscow) he was the guest of Tsar Nicholas II. In Stockholm he was given a lavish reception since his visit coincided with the jubilee of King Oscar II. From Copenhagen, Rama V sailed to England. After landing in Portsmouth, he visited London and then moved on to Scotland. Back on the continent, Chulalongkorn visited Germany, stopping at Dresden and Potsdam and meeting Bismarck in Berlin, as well as the Netherlands and Belgium en route to Paris. Rama V spent one week there, at the time of the lowest ebb in Franco-Siamese relations. From Paris he went back to England, visiting Windsor Castle, Oxford, and Eton, and celebrating his forty-fourth birthday with his sons at Taplow Court. Encounters with the sovereigns of Spain and Portugal completed Rama V's familiarization with European royalty. The second journey, undertaken as a private tour, took place from 27 March to 17 November 1907. From Singapore, the royal suite traveled to Europe on a German mail steamer whose entire first class had been reserved. The eight-month journey was punctuated by informal encounters with members of Italy's House of Savoy, the French president Fallières, King Edward and Queen Alexandra, Kaiser Wilhelm II, and the sovereigns of Denmark, Norway, and Spain.

Usually commended for boosting Siam's prestige abroad and inspiring domestic policies of modernization, Chulalongkorn's European journeys were also shopping sprees on a veritable royal scale. Reading Rama V's letters written from overseas,[34] one is left with the impression that as much as fraternizing with European monarchs, a highlight of these travels was the acquisition (through purchase and gifts) of luxury goods such as paintings and sculptures in Florence, porcelain sets in Sèvres, Tiffany vases in London, Fabergé *objets* in St. Petersburg, and jewelry in Berlin. The reputation of "big spender" earned by the king during his overseas trips also ensured continuous attention by European commercial firms and prestigious retailers.[35] Money was spent on travel, accommodation, and luxury goods as well as on smaller items, such as the portraits taken by professional photographers in most of the places visited.

A group picture of the royal household in the Fourth and Fifth Reigns may help to put in context the court's new consumption patterns. King Mongkut fathered eighty-two children (thirty-nine princes and forty-three princesses) with thirty-five wives, and Chulalongkorn seventy-six children (thirty-two princes and forty-four princesses) with thirty-six wives. One can thus guess that many of the luxury items purchased from Europe were for the female members of the court. Dr. Smith calculated that at the beginning of the Sixth Reign (1910), the time of maximum expansion of the royal household, a gathering restricted to members bearing the title *momchao* (a prince's offspring) numbered about five hundred people.[36] During the Fifth Reign all royal wives and children received emoluments from the treasury. Annual allowances for the king's wives varied from a minimum of 240 baht (equivalent to the yearly salary of a junior clerk in the bureaucracy) to a maximum of 20,000 baht for those who had borne the king children with senior titles.[37] Emoluments for the king's progeny began at birth and were doubled upon assumption of full titles. In the early 1910s, the annual allowance for a royal prince of the highest rank (*chaofa*) was about 52,000 baht (roughly equivalent to 4,000 pounds sterling); this sum was usually compounded by additional incomes deriving from government offices and the rental of real properties.[38]

The outcome of the royalty's privilege is acknowledged even by David Wyatt, an otherwise staunch admirer of Rama V's achievements: "one might hazard the guess that the social distance—created by education, wealth, lifestyle, exposure to the outside world, even language—between the urban, educated elite and the peasant mass of Siamese society was never greater than it was at the end of the Fifth Reign."[39] In fact, the Westernized taste of the modernizing elite underscored social distinction domestically as much as it invoked an image of them as civilized individuals in the eyes of the transnational elite of the Victorian ecumene. The wider context of the refashioning of the Siamese elite's consciousness encompassed major political changes that affected the international and domestic arenas in the 1870s and 1880s: the advent of direct colonial rule in South and Southeast Asia and the imposition of a central royal authority over the newly bounded Siamese state. Along with a cultural—one could almost say anthropological—dimension, the refashioning of the Siamese royalty's image reveals thus a sociological dimension as well, involving repositioning vis-à-vis foreign as well as indigenous prestige groups. The cultural and sociological dynamics underlying the emergence of novel modes of courtly consumption in Fifth Reign Siam are examined in the remainder of this chapter.

Westernized Taste, Symbolic Capital, and Social Identity

In the Introduction mention was made of O. W. Wolters' concept of localization—the process whereby themes and motifs from Indic mythology, religion, poetry, and the visual and performing arts were appropriated and transformed into constituents of the cultural identity of the indigenous elites in Southeast Asia. A paradigmatic case of localization is the recasting of the Indian epic *Ramayana* as the Thai *Ramakian,* which in turn furnished the subject of the masked court performance (*khon*), also derived from Indian temple rituals. Because of the material losses incurred in the fall of Ayutthaya, a revival of elite culture was promoted in the first and second Bangkok reigns. Thus the court poets under the direction of the founder of the Chakri dynasty composed a new version of the *Ramakian,* also reworked and abridged by his successor. Yet the rectification by Rama I's order early in his reign of what he perceived to be unorthodox—in fact, Brahmanic—court rituals suggests that other elements of the elite's Indic cultural heritage had become unintelligible or had perceivably lost performative power by the beginning of the Bangkok period.[40] This hypothesis is supported by the inconsistencies in the supposedly cosmographical layout of the Chakri's seat, Rattanakosin City (discussed in chapter 3), and by the stylistic stagnation of architecture and the plastic arts.

Balancing the partial loss of significance of the Indic heritage in the first half of the nineteenth century was the growing Sinicization of courtly taste resulting from the revival of the tributary trade with China. The massive consumption of Chinese material culture might have promoted an interest in Chinese culture *tout court.* Literature provides a significant example. Along with the rewriting of the *Ramakian,* another undertaking of the First Reign court officials was the translation of the Chinese historical novel *The Romance of the Three Kingdoms* (*San guo yanyi,* which in Thai became *Sam kok*). In his brilliant analysis of the various social incarnations of *Sam kok,* Craig Reynolds quotes Prince Damrong's statement that the novel was translated because of its "usefulness in conducting the affairs of state,"[41] by which Damrong presumably meant it offered exemplars of leadership qualities such as strategy and martial prowess. Now, the establishment of the Chakri dynasty was due to such abilities as much as to the decisive support of the Chinese merchants who were business partners, if not relatives, of the royalty. Rama I's appointment of the head of the treasury (*phrakhlang*) to supervise the *San guo*'s translation highlights the intersection of power, wealth, and cultural production in the early Bangkok period.[42]

From the viewpoint of the hegemonic center, the Qing court in Beijing, the tributary system represented an instrument of imperial diplomacy the purpose of which was the expansion of its civilizational sphere. In Chinese political thought, civilization (*wenming*) was understood to spread spatially via proximity (*jin*), from the emperor in the center to those outside the Middle Kingdom; accordingly, the presentation of tributes to the Son of Heaven signified acceptance of his lordship and implicitly of *wenming;* in return peripheral rulers obtained imperial recognition.[43] The founder of the Chakri dynasty was acknowledged ruler of Siam with the name of Cheng Ho following a mission of tribute in 1784, and even Siam's last tributary mission in 1854 was sent to reciprocate the imperial investiture of King Mongkut.[44] The consequence of the Bowring Treaty (1855) was not only to terminate this pattern of trading and diplomatic relations but also to replace Britain for China as Bangkok's chief commercial partner. Similar to the way participation in the tributary system entailed acceptance of the Chinese concept of civilization, signing of the Bowring Treaty too implied acknowledgment of the diplomatic and even legal and philosophical premises of Britain's trading policy.

This culturalist perspective on the shift of Siam's trading partnership corroborates the well-established argument that it took someone like King Mongkut, who had been acquainted with European and American missionaries since his youth and studied Western humanistic and scientific culture, to initiate an "open policy" toward the West.[45] The keen interest that Mongkut and a few other princes took in Western notions of time and space—and consequently of human action, which takes place in time and space, and history, which represents past human action—have also been pointed out.[46] Time, space, and action are fundamental mental categories that inform both individual and collective worldviews; reconsideration of these categories in the light of Western ideas underscores the emergence of a modern kind of cultural consciousness. Historians, however, have tended to single out the threat of colonialism as the catalyst for the implementation of modernizing policies. This view has led to laying emphasis on the preservation of national independence—or, from a revisionist perspective, the elite's power—as the central objective of modernization in late-nineteenth-century Asia. According to Yoneo Ishii, the ruling elites of Siam as well as Japan accomplished this objective by divorcing the material culture of the West from its "moral culture" and appropriating the former while refusing the latter.[47]

Ishii's argument has the merit of accounting for the technologically driven vision of modernity advocated by many East and Southeast Asian governments in the postcolonial period; yet it is also unsatisfactory in that it explains modernization in Asia as a process both derivative and essentially keyed to the domain of politics. On this account, even when modernization is assessed critically as organic to the reproduction of elite power, its effect on elite sociocultural values is largely ignored. In fact, the appropriation of Western material culture and social and cultural practices by the Siamese royalty occurred at a historic juncture when the cosmological, institutional, and behavioral frameworks that had defined their role and identity in the Indic civilizational sphere and (since the late eighteenth century) the partly overlapping Sinic civilizational sphere appeared no longer capable of empowering them by means of connection to the source of "civilization," be it *arayatham* or *wenming,* as this source was now perceived to be located elsewhere—Europe. The early intimations of a Westernized taste in the Fourth Reign, exemplified by the neoclassical style of royal architecture and the collecting of scientific instruments, is thus as telling of the dynamic of cultural change as Mongkut's well-known interest in modern astronomy.[48]

Pierre Bourdieu's concepts of cultural and symbolic capital can be employed profitably here.[49] Keeping in line with Bourdieu's terminology, I shall invoke a situation in which the Siamese elite's traditional forms of cultural and symbolic capital, which enjoyed currency across the whole of Indianized Southeast Asia, were dramatically depreciated as a result of the new hegemony of the Western civilizational sphere. In this situation a "recapitalization" was required, and one must admit that the appreciation of this imperative is proof of the Siamese royalty's farsightedness. Recapitalization was achieved, perhaps most significantly, by investing economic capital—at the monarchy's disposal in larger amount than ever before from the 1880s onward thanks to the progressive monopolization of taxation—into the field that above all yields cultural capital: education. Following the erratic tutoring of princes by Western teachers and missionaries in the Fourth Reign, the Fifth Reign saw the enrollment of royal princes in European colleges and institutes, mostly in Britain but also in Germany and Russia. The first Siamese overseas students were Chulalongkorn's four elder sons who arrived in Britain in 1885 and, once back in Bangkok, were given key government offices (especially in the Ministry of War). The presence of the Siamese princes and noblemen in educational institutions abroad also promoted public perception of the Chakri dynasty as a number of the world royalty—on occasions such as Crown Prince Vajiravudh's participation, along with the scions of European royal houses, in the celebrations for Queen Victoria's Diamond Jubilee.

Overseas travels by senior members of the royal household in Asia, Europe, and America were at least as important as the education of young princes and noblemen abroad for the accumulation of cultural as well as symbolic capital. Chulalongkorn's own "kingly" education came from the tours of colonial Asia (Singapore, Java, and India) accomplished in the early years of his reign (1871–1872), which historians, following Prince Damrong's memoirs,[50] have linked to the beginning of reforms. The most significant of these grand tours were of course the two journeys to Europe undertaken by Rama V in the company of some of his brothers and sons. He described the main purposes of the first visit in the following terms: "First, to see how life in Europe is; second, to study how wealth and goods originate; third, to fathom their strength, were they to attack us; fourth, to enjoy myself as well."[51] Following his previous visits in 1871 and 1896, in 1901 Rama V went to Java for the third time; but, after the sight of Europe, the colonial world of Southeast Asia had apparently lost for him much of its appeal. In May 1907, while on holiday in Italy, Chulalongkorn wrote to Damrong,

> *I was deeply bored in Singapore. I am considering saving time on the way*
> *back and spending in Singapore something like three hours so to stay longer*
> *in Europe. I enjoy myself only when I am here; all the way through is a*

terrible tedium. . . . If I do not go to Russia and Turkey, I might have
extra time to travel to America. I have a great desire to visit it.[52]

By expressing a desire to see and experience more, a desire stem-
ming from a quest for self-fulfillment, Chulalongkorn revealed an eminently
"modern" attitude.[53] Traditional courtly prestige expenditure, in Siam as
elsewhere, served mainly to signify social status. Instead, the elite's novel
patterns of consumption, from massive purchase of luxury goods to residential developments, promoted self-definition via the adoption of a desired
lifestyle as much as they amounted to symbolic statements about the prestige of the Bangkok court vis-à-vis European royalty. The royal houses of
Europe had been for centuries forging links and alliances by means of
wedding policy. But since racial prescriptions and social conventions
prevented the establishment of blood ties between the House of Chakri
and European royalty, the only way to join the family of the Windsors,
the Habsburgs, the Romanovs, and the rest was to develop a familiarity
with tastes and consumption patterns that had constituted a means of self-
identification common to this class since the early modern period: "The
members of this multifarious society spoke the same language throughout
the whole of Europe . . . they read the same books, they had the same taste,
the same manners and . . . the same style of living."[54]

The psychological dimension of the Siamese royalty's identification with European courts is captured in the following comment on Queen
Saowapha by her British physician: "Her knowledge of the surviving royal
houses of Europe was astonishingly complete. She knew their family-trees
far better than I did, and spoke of some of the people almost if they were
her own relations."[55] King Chulalongkorn's own explanation of his com-
pulsion to buy expensive local porcelain in Denmark is revealing of the
way conspicuous consumption afforded the means for such an identification: "It has become fashionable because Alexander III [tsar, 1881–1894]
loved to buy many things made in his wife's country [Denmark], and now
that it is in vogue everybody is compelled to follow."[56] Likewise, in need
of rest before setting off on his 1907 tour of Europe, Rama V relaxed for a
couple of weeks in the Italian seaside resort of Sanremo, on that stretch of
Mediterranean coastline—la Riviera—that was then fashionable among
elite holiday-goers, in particular the British and Russian nobility.

While promoting the construction of a modern self, the lifestyle
of the modernizing elite continued to have a representational function too.

Rama V's consumer habits made him a tastemaker within the court as much as they defined his public persona; announcing his second trip to Europe, Bangkok's English-language press glossed, "King Chulalongkorn is an enthusiastic motorist, and it is expected that he will make large purchase of cars in France and England."[57] In the 1880s and 1890s, an increasing number of foreign guests (travelers, diplomats, and government advisers) were admitted to court, and some of them later published accounts of Bangkok courtly life. Etchings and, later on, photographic illustrations in books and magazines were crucial in showing people in Europe and America the dress, furniture, habitations, and other aspects of the Siamese royalty's taste and lifestyle.

Before the construction of a modern residential suburb in the first decade of the twentieth century, the favorite place for the enactment of the royalty's civilized self was the summer palace at Bang Pa-in, near the ruined royal city of Ayutthaya. The site of the seventeenth-century palace was identified by King Mongkut, who had temporary buildings erected there. Between 1872 and 1889, Chulalongkorn transformed it into a recreational space for the court by adding exotic edifices, including a neoclassical throne hall, a no longer extant "Oriental" pavilion (akin to that in Brighton), Alpine-style chalets, and even a marble cenotaph commemorating Queen Sunantha, who had drowned in a boat accident on the way to Bang Pa-in in 1881. A Siamese-style pavilion was also placed in the middle of the central pond to complement this exoticizing built environment, redolent of the architectural displays of international exhibitions that Siam had been attending since the 1870s. A few years later, a Chinese-style mansion, assembled in sections shipped from China, was erected, as a present to the king by the precursor of the Chinese Chamber of Commerce.[58] In the late 1870s, on the riverbank opposite the palace, Rama V had a foreign contractor build Wat Niwet, whose incongruous neo-Gothic ordination hall accorded with the exhibition-like architectural exoticism of the summer palace.

The court stayed regularly at Bang Pa-in, and because the palace served as a base for excursions to the Ayutthaya ruins, foreign guests were often taken there. The Belgian Charles Buls, a former mayor of Brussels who visited Bang Pa-in in 1900, penned a dismissive account of the palace as containing "a villa in poor Italian style . . . decorated with mediocre Siamese paintings . . . a small, poor park . . . with rare, suffering trees . . . stuffed with tasteless pavilions without architecture." The king's residence, a two-storied wooden chalet, Buls found "heavy, pretentious, stuffed with massive furniture and objects from a bazaar of Italian, German and English making."[59] Buls' ruminations at the sight of the royal chalet's interior are worth quoting at length:

> *I often asked myself where do all the horrors which are exposed in the World Expos end up. I imagined that they would furnish the castles of our upstarts. The visit of the summer palaces of the King of Siam and the Sultan of Johore revealed to me that it is to the poor Asian princes that the unscrupulous industrialists sold, doubtlessly for double or triple their value, the pendulum with a power hammer or in the form of the Eiffel Tower, crystal candelabrums, colored negroes, chairs in twisted wood, statues in gilded zinc, vases in sculpted alabaster.*[60]

The Siamese royalty was by no means alone in building replicas of Tudor castles and Renaissance villas and stuffing them with furniture in some revival style, imitations of classical statuary, and assorted bric-a-brac. Had Buls visited India's princely courts he would have seen, inside palaces whose style ranged from neoclassical to Beaux Arts, far more extravagant items such as the electrically illuminated rock garden and the miniature silver train running on the dining room table in the mansion of the Maharaja of Gwailor.[61] Moreover, not all guests were dismissive of the summer palace of Bang Pa-in. A Russian prince in the suite of the tsarevich (later Tsar Nicholas II) that toured Siam in 1891 described the same chalet despised by Buls as being "furnished luxuriously and with refined taste and comfort."[62] Only the Chinese mansion reconciled the tastes of the Belgian bourgeois and the Russian aristocrat, proving Europeans' enduring fascination with Chinoiserie; according to Charles Buls, it was the only "beautiful and interesting thing in the park," and Prince Ookhtomsky somewhat naively remarked, "The emperor of China himself can scarcely have a palace much finer than this."[63]

The omnivorous aesthetic that informed the furnishing and decoration of Fifth Reign royal residences was indeed typical of late-Victorian consumer culture, which embraced that universe of mass-produced commodities encompassed by the term "kitsch."[64] Kitsch, on global circulation from upper-middle-class homes in the metropole to princely and royal households in South and Southeast Asia, was pivotal for the formation in the mid-nineteenth century of a global elite united by their common tastes and consumer habits.

Another important outlet of courtly conspicuous consumption in the Fifth Reign was the patronage of Western artists. Here, again, royal taste coincided with the dominant taste in Europe at that time: academic, or Salon-style, painting. Besides the several portraits of members of the royal family that had been painted by European artists since the early 1870s, many artworks were purchased during the two royal tours of Europe. King Chulalongkorn's correspondence from overseas contains several comments on art and architecture that reveal his delight in presenting himself back home as being acquainted with Europe's artists no less than with its crowned heads.[65] Complaisant to Rama V's self-image as an art connoisseur, Apinan Poshyananda hails him as "modern monarch and patron of the arts" in his history of modern art in Thailand, stating, "Showing visitors a royal collection of Western art treasures was part of the king's modernization program."[66] But while, on the one hand, Apinan assigns Chulalongkorn a prominent place in Thailand's art-historical narrative for spurring stylistic rejuvenation, on the other, royal taste for European paintings (hardly any of which, it must be noted in passing, would qualify as a "treasure" according to current scales of artistic or market value) is still accounted for from the prescriptive viewpoint of modernization as a political project. The formation of a collection of Western paintings is better understood as one of those emulation-driven acts of consumption whereby the Bangkok royalty was able to identify with its Western counterparts.

Although patronage of craftsmen was common in the Ayutthaya and the early Bangkok courts, the formation of an art collection was a novel pursuit in late-nineteenth-century Siam because the very idea of an objectified artwork was novel in that context. The collecting of aesthetically satisfying objects, later ennobled as "works of art," emerged as a pursuit distinct from the accumulation of valuables in early modern Europe. Following the conceptual integration of art collecting and patronage by Italian humanists into the doctrine of magnificence underpinning the political ascendancy of merchant families such as Florence's Medici, the relationship between these practices and political authority fully unfolded in the seventeenth century at the courts of the modern European monarchies —in particular Vienna and Versailles, where extensive royal art collections were assembled.[67] Art historian John Clark argues that the art collection of the Thai royal household reveals, however, "the apparent indifference of the patrons to systematic considerations of taste."[68] "Collection" may thus be somewhat of a misnomer since a collection is, by definition, based on selective acquisition.[69] This is not to say that European monarchs in general displayed better taste or a deeper understanding of art; in fact, the main role in the establishment of European royal households' art collections was played by advisers who tended to be of commoner rather than aristocratic background.[70]

King Chulalongkorn's purchase of artworks reflected, instead, his personal taste or, at the most, the taste of the princes who traveled with him (Sapphasat Supakit, Charun Kridakon, Rapi Pattanasak, and Boriphat Sukhumpan).[71] Along with copies of Renaissance masters, the paintings purchased abroad tended to be the work of artists who enjoyed mainstream approval and (possibly) well-known patrons, like those who exhibited at official art venues such as the Venice Biennale, visited by Rama V in 1897 (its second edition) and again in 1907. His overseas letters reveal a keen appreciation of artworks as both commodities and status symbols. In informing his daughter of his intention to shop for paintings in Florence and Venice in 1907, Chulalongkorn remarked that he must do this "before the summer arrival of the American millionaires eager to buy everything"[72] and that the Florence mayor would purchase at a special price on his behalf two bronze sculptures he had seen at an exhibition there, "with many good pieces at affordable prices, many of which, however, were already reserved for the king [of Italy]."[73]

Two episodes demonstrate the degree of symbolic capital Chulalongkorn had accumulated by the later years of his reign. On 12 April 1908, the *New York Times* announced that Rama V was considering having the letters he had sent from Europe to his daughter, Princess Nipha (later collected under the title *Klai ban*), published in Bangkok; four days after this announcement, a New York publisher, Hubert Bancroft, proposed to the king the publication of an English version of his "travel diaries." Bancroft's proposal, as he explained, stemmed from his "belief that the volume would be interesting to the world at large."[74] One year earlier, precisely on 25 June 1907, Chulalongkorn's symbolic capital had already received a major boost with the conferral of the Doctorate in Civil Law *honoris causa* by the University of Cambridge during his stay in England.[75] There was a twofold reason for this honorary academic degree: the financial contribution to the compilation of the *Sacred Books of the Buddhists,* accomplished at Oxford under the direction of renowned Indologist and historian of religions, Friedrich Max Müller (a German by birth but naturalized British), and the support given to the 1889 Cambridge expedition in northern Malaya, which had resulted in *The Pagan Races of the Malay Peninsula,* published in 1906.[76] At the conferral ceremony, which was attended by the Prince of Nakhon Sawan, the officers of the Siamese legation in London, and the British financial adviser to the Siamese government (C. Rivett-Carnac), the public orator proffered a speech in Latin in which he lauded the *Sacred Books of the Buddhists* as "*munificentiae regiae monumenta*" (monuments of royal munificence) and Rama V as "*virum in Academiam nostram liberalissimus*" (a most generous man to our university).[77]

In a sense, the financial support for the translation of the Buddhist scriptures, whose definitive edition in a thirty-nine-volume set was printed in one thousand copies for distribution to libraries across the world, complemented the project initiated in 1888 with the convocation of a council to revise the Theravada canon.[78] These initiatives harked back to the rationalist reform of Siamese Buddhism initiated in the 1830s by Mongkut while a monk, a reform that had laid the basis for the institutionalization of the *sangha* in the Fifth Reign.[79] At the same time, the manifestation of Chulalongkorn's patronage of Buddhism was not limited to the Indic civilizational sphere, encompassing South and Southeast Asia only, but extended to the whole Victorian ecumene; as a result, it took on a novel resonance. The study of Buddhism at the turn of the nineteenth and twentieth centuries was carried out by Western scholars in the libraries and universities of imperial metropoles.[80] In this sense, Buddhist studies were fully embedded in that "Orientalist empiricism" that produced knowledge about Asian societies within the political and ideological framework of imperialism.[81] Rama V's association with the production of Orientalist scholarship may be taken as a further proof of his (and his advisers') political acumen. But the dispute that had marred his encounter with the *sangha* in Ceylon (Sri Lanka) back in 1897 suggests that, rather than adopting it as a mere instrumental pose, Chulalongkorn internalized Orientalism's empirical stand in the construction of his self-image as a modern individual.

Relations between the monastic communities of Siam and Ceylon, from which Theravada Buddhism had spread to mainland Southeast Asia, dated back several centuries. In the fifteenth century monks from the Thai kingdom of Chiang Mai traveled to Ceylon to be reordained and, on their return, founded a Sinhalese sect; two and a half centuries later, a reverse regenerative act took place when monks journeyed from Siam to Ceylon to perform an ordination ceremony as part of the Buddhist revival initiated on the island under Dutch colonial rule.[82] In the Bangkok period, ten monks headed for the Temple of the Holy Tooth in Kandy with offers following the cremation of Rama III in 1852.[83] Chulalongkorn himself, abiding by his institutional role of "defender of the faith," had presented the Sinhalese *sangha* with gifts and a monetary offer for the restoration of a shrine (the Mirisaveti *cetiya* in Anuradhapura) after his enthronement. Three days were, however, sufficient to undermine this secular relationship when Rama V finally visited Ceylon, en route to Europe, from 19 to 21 April 1897.

While for the British colonial authorities Chulalongkorn was a foreign sovereign on an official visit, for the Sinhalese population he stood as the living embodiment of the "universal monarch" (*chakravartin*) of the Indo-Buddhist tradition. In the city of Colombo, the day after his arrival, Rama V was given a warm reception by the local Buddhist community, whose banner proclaimed "Welcome to the Protector of Our Religion." However, the welcoming ceremony was compromised by an awkward slippage of cultural and linguistic idioms. The conversation between the local monks and Chulalongkorn, in full Western dress, was hesitantly conducted in Pali (the language of the Theravada canon) up to a point when he asked them, in English, "Do you understand me?"[84] To Queen Saowapha, the king confessed in writing that he was unable to understand whether the monks spoke Pali or Sinhalese.[85] The following day, Rama V visited the Temple of the Holy Tooth, home to a famous Buddhist relic. There he asked, probably to the surprise of those present, to hold the relic in his hands only to have his request refused by a temple monk in spite of his overwhelming authority. As a result, Chulalongkorn left the temple at once, withdrew his offerings, and even returned the gifts the Sinhalese monks had presented to him. The enquiry immediately set up by the colonial authorities to investigate the episode conveniently found the interpreter, one poor Mr. Panabokke, responsible for the misunderstanding that had caused offense to the king of Siam.[86]

In relating the Kandy incident to Queen Saowapha, Chulalongkorn stigmatized the lack of courtesy and disrespectful attitude of the monks and even cast doubts on the relic's authenticity.[87] A significantly different version of the incident is found in the memories of a Belgian adviser to the Siamese Ministry of Justice from 1898 to 1900, Émile Jottrand, who reported a confidence Rama V had allegedly shared with his general adviser, Gustave Rolin-Jaequemyns (countryman of Jottrand and his source). According to this version, believing the relic to be an alligator's tooth,

Rama V had simulated his feelings of devotion with the real intent of exposing it as a forgery though his plan was eventually foiled.[88] Although this version of the episode has a somewhat apocryphal ring, it suitably illustrates Chulalongkorn's self-image as both a Buddhist leader and a champion of rationalism. A few months after the Kandy incident, alleged relics of the Buddha were discovered at his birthplace, Kapilavastu; the British viceroy of India offered them to Rama V as the only *remaining* Buddhist monarch (the Buddhist kings of Laos and Cambodia, *souverains protégés* of the French, notably being accorded no consideration), provided he would share them with Buddhists in Burma and Ceylon.[89] In this legitimating triangulation, the British underscored King Chulalongkorn's symbolic capital as the world's leader of Buddhist believers (at least those of Theravada persuasion) by placing their colonial subjects under his moral authority; Rama V, on his part, provided financial support for the translation of the Buddhist scriptures undertaken at the academic epicenter of the empire, thus acknowledging the discursive authority of Orientalist scholarship over Buddhism.

In short, even though the refashioning of the royal elite's identity encompassed a variety of social and cultural practices, it was by developing a familiarity with the tastes and habits of consumption of Western elites (the aristocracy as much as the haute bourgeoisie) that the Bangkok court was most readily able to experience affiliation with the civilizational vanguard of the Victorian ecumene. The competences required by these novel modes of consumption were both denotative of the kind of cultural capital and augmentative of the kind of symbolic capital that enjoyed validation within the Euro-centered civilizational sphere. However important this transnational dimension was, the modernizing elite's new consumer habits needs also to be considered from a domestic angle, as their emergence was concurrent with the establishment of royal absolutism in Siam.

Conspicuous Consumption and Royal Absolutism

Following the sociological approach to seventeenth-century absolutism pioneered by Norbert Elias, who theorized the elaboration of good manners and the cultivation of taste within the environment of the court as central moments of the "civilizing process," I shall draw a comparative examination of the import of courtly patterns of consumption in Fifth Reign Siam and European courts in the age of absolutism. The examination is prompted by Elias' own realization that the civilizing process brought about not only self-control and the refinement in manners (in terms of which the Siamese may have been more ahead of the Europeans) but, ultimately, the centralization of political power.

The first analogy to be explored is the reign of Louis XIV (1643–1715), the self-proclaimed embodiment of monarchical absolutism. Leaving aside for the sake of comparison the differences in the dimensions of their respective households and in the scale of consumption indulged therein, one might argue that Rama V, like the Sun King, took on the undisputed role of arbiter of taste within a court whose lifestyle was far removed from that of the majority of the populace. Another intriguing analogy is that they both ruled for a considerable length of time after having experienced, early in their reigns, internal rebellions fomented by factions within the court that highlighted the fragile basis of royal power and the need to strengthen the sovereign's grip over the nobility: the Fronde, which broke out in 1648 during Cardinal Mazarin's regency and lasted until 1652; and the Front Palace Incident of 1874–1875, which was caused by the claim to power of the *uparaja,* a rank later abolished by Chulalongkorn.

In *The Court Society* (1969),[90] Elias proposes that Louis XIV gained control over the fractious French aristocracy by making his court the center of competition for prestige and status. By subjecting the nobles to Versailles' demanding lifestyle, a condition expressed by the phrase "noblesse oblige," Louis XIV caused their financial resources, already strained by the changes over the previous century, to shrink further, and thus increased their dependence on royal goodwill. Courtly conspicuous consumption was thus instrumental in effecting the long-term shift of power from the feudal nobility to an absolute monarch in early modern France. The Sun King perfected his strategy of subjection by manipulating the status of individual nobles at court while, at the same time, awarding remunerative government offices to the bourgeoisie's top layer and allowing them to satisfy their craving for status through the purchase of titles of nobility. As a result, proximity to the king replaced lineage as the foremost mark of individual status at court.

My intention here is not to engage Elias' conceptualization of Louis XIV's court as a "cage" for the aristocracy[91] but to ascertain whether such a model, as it stands, is of any relevance for sociopolitical change in Fifth Reign Siam. There too royal absolutism was able to assert itself because of the decline of the nobility (*khunnang*), whose many privileges included the collection of revenue and the control of manpower through a master-client relationship, the *phrai* system, that gave the nobles both a political and an economic base. In the early part of the Fifth Reign the *khunnang* had appropriated so large a share of the revenues collected that, as Chulalongkorn recalled years later, the royal household had suffered a shortage of income.[92] Such conduct by the *khunnang* was probably due to the decline in their other main source of revenues, their share in the royal monopoly system, which had vanished in the 1850s with the conclusion of the commercial treaties with Western countries.[93] The aims of asserting the throne's authority and placing it in control of the country's financial resources went thus hand in hand in the minds of the modernizing elite.

Although the two factions that opposed the king's authority in Bangkok, the regent's and the *uparaja*'s parties (known respectively as Conservative Siam and Old Siam),[94] disbanded in the early 1880s at the death of their leaders, the curbing of the provincial nobility's power was achieved only a decade later with the centralization of the administration, tax collection, and military draft by the *thesaphiban* system.[95] Only then were most provincial *khunnang* demoted to the rank of state officials (*kharatchakan*, "king's servants" in a rather literal sense). After the co-option of his many half-brothers through appointments in the ministerial cabinet formed in 1892, Rama V achieved "absolute" power, which incidentally entailed absolute spending power—a condition quite unlike that of any previous Chakri monarch. The centralization of tax collection was crucial in bringing about the growth in revenues that made possible the already mentioned threefold increase in royal household expenditures between 1892 and 1910 (from 3.75 to 10.37 million baht). Moreover, after the establishment of the Privy Purse in 1890, the royal household increasingly invested its private wealth in various profit-making activities, such as real estate speculation, manufacturing industry, and joint-venture partnership with foreign firms. The enormous amount of revenues that the court was able to appropriate to its own advantage warrants the definition of "absolute monarchy" for turn-of-the-century Siam in spite of the judicial and administrative limitations on its sovereignty resulting from the "unequal treaties" signed with Western countries.

Therefore, whereas the increased level of courtly consumption in Louis XIV's France was a key determinant in the decline of the nobility, in Fifth Reign Siam such an increase was made possible by the nobility's losing out financially to the royalty. Seksan Prasertkul maintains in his dissertation that besides the loss of financial resource, another factor that contributed to the decline of the *khunnang* as a class was the royal elite's changing view of themselves, which resulted in an unprecedented consciousness of the status divide between royalty and nobility. Seksan simply suggests that the royalty's new self-awareness was due partly to the internal political situation and partly to European cultural influences.[96] The construction of so grand a building as the Chakri Throne Hall at a time, the late 1870s, when the royal household's financial condition was not particularly rosy can be taken as a clue to the linkage between increasing prestige expenditure by the court and the inflation of the royalty's social identity early in the Fifth Reign.

In *Die Rolle des Hofes im Absolutismus*, J. F. von Krüdener proposes that European sovereigns used courtly splendor to impress their subjects as much as other monarchs. As Krüdener's argument is summed up by Jeroen Duindam, "In the battle for prestige among the rulers of Europe, the size and magnificence of courtly households, palaces and gardens contributed to the outcome."[97] In other words, self-representation by means of conspicuous consumption in the absolutist courts was creative more than reactive, expressing not just a sovereign's actual power but his pretension to it vis-à-vis the perceived power of foreign rulers. Peter the Great (1682–1725), who closely modeled his self-image and self-aggrandizement policies on Louis XIV's,[98] is an example of status competition among absolutist monarchs. However, Peter's emulation of the French court lifestyle, following his visit to Versailles in 1717, served a different purpose. In Richard Wortman's words, "Having given the Russian state the semblance of a Western administration, Peter set about creating a Western court culture to unite and educate his servitors."[99] The political use of conspicuous consumption by Peter the Great strikes thus a closer analogy with Chulalongkorn's than does the Sun King's, particularly in the light of Wortman's comments about the "symbolic meaning" of Peter's reforms, which put in place "governmental institutions that resembled those of the other major powers, a state to befit a European monarch."[100] Likewise, external perception of Siam as a modernizing country can be said to have depended on the court's adoption of a civilized lifestyle as much as on the implementation of governmental and juridical apparatuses patterned after Western institutions.

One crucial historical factor made conspicuous consumption in the absolutist court of Europe different from that in Fifth Reign Siam: not the sovereign's authority, since even those most illustrious absolutist kings such as Louis XIV and Peter the Great had in fact to negotiate their power amid clashing factional interests and defend it militarily from foreign rulers, but the shape and reach of the marketplace in which the luxury goods constitutive of high social status were produced and circulated. Not any longer sustained by royal factories and regulated by sumptuary laws, ostentatious consumption too was tied in the nineteenth century to the mass production of commodities and their global distribution via an imperial trade network. The outcome of this situation was clearly expounded by two acute contemporary observers: "The bourgeoisie has through its exploitation of the world market given a cosmopolitan character to production and consumption in every country."[101] In representing themselves as modern, civilized individuals by means of consumption practices, the Siamese royalty could only abide by bourgeois taste—while indulging in it with virtually no financial constraints, as in a true absolutist regime.

Chapter 2

Presentation and Representation
of the Royal Self

The conviction that a modern self could not be disjointed from a perceivably civilized body made bodily and clothing practices central to the re-fashioning of the Siamese monarchy's image. The relations entertained with Southeast Asia's colonial elites since the early 1870s awakened the Siamese royalty to the importance of a presentation of the self adequate to the status and authority they were claiming within the Victorian ecumene; hose and shoes came thus into use despite their dubious convenience in Bangkok's tropical climate, while the time-honored shaved haircut was abandoned. Reformation of the body natural of the king and the royalty anticipated by some two decades the reformation of the Siamese body politic in the early 1890s; indeed, the royalty's reformed body natural served as a living—even more, traveling—advertisement of the modernizing mission by which the Siamese ruling elite laid claim to legitimacy in the international arena.

Although most innovations evidently accorded with contemporary Western norms of decorum, the bodily self of the modernizing elite was still negotiated on an ad hoc basis. The approach to betel chewing, a habit that spanned the whole spectrum of Siamese society but whose effect was repugnant to Western decorum, is instructive in this regard. The Belgian Émile Jottrand, struck upon his arrival in Bangkok in 1898 by the blackened teeth of princes and officials, remarked in his diary, "We have come to learn that they only clean them when they want to be photographed, and then we see their admirable white teeth!"[1] Appreciation of the value of photographic portrait as purveyor of an improved image of one's self justified an even stricter, if temporary, disciplining of the body than the new mode of self-presentation modeled on Victorian norms. Jottrand's comment highlights also the critical role played by photography in the construction, rather than the mere projection, of the Siamese monarchy's modern public image, so that reformation of the "clothes-body complex"[2] of the royalty and visual representations of it can be understood as complementary processes.

The Siamese court lacked a tradition of royal portraiture, since depiction of someone's likeness was considered to be a threat to their life spirit. The general taboo on representation extended to the very vision of the royal body: commoners were forbidden to cast their eyes on the king's person at public ceremonies, and he concealed himself behind a curtain or in a dim light when receiving foreign representatives, as described by John Crawfurd in his account of his audience with Rama II in 1822.[3] Aware of the importance that the ruler's image had in the Western symbolics of power, King Mongkut foregrounded new modes in the presentation and representation of the royal self by making himself approachable by foreigners and having portraits done in painting, sculpture, and photography —the newest, yet in a sense most magical, representational medium of all.[4] Such a change of attitude was to be of critical import as printing and photographic techniques improved considerably from the late nineteenth century to the early twentieth. Inventions such as dry-plate photography, which in the mid-1870s replaced the more time-consuming wet-plate process, and the steam press, which made it possible to print engravings in books and magazines, brought about what Daniel Boorstin has termed the "graphic revolution,"[5] one result of which was to give heads of state and other public figures for the first time a global audience. Indeed, the earliest engraving portraits of the Siamese royalty drawn from daguerreotypes appeared in the English-language edition of the travel diaries of French explorer Henri Mouhot (1864); also illustrated were the fictionalized memoirs of Anna Leonowens (1870), the English tutor of King Mongkut's children, and the early travelogue by American businessman Frank Vincent (1873).[6]

This chapter details the transformation in the royalty's bodily and sartorial self accomplished in the latter decades of the nineteenth century and then moves on to examine how the new mode of self-presentation was appraised by foreign observers and given iconic status by European artists; finally, it considers the dissemination of King Chulalongkorn's image via effigy on medals, coins, and stamps, which in the West had long functioned as carriers of the rulers' icon but in Siam were introduced only in the Fifth Reign.

Refashioning Civilization's Accoutrements

As in other Indianized courts of Southeast Asia, self-presentation—from dress to language and demeanor—was a highly refined and ritualized practice in Ayutthaya and early Bangkok. Foreign visitors to Siam, from Simon de la Loubère in the late seventeenth century to John Bowring in the mid-nineteenth, attest to the observance in the central Thai courts of sumptuary regulations prescribing the kind of dress suitable to one's social status and position even though in Siam, unlike in the Malay world, such regulations apparently were not codified.[7] Bowring in particular noted that, while "there is universal passion for jewelry and ornaments of the precious metals," "the law forbids the use of certain garments to any but persons of elevated condition."[8] The principal items of dress reserved for the aristocracy in the late Ayutthaya and early Bangkok periods were silk and cotton cloths with decorative patterns denoting rank (*pha laiyang*), which were produced in India according to the specifications provided by the Siamese court. At the beginning of the Fourth Reign a civilizing regulation was also introduced, whereby those attending royal audiences were required to wear shirts.[9]

Daguerreotypes dating to the mid-1860s show Siamese noblemen still abiding by the fashion, whose origins dated to the time of Southeast Asia's commercial and urban growth from the fifteenth century to the seventeenth, of wearing jackets of Persian or European manufacture over a silk lower garment (*phanung*).[10] The same noblemen sported the customary indigenous hairstyle with close-shaved sides and a tuft of hair on top of the head (*mahatthai*), which women too followed in a slightly less drastic fashion (*phomthat*). An extant daguerreotype and engravings, however, show the Siamese envoys received by Queen Victoria at Windsor Castle (on 19 November 1857) with shoulder-length hair.[11] According to Prince Damrong, it was the first time the *mahatthai* was dispensed with in favor of Western fashion.[12] Damrong's claim is somewhat puzzling, since the Siamese envoys' hairstyle had long been out of fashion in Europe: eighteenth-century visitors to Ayutthaya might have sported it, but certainly not those Westerners who had been coming to Bangkok since the 1820s. The change in hairstyle was, in any case, only a temporary measure: the envoys, Damrong points out, resumed the *mahatthai* after their return home.

The earliest extant daguerreotype image of a Siamese monarch (today in the collection of the Smithsonian Institution, Washington, D.C.) dates to the early 1850s. It shows Mongkut, bareheaded and wearing a simple robe over a shirt, next to Queen Thepsirin (Chulalongkorn's mother), who is wearing an embroidered breast-wrap (*sabai*) over the *phanung* and sporting the *phomthat* hairdo and jewelry. The daguerreotype accompanied the missive and presents sent to U.S. president Franklin Pierce in July 1856 in return for the gifts presented by the American envoy who had negotiated the commercial treaty in Bangkok. Rama IV was aware that foreign heads of state had their portraits circulated for public relations purposes: Bowring saw portraits of the pope, Queen Victoria, the U.S. president, and the Chinese emperor on display in the Grand Palace's audience hall.[13] The portrait of Mongkut and Thepsirin was probably taken by either Bishop Pallegoix or his aide, Father J. B. Larnaudie, who, fulfilling Pallegoix's request, had brought a daguerreotype camera to Bangkok in July 1845, six years after its invention and two years after photographic portraiture had become commercially available in Singapore.[14] The photographer's alertness to the democratic ideals and puritanical ethos of the addressee may explain the absence, in the picture, of crown, regal attire, and other symbols of royalty (Rama IV appears grasping a simple stick), as well as the evocation of monogamy resulting from Mongkut's and Thepsirin's sitting next to each other.

In 1856 the British envoy sent to Bangkok for the ratification of the Bowring Treaty, Harry Parks, presented Rama IV with gifts, including a daguerreotype camera with which more portraits of the royal couple were taken by Luang Wisut Yothamat (Mot Amatyakun), the director of the mint and arguably the first Thai to master photography (his name was even mentioned in a short report, "Photography in Siam," by one Patterson Dubois, published in the September 1865 issue of the *Philadelphia Photographer*).[15] Two daguerreotype portraits probably taken by Luang Wisut— one showing Mongkut in full regal attire, the other him and Queen Thepsirin holding on their laps two of their toddlers—were presented to Queen Victoria in 1857. Separate portraits of Mongkut and Thepsirin were also presented by the Siamese embassy to Pope Pius IX in March 1861 and Napoleon III the following June,[16] during a reception at the Palace of Fontainebleau that was celebrated in a large canvas by the Second Empire's leading artist (and major exponent of Orientalist painting), Jean-Louis Gérome.

In most of his later photographic portraits, King Mongkut appears wearing various dress uniforms with gold-leaf embroidery, similar to those of French admirals and generals, matched by a bicorn hat and the Légion d'Honneur decoration bestowed on him by Napoleon III (figure 1). The "second king" too, Prince Chutamani, was photographed in uniform and bicorn albeit without sash.[17] The Siamese envoys at the British and French courts could not have failed to notice that both Prince Albert and Napoleon III wore not the robes and ermines distinctive of early modern royalty, but dress uniforms. The progressive adoption of military uniform as formal male dress in most European courts over the period 1760–1830 has been interpreted as a signal of their militarization in a revolutionary age and even of the resurgence of the Roman ideal of the ruler as a military leader.[18] But as far as King Mongkut and Prince Chutamani were concerned, their reason for posing in Western-style uniforms arguably lay in the desire to identify with powerful sovereigns whom they knew to wear uniforms for public presentation.[19]

The two earliest portraits of Chulalongkorn, taken when he was about eight years old by an anonymous photographer, show the future modernizer barefoot and with heavy anklets.[20] During his stay in Bangkok late in 1865, pioneer Scot photo-reporter John Thomson (1837–1921) took a series of shots of Chulalongkorn in the royal palace shortly before his tonsure ceremony (figure 2).[21] Photographs of Chulalongkorn as a teenager, and probably also those of his first coronation ceremony in November 1868, were the work of Siam's first commercial photographer, Chit Chitrakani (1830–1892).[22] Under his Christian name, Francis Chit, he had established in 1863 a photographic studio on a floating house near the St. Cruz church, in Thonburi. Chit's business was widely advertised in Bangkok's early English-language papers, the *Bangkok Recorder* and the *Bangkok Summary*. An advertisement, published in January 1865, announced, "He has on hand, for sale, a great variety of photographs of palaces, temples, buildings, scenery and public men of Siam." Chit became, as the logo of his studio proclaimed, the first "appointed photographer to His Majesty the King of Siam" and was eventually granted the title of Luang Akhani Narumit for his services to the royal household.[23]

The major restyling of the elite's clothes-body complex took place during the decade and a half between Chulalongkorn's trip to India in 1872 and his first visit to Europe in 1897. Usages that most evidently jarred with prevailing Western norms, such as the cropped hairstyle and the exposure of body parts, were dispensed with; but Western-style dress did not become the sartorial norm at court. Tellingly, sartorial reform applied to men first, insofar as only the king and princes were exposed to the gaze of foreigners. As David Wyatt writes, with implicit value judgment, of Rama V's first trip abroad in 1871, "The king and regent had no desire to appear in Singapore and Batavia as barbarians."[24] The innovations brought to the royalty's clothes-body complex were longer hair as well as mustaches (in line with contemporary Western fashion), and more, and partly novel, clothes and accessories, such as hose and shoes. Photographs taken on the occasion of Chulalongkorn's visits to Singapore and Java (March–April 1871) and Burma and India (December 1871–March 1872) show the young king and his entourage wearing jackets of various shapes, and even frock coats, over the *phanung* folded to look like knickerbockers (and called in this guise *chongkrabaen*) with hose underneath.[25]

Following Rama V's visit to Calcutta, the owner of a local tailoring establishment moved his business to Bangkok, probably in the hope of increasing his profits in a city where services catering to the Western community had just started developing. This led to the establishment of the Ramsey Firm, on Bamrung Muang Road, which tailored both men's and women's Western-style garments.[26] An insight into the Bangkok tailoring market of the early 1870s is afforded by the autobiography of Prince Wachirayan Warorot (1860–1921), one of Chulalongkorn's half brothers and the future supreme patriarch of the Siamese *sangha*. After two and a half months spent as a novice monk, thirteen-year-old Prince Wachirayan was given by his older brother the considerable sum of four hundred baht to purchase clothes and other personal items. Wachirayan thus found himself considering the options available to someone of his station:

> To have my clothes tailored at a Chinese shop would have been inappropriate for me, as they say. There was plenty of clothing, but I was ashamed to wear it. Tailoring at European stores cost more, so my first inclination was to go there. . . . I was also unhappy about using the Indian shops as they were not as prosperous looking. Furthermore, the Indian shops required cash payment. In the European stores I could make the purchase myself. They granted me credit and I did not have to pay cash . . . I only had to sign my name. When the debt grew large, they would periodically send a bill requesting payment. The goods they sold were well-made and one could display them with pride. One could identify these goods from their beauty, even if the Indian shops had similar goods.[27]

By his own admission, Prince Wachirayan based his consumer choice on the recognizability of the garments' European manufacture as well as the shopkeeper's offer of open credit, both of which at once reflected and reinforced the prince's status and self-image. His comparison with the Indian shops that sold "similar goods" to the European ones is especially telling of the change in the taste and sense of propriety of the royal elite: until only two decades earlier Indian cloth imported for the court's exclusive use had expressed royal status.

*Figure 1. King Mongkut photographed by John Thomson, ca. 1865
(Sakda,* Kasattri lae klong, *p. 78).*

*Figure 2. King Chulalongkorn photographed by John Thomson, ca. 1865
(Sakda, Kasattri lae klong, p. 80).*

Figure 3. King Chulalongkorn photographed by Robert Lenz, early 1890s
*(*Samut phap ratchakan thi 5*, p. 14).*

Figure 4. Royal procession to Wat Bowon Niwet for the kathin *ceremony, late 1890s* (Samut phap ratchakan thi 5, *p. 133).*

Figure 5. Queen Saowapha, photographed by Francis Chit (Sakda, Kasattri lae klong, *p. 145).*

Figure 6. Children of King Chulalongkorn and Queen Sawang (Samut phap ratchakan thi 5, p. 163).

*Figures 7 and 8. King Chulalongkorn and entourage photographed at Lenz's studio, Singapore, 17 May 1896 (*Samat phap ratchakan thi 5, *p. 174;* Sakda, Kasattri lae klong, *p. 90).*

Figure 9. Odoardo Gelli, The Royal Family *(1899). (Bureau of the Royal Thai Household)*

Figure 10. C.-E.-A. Carolus-Duran, Portrait of King Chulalongkorn (1907). (Bureau of the Royal Thai Household)

Photographic sources indicate that a formal court attire came into use in the 1870s. This attire, common to king, princes, and court officials, consisted of a high-collar white jacket with five center-front buttons (called *ratcha pattaen,* "royal pattern") and blue silk *chongkrabaen,* worn with white hose and leather shoes. This court dress, still worn today by court officials on ceremonial occasions such as the Ploughing Ceremony, is a clear example of invented tradition. By having every male at court dressed in the same way, this semiofficial attire arguably fostered in-group identification at the same time that it established the elite's respectability in Western eyes. The sartorial uniformity that the court attire effected around the person of the king also prefigured the administrative unification of the kingdom under a centralized—as well as uniformly clothed—modern bureaucracy later in the reign. By contrast, the move to Westernize military uniforms seems to have been carried out more haphazardly. Custom-made uniforms were imported from India as early as the Third Reign.[28] John Bowring attested, in 1855, to "costumes as multifarious as the tribes and tongues of their wearers."[29] Some thirty years later Carl Bock noticed that the infantry, the marines, and the newer royal page corps wore Western-style uniforms while the older page corps retained colorful jackets and large round hats, and commented, "The Chinese and European army tailors are continually hitting new designs and patterns for the clothing of the army in which . . . there must be an endless number of regiments, if the variety of uniforms is to be taken as a guide."[30] Siamese uniforms in the late 1800s were described as being "imitated from the soldiers of the 1830s, shoulder-belts crossed over their breasts, hats extended upwards."[31] Photographs of Chulalongkorn in dress uniform taken in the 1870s and 1880s show that, over this period, the early elongated jackets were shortened, the patent-leather pumps replaced by laced shoes, and a Prussian-style pointed helmet added to the feathered one; yet the *chongkrabaen,* rather than trousers, still constituted the lower garment.

This hybrid outfit magnified the purely ceremonial function of military dress (figure 3). Judging from photographs, only in the mid-1890s was the *chongkrabaen* replaced by trousers, a change possibly linked to the need to boost the image of the Siamese army after the humiliation suffered at the hands of France in 1893. From the late 1890s onward, Rama V took to wearing dress uniform in place of the royal ceremonial garb both when posing for official portraits and when attending state rituals such as the *kathin,* the visit made to temples for distributing new robes at the end of the Buddhist Lent (figure 4). At least in the eyes of Westerners looking for the exotic, such a change constituted, however, an impoverishment of the ceremony's evocative power. "There is very limited religious aura," wrote Émile Jottrand, "the moment the King appears in an European military uniform with a helmet adorned with feathers."[32]

By that time, the clothes-body complex of female members of the court had too undergone restyling. Two innovations stood out above all: hair was grown longer and combed backward (a hairstyle called *dokkra-thum* or *phomsan*), and the body was entirely clothed, perhaps in accordance with Victorian standards of morality and certainly in contrast with previous usage, which left bare the neck, the right shoulder and arm, the lower left arm, and the feet. The female court costume in use from the early 1880s throughout the end of the Fifth Reign consisted of a high-necked blouse trimmed with lace (*sua lukmai*), with the old *sabai* worn over it as a decorative shoulder-shawl (later replaced by a decorative sash), a silk *chongkra-baen* (often woven in Europe); European stockings, and high-heeled shoes.[33] On special occasions, such as when sitting for a photographic portrait, a woman smartened this basic outfit by wearing a brocaded instead of a plain silk cloth for the *chongkrabaen,* a more elaborately frilled blouse (and, in the early 1900s, the model with large puffed sleeves made popular by Queen Alexandra), and jewels of Western manufacture such as rings, bracelets, necklaces, and occasionally earrings (figure 5). Children were not left out of the reclothing fad. Whereas in the Fourth Reign the royal children still wore two basic garments (a shirt and a *phanung*), Chulalongkorn's own children were clad, at least for portraits, in fashionable clothes—from frocks and velvet suits to miniature uniforms—that emphasized, in spirit if not exactly in style, the aristocratic status they shared with their European "cousins." However, traditional ornaments like bangles and anklets were still appreciated as status symbols and apparently worn over the "civilized" socks (figure 6).

To a certain extent, the refashioning of the royalty's clothes-body complex in the latter decades of the nineteenth century followed the long-established pattern of blending indigenous and exotic clothes to create a distinctive dressing style. Not unlike the garments constitutive of royal status imported from India and other places in Asia up until the mid-nineteenth century, Western-style clothes were integrated into a hybrid ensemble signifying the Siamese elite's connection to a foreign civilization that was instrumental to the definition of their own identity and yet distinct. As a result, different modes of self-presentation—one for the colonial stage, one for the domestic stage, one for the private realm—came into play, allowing for the negotiation of external expectations and personal tastes. One can see a parallel here with the experience of the Bengali elite, who also relied on distinct "sartorial identities" to negotiate the simultaneous needs to appear modern and yet visibly different from the colonial masters; but their attempt was first frustrated by the British elite, who tightened "sartorial correctness" to escape imitation, and then nullified by the independence movement, which polarized Western-style and Indian clothes as symbols of foreign domination and the struggle against it.[34] In Siam, the function of Westernized clothing as a civilization marker was far less contentious: on the one hand, the sartorial legitimacy of the court's eclectic dressing style escaped questioning by European arbiters of taste; on the other hand, the association of Western dress with civilized status went also undisputed, and thus was never impugned as an ideological banner.

What did change in Siam was the way dress helped define elite identity. The arrival of commercial tailors in 1870s Bangkok marked the definite demise of sumptuary regulations because now the sole condition for appropriating Western-style clothes, and the civilized aura emanating from them, was wealth; thus style—in dressing as in other matters of consumption—no longer ensued from status but determined it. The new opportunity was appreciated by urbanites of commoner rank such as Thianwan (1842–1915), a merchant and practicing attorney famous in his day for his progressive ideas as much as for his fashionable clothes. Thianwan prided himself on having been the first Siamese to sport a Western hairstyle, grow a beard, and eschew the habit of betel chewing (which was still practiced at court).[35] In light of his being jailed for seventeen years for contempt of the court during Chulalongkorn's reign, Thianwan's claim to pioneering a civilized body may well have carried a polemical intent. But if being modern clearly entailed very different views on civil liberties for Thianwan and the judiciary that condemned him, both concurred in acknowledging Western-style clothes as an index of *siwilai*.

As a matter of fact, the great majority of Bangkok's inhabitants immortalized in turn-of-the-century photographic vistas appear to be wearing just a baggy shirt and, if women, a shawl (*phahom*) thrown over their *phanung*. Some might have worn even less clothing judging from a decree issued in January 1899, in preparation for the forthcoming visit of Prince Henri of Prussia. The decree, advertised all over Bangkok, established that the *phanung* worn by men should cover the knee (with the exception of those returning from bathing in the canal); that all women, without exception, must have their breasts covered in public; and that children could not go around naked except when bathing (parents would be held responsible for those under fifteen years of age). Fines of one baht for first-time offenders, four baht for second-time offenders, and twelve baht for recidivists were imposed, even though only few were meted out in the first two weeks of the decree's enforcement.[36] Such a royal decree stands as a notable precedent for the cultural mandates (*rattaniyom*) issued by the government of Phibun Songkhram in the early 1940s, which aimed at modernizing the lifestyle of the Siamese by having them stop chewing betel and start wearing Western-style clothes, hats, and especially shoes.[37]

Presenting and Representing the Modern Royal Self

Because of the taboo on the representation of the self, the earliest painted and sculptural portraits of Siamese kings date, like photographic ones, to the Fourth Reign. Since this taboo applied even to the dead, Buddha images dedicated to individual monarchs were executed posthumously in lieu of portraits and statues as late as the Third Reign to allow for their worship, continuing a practice inherited by the Khmer royalty.[38] Although portraits of Western monarchs tend to possess an iconic quality whereby the individual's facial features appear frozen into a mask, the absence of a portraiture tradition in the cultural makeup of the Siamese royalty until the mid-nineteenth century arguably entailed a lesser degree of familiarity with their own image than their European counterparts had. The condition of the Siamese elite thus resembled, even though for entirely different reasons, that of ordinary Europeans who could not afford a painted portrait but, from the 1840s onward, were able to enhance their self-awareness of deportment and facial expressions by posing in front of the camera and then scrutinizing their own printed image.[39] When approached from a perspective informed by Michel Foucault's emphasis on body disciplining as the central objective of the project of modernity, the nineteenth-century "democratization of portraiture" may also be read as a phenomenon that was itself constitutive of modern selves.[40] Despite their different appraisal of the social import of photography, both these approaches help in conceptualizing the Siamese royalty's experience. When compared to the stiff postures and stares of photographic portraits of the Fourth Reign, the poise displayed by members of the court in both formal and informal shots taken in the Fifth Reign points to a growing mastery over self-presentation. Western prevailing representational modes, which prized formality but on occasion also the acting out of affection and intimacy, arguably helped mold the Siamese elite's modern image, too: in the early 1880s, Chulalongkorn had several photographs taken with his small children in tender paternal poses, one of which was rendered into an illustration for Carl Bock's *Temples and Elephants*.[41]

Between May and August 1896, Rama V toured Singapore and Java with a following of twenty-five people. Full Western dress was opted for; and a contemporary witness put the cost of dressing the whole royal retinue, attendants included, at 20,000–30,0000 baht.[42] The three-month visit, the various stages of which were recorded by photography,[43] indeed represented an occasion for rehearsing self-presentation on the colonial stage in preparation for the visit to Europe the following year. The 17 May entry on Rama V's travel diary reads, "Today is Sunday. I would have loved to lie lazily in bed but it was not possible. I had to get up earlier than usual because there are few days left [in Singapore] and we had to sit for the taking of photographs at Mr. Lenz's [studio]. The heat almost made me dizzy when we arrived at 9 o'clock."[44] At Lenz's studio several portraits were taken of the king alone and also with the male members of the entourage, who were immortalized dressed in the typical male outfit of the time (trousers, frock coat, waistcoat, bow tie or necktie, top hat, and walking stick) as well as in the most recent style: a homburg hat, whose vogue had been launched by the Prince of Wales, and a light-colored three-piece suit (figures 7 and 8).

The public reaction to his arrival in Bangka (Java), on 23 May, induced in Chulalongkorn this smug observation: "I was surrounded by the crowd, but they retreated as I proceeded. It is an advantage for me to wear Western dress because the locals fear Europeans."[45] In an outdoor photograph taken at the palace of the sultan of Solo, he and the Siamese monarch appear standing arm in arm—the sultan sporting an embroidered velvet jacket over a sarong and Chulalongkorn, in contrast, in full Western-style dress uniform, white gloves included. As in Europe the following year, in the course of the tour Rama V alternated civilian dress and uniform while Queen Saowapha and a minor consort, who were part of the royal retinue, wore both fashionable morning dresses (complete with hats and fans) and the hybrid court costume of a lace blouse and *chongkrabaen*.

Self-presentation was of course very important in the course of the 1897 tour of Europe, and contemporary reports indicate that it won Rama V and his retinue considerable favor. His presence unsurprisingly aroused public curiosity and received press coverage in all the countries he visited. Although Chulalongkorn's public image as a reforming, if absolutist, monarch keen to civilize Siam had been enjoying currency even before the visit, the press appreciation of his manners, look, and personality boosted further the aura of modernity surrounding the Siamese monarchy. In the Western worldview, beauty has been associated with moral virtue long before the birth of movie stardom early in the twentieth century—for the ancient Greeks, heroes were by definition "handsome and kind." The unitary vision of moral and aesthetic value underlay comments like that of the *National Geographic Magazine,* which in a story on elephant riding at Ayutthaya published in 1907 described Chulalongkorn as "one of the most kindly looking men now gracing a throne," adducing in its support that foreign diplomats called him "the handsomest man in Asia."[46]

Even a cursory review of the press comments in three of the countries visited may suffice to illustrate the overall responses to Rama V's visit. The British public, for reasons having to do with the empire as much as with its special fascination with royalty, was probably the most familiar with the Siamese monarch. An engraving portrait of Chulalongkorn had appeared in the *Graphic* as early as 1872,[47] and most nineteenth-century travelogues on Siam were published in London. The British Press Association announced Rama V's imminent visit, suggesting that he was to take up residence in the neighborhood of London and that his stay was likely "to extend to at least one year."[48] British magazines had engravers depicting the various stages of King Chulalongkorn's visit, including his disembarkation at Spithead, arrival at the London railway station, and luncheon with Queen Victoria at Osborne House. His clothes too, perhaps unsurprisingly, came under the scrutiny of the leading trade journal, *Tailor and Cutter:*

> *It can be seen at a glance that his clothes were made by an English tailor. The King, judged by his dress, looks like a typical English gentleman. Perhaps the silk-facing on the lapel of his neatly-fitting coat is a little too heavy for the real West-End article, and, in one or two small matters of details, criticism might be justifiable; but taking the dress as a whole, it does credit both to His Majesty's good taste and to the tailor who produced the garment.*[49]

By the time of his visit, Rama V was well known as being a fervent anglophile: in no other country touched by the 1897 tour did he spend so long a time as in England, where eleven of his sons were studying at that time together with several noblemen.[50] Yet the *Tailor and Cutter* article did more than endorse the established view of Chulalongkorn as an educated, well mannered and even handsome Oriental sovereign: it granted him the anthropological status of "same" ("a typical English gentleman") by virtue of his clothes while at the same time questioning his taste, and thus implicitly his credentials as world-class royalty, through the punctilious scrutiny of sartorial details ("too heavy for the *real* West-End article"), the true mark of social distinction. Ten years later, again in Britain, the conferral of the honorary doctorate by the University of Cambridge gave Rama V the opportunity of cladding himself with the ultimate accoutrement of Western civilization—the academic gown—in which he was immortalized in a full-length portrait taken at the studio of W. and D. Downey, "court photographers."

France was the only European country that had notable historical precedents in diplomatic relations with Siam: the exchange of embassies in 1685–1687, at the time of the reigns of Louis XIV and Narai. But because of the tense state of relations between the two countries in the 1890s, the French press' comments predictably had an ambivalent tone. An article in the magazine *Les Annales,* published a few months before his visit, described Rama V as "very intelligent and learned . . . a polyglot equally at ease in speaking French and English," but then concluded on a gruesome note by contrasting his advocacy of reforms to the punishment purportedly meted out to an unfaithful woman of his harem: death by starvation.[51] Chulalongkorn's self-presentation upon his arrival in Paris, on 11 September, somehow mirrored these inimical attitudes. Not only did he show up in dress uniform, as on most public occasions in the course of the tour, but he also responded to the crowd's ovation with a military salute, a gesture whose significance was not missed to local reporters.[52] The French press was in any case prodigal of attention: the illustrated supplement of *Le Petit Journal,* which already at the time of the Franco-Siamese incident of 1893 had featured Rama V and Queen Sawang on its cover, came out with an idealized engraving portrait of the king.[53] Popular magazines also provided graphic illustration of Chulalongkorn's visits to Napoleon's tomb and the recently built Eiffel Tower. It is worth noting that, either because of courtesy or representational conventions, the illustrations in French and British periodicals minimized the considerable height disparity between Rama V and most of his hosts, even though it could have been easily exploited as a visual metaphor of Siam's military inferiority.

As for the Italian press, the Venice newspaper *La Gazzetta di Venezia,* after noting that everybody in the king's entourage wore Western dress except the two aides-de-camp, went on to describe Rama V as "an extremely cultured man, also in the European sense, full of intelligence and political skill." Florence's paper, *La Nazione,* praised the king's passionate conversation about art and his "agreeable and sharp observations particularly in front of paintings of women," remarking that, on hearing the name of Pauline Borghese, "the king, who is very knowledgeable about European history, wittily touched on episodes in Bonaparte's life." Even the press' unavoidable dash of Orientalist fantasy, a harem housing "800 odalisques," was accommodated to suit Chulalongkorn's gentlemanly image: "The king has not stepped in it for years as he is in love with Queen Sawang."[54] A correspondent from Florence for the *Journal de Genève* captured an important aspect of the visit, the patronizing of artists' and photographers' studios: "For the ten days that he [Rama V] has been with us, his chief desire seems to have been to have himself painted, and represented in sculpture, and also photographed . . . and not content with so many portraits and busts, as he is a model husband, he has had portraits painted and busts sculptured of his wife. Here people like him very much, because he is simple, cordial, in a word *alla mano* as we say."[55] Indeed, besides the encounter with foreign royalty and heads of state, the European tour also gave Chulalongkorn the opportunity to experience the "embrace of the crowd," not yet a feature of the Siamese theater of power.

The most renowned of the Florentine artists patronized by Rama V was Odoardo Gelli (1852–1933), the painter of the group portrait *The Royal Family* (figure 9). Gelli had spent three years as a court painter in Vienna and had to his credit "fifteen portraits of various kings," as Chulalongkorn pointed out in a letter to Queen Saowapha. This letter indicates that Gelli was given the commission for the group portrait before Rama V's visit to Florence, as at that time he had apparently already started working on it.[56] *The Royal Family,* which since its delivery has hung in the Chakri Throne Hall's private room, portrays Chulalongkorn and Saowapha with their five sons (from youngest to oldest): Prajadhipok (the future Rama VII), Chuthathut, Atsadang, Chakrabongse, and Crown Prince Vajiravudh. At the center of the composition, sitting on gilded armchairs, are the king and the queen: he in the dress uniform of an army field marshal, with a plumed helmet on his right knee, she in a composite costume combining a puffed-sleeve blouse with a long silk brocade skirt (reminiscent of the tubular *phanung* of northern Siam, the *phasin*). The two oldest royal sons, Chakrabongse and Vajiravudh (standing alone between his parents), are clad in dress uniform; the youngest wear, instead, the sailor suit then fashionable in Europe.

Following a practice common even among the best portrait artists by the 1870s,[57] Gelli relied on a photograph taken, arguably for this purpose, at the Lenz studio in Bangkok.[58] Initially based in Singapore, the German Robert Lenz had opened a branch in Bangkok early in 1894, following the lead of fellow countrymen (G. R. Lambert, H. Schüren, W. K. Loftus, F. Schumann) whose photographic studios catered to both the foreign and the Siamese elites since the 1880s.[59] The Lenz studio became the royalty's favorite: most of the portraits of Rama V and Queen Saowapha after 1894 were taken there. Gelli followed closely the arrangement and the postures in the photograph—notably, Queen Saowapha's curious pose, looking obliquely away from the viewer's gaze, is drawn from it—but he substituted Chakrabongse and Vajiravudh for their half brothers, Chiraprawati and Sommatiwong, who had posed in their stead at the Lenz studio,[60] and restyled the setting. The studio props and painted background were replaced by a stately interior, presumably that of the Chakri Throne Hall, whose décor includes a classical marble statue on pedestal, a column-framed doorway with hanging curtain, stands for vases at each side of the doorway, parts of a sofa, and a framed painting; the lion skin lying in the foreground, however, was apparently inspired by the tiger skin prop in the photograph.

Gelli's lifeless rendering of his subjects emphasizes, by contrast, the things surrounding them, which are also exalted by the oil medium, "especially good at rendering the high-grade and expensive materials which are part and parcel of our ideas about quality: the furs, silk brocades, and marbles."[61] Significantly, the setting of the painting is entirely Western in taste but for the queen's hybrid costume, itself the product of the recent refashioning of court dress (Gelli, unhappy with the way her garments looked in the photograph he was relying upon, asked Rama V to have them sent from Bangkok).[62] But if, iconographically speaking, *The Royal Family* fits unimaginatively the genre of celebrative portraiture, can the same be said of its representational function? Portraiture of European royalty, often reproduced for circulation in engravings and later prints, partook of the "domestication of majesty" that started in the eighteenth century and greatly accelerated after the end of the Napoleonic Wars.[63] By shedding the Olympian image of ancien régime dynasties in favor of a domestic ethos, the royal houses of Europe paid symbolic tribute to the family values of the bourgeoisie, to which they increasingly owed their legitimation and survival after 1815.

In fact, as Simon Schama caustically comments, "the nineteenth-century royal families were . . . the very opposite of the image they projected," carrying on with arranged marriages for dynastic reasons in patent contrast to the modern values of individual freedom and romantic love.[64] As for the Siamese royal family, it goes without saying that the familial cliché invoked by Gelli's painting—father, mother, and five sons—was at odds with the actual situation: Chulalongkorn had dozens of wives, the three highest in rank (Sunantha, Sawang, and Saowapha) being also his own half sisters,[65] and fathered seventy-six children. Gelli's painting visualizes the dynastically relevant nucleus of this extended royal household. Following the death in 1895 of Crown Prince Wachirunhit, the son of Queen Sawang, the line of succession had switched to the oldest son of Queen Saowapha, whose special status as mother to the heir to the throne was signified by a new title (*somdet phraparama ratchani*) and stressed by her designation as regent during the king's visit to Europe in 1897. In other words, Schama's interpretive framework does not make much sense in this case: not only was the Bangkok middle class politically uninfluential at the turn of the century; it too widely practiced polygamy. Therefore, the need for the Siamese monarchy to pay lip service to a bourgeois family ethos simply did not exist. Indeed, unlike domestic images of European royalty, *The Royal Family* was not rendered into engraving for circulation in prints.

If a demotic image of the royal family for the Siamese public's sake was not demanded, the reason for commissioning such a painting must be seen in Rama V's self-image as a modern monarch and a person of good taste. Having a group portrait done by an artist famous for his royal patrons represented one of those acts of consumption whereby the Bangkok royalty identified with their Western counterparts. Ten years later, another "establishment" artist, the Frenchman C.-E.-A. Carolus-Duran (1838–1917), was commissioned to paint a full-length portrait of Rama V (figure 10).[66] Sketched at a friend's studio while the king was holidaying in Sanremo in May 1907, the portrait was finished by Carolus-Duran in Paris and exhibited for a week, with the patron's approval, at that summer's Salon before being shipped. Fortuitously enough, the public exhibition of Rama V's portrait followed the ratification of the Franco-Siamese settlement over the disputed Indochinese border, a copy of which was handed to King Chulalongkorn in Paris in July 1907.[67] Given Carolus-Duran's close connections to the Third Republic's political establishment, it is unlikely that the exhibition and the ratifications were coincidental. The French were too adroit at using art for political ends to miss a public-relations exploit that spread the luster of their national genius on their newfound "friend," leaving him to pay the bill.

The Image of Chulalongkorn in Siamese Eyes

So far, this examination of the new modes of presentation and representation of the royal self has privileged the gaze of the selected domestic audience, which included high-ranking officials and the Bangkok foreign community, as well as the European public. But what image did Rama V's ordinary subjects have of him?

Writing about the symbolics of the French monarchy, Anne-Marie Lecoq distinguishes between a "symbolic image" of the sovereign, expressed by emblems and heraldic figurations, and a "historic image," featured in portraits and effigies.[68] The first flat coins minted in Siam in the Fourth Reign were engraved with royal emblems, such as the *chakr-tri* (symbol of the dynasty) and the conical crown. Chulalongkorn was the first Siamese sovereign to have his likeness represented on commemorative medals (1871),[69] coins (late 1870s),[70] and postage stamps (1883).[71] The different effigies on subsequent coin and especially stamp issues (five between 1883 and 1910) show him growing into maturity with reliable accuracy unlike, for instance, the perennial youthful image of Queen Victoria's effigies. Chulalongkorn's effigy and insignia, imprinted on luxury objects made in Europe for court use and as gifts for foreign guests and authorities,[72] were also by the early 1900s engraved and printed on cheap goods (cups, spoons, pens), which were reportedly manufactured in Germany.[73]

Given the long-observed taboo on the vision and representation of the royal self, one might assume that the initial response to the king's effigy on coins and stamps was one of bewilderment. Hypothetically, these carriers of the king's historic image placed the user in a dilemma, since their handling would contravene the taboo of the approachability of the royal body (even if in iconic form). In fact, there is no reason why the iconic value of coins and stamps should have proven inhibiting to the Siamese people; neither should one exaggerate their importance in making Chulalongkorn's image known to the population at large, since even in the Fifth Reign's later years the baht hardly circulated outside the Central Plains region, and the diffusion of postage stamps outside Bangkok must have also been very limited. Though somewhat legendary, the incognito visits made by Rama V to the countryside during the last decade of his reign indicate that his face was relatively unknown.[74] People in Bangkok had of course more chances of having a glimpse of King Chulalongkorn's person, particularly in the reign's last decade, on occasions such as his daily outings in landau from the Grand Palace to the construction site of the Dusit Palace and the annual fair held since 1899 at Wat Benchama Bophit, where the king and the members of the royalty ran stalls.[75] For the fortieth anniversary of his reign, in November 1908, Rama V attended public celebrations for a whole week including the unveiling of his equestrian statue (whose genesis is detailed in chapter 4), which made his image a perennial feature of the cityscape.

In the last three or four years of the Fifth Reign, another carrier of the king's historic image became available in Bangkok: picture postcards. The most ephemeral of objects, postcards were probably the most far-reaching of the preelectric mass media. Although picture postcards, a German invention, had first become popular as a result of the Franco-Prussian War, they surged to a mass fad in the two decades leading to World War I.[76] Picture postcards of Siam were printed in Europe and featured the typical range of subjects: landscapes, buildings, ceremonies and local customs, human types and beauties, as well as the royalty.[77] It is possible to see from extant specimens that postcards carrying portraits of Chulalongkorn and Vajiravudh were sent from Siam by travelers and foreign residents, as well as relatives of the few Thais then living abroad.[78] But besides popularizing the images of the Siamese royals, picture postcards promoted the demolition of the taboo concerning the king's physical and iconic body; some senders penned their messages all over the postcard's pictured side (the other side was reserved for the address by International Postal Union regulations), running the risk of "defacing" royal images like unwilling iconoclasts.

The European manufacture of the whole gamut of visual representations of Rama V—equestrian statue included—support from a different perspective Tambiah's argument that the paradoxical effect of Western economic interests in Siam was to provide the throne with the financial resources it needed to fend off the imperialist threat and assert its political authority.[79] Western representational practices and printing technology can be judged to have been equally crucial in establishing King Chulalongkorn's historic image as the preeminent symbol of the modern Siamese state, first in the eyes of Westerners and eventually in those of his subjects as well. But as European rulers knew only too well, visual representations of the sovereign could be in the service of both royalist propaganda and its opponents'. By the early 1920s, Rama VI had been made into an object of public scorn in various Bangkok publications by caricatures that ridiculed him as a plump and balding boy.[80] Not even remotely as photogenic as his father was, Vajiravudh generally had his portraits taken in some variety of dress uniform or even in stage costumes: unable, in any case, to play the king's role for real.

Part II
SPACES

Chapter 3

Suburban Playgrounds

The refashioning of the Siamese monarchy's image could not leave out the private space in which the court's daily life unfolded and the urban landscape in which royal authority was manifested by means of layout and architecture as well as pageantry. During most of the Fifth Reign, however, new buildings representative of the court's Westernized taste were accommodated within the walled compound of the Grand Palace, built by the founder of the dynasty and added to by the following four sovereigns. It was only in the last decade of the nineteenth century, when the political survival of the dynasty had apparently been secured and the royal princes started coming back from Europe, that the court moved out of the Grand Palace to a new district built in Bangkok's northern outskirts. The residential complex of Suan Dusit (Celestial garden)—Dusit Park in the Anglicized form then used by the press—was first linked by a new thoroughfare to the Grand Palace, where state ceremonies continued to be conducted, and later endowed with a monumental urban tableau befitting the modernizing monarchy's ceremonial and representational needs. The progressive expansion of the Dusit residential complex was reflected by the changes in its denomination: first designated as *wang* (any princely palace), then *phraratchawang* (royal palace), Dusit had the prefix *suan* dropped at the completion of the Ananta Samakhom Throne Hall and its official name established as Phraratchawang Dusit.[1]

Because of their concomitant foundation in 1782, the histories of the Chakri dynasty and the city of Bangkok are often subsumed in a single narrative, at least until the overthrow of the absolute monarchy in 1932. For example, in her recent glossy book architectural historian Naengnoi Saksi argues that the construction of royal palaces in the period from the First Reign to the Sixth provided "an impetus to urban expansion."[2] The early stage of Bangkok's modernization in particular tends to be construed as a subplot in the narrative of progress effected by the throne. With the extension of the city's road network in the last quarter of the nineteenth century, novel means of conveyance came into use, including carriages; rick-shaws (imported from Swatow, in southern China, in the early 1870s); a horse-powered tram, instituted in 1888 and electrified in 1894; and, from the outset of the twentieth century, automobiles, owned largely by the aris-tocracy.[3] The dynasty associated itself with urban modernization by means of the "birthday bridge" program, initiated by Rama V in 1894 and car-ried on by Rama VI until 1916, whereby the king donated money on his birthday for the construction of ferroconcrete bridges both to replace wooden structures and to provide new crossings. Overall, sixteen bridges were built under this scheme.[4]

The modernization of Bangkok during this period might appear to be part of the global trend of embellishment and monumentalization of urban spaces that was carried out on an unprecedented scale in the half century preceding World War I both in Europe and in its colonies.[5] In the wake of Prefect Haussmann's rebuilding of Paris in the 1850s, many muni-cipal administrations undertook renewal projects to solve the hygienic and social shortcomings that in the first half of the nineteenth century had pre-cipitated periodical outbursts of urban plagues and urban revolts.[6] Nation-alism was not extraneous to this global trend of urban renewal. Both the capital cities of newly unified nations, such as Rome and Berlin, and archi-tecturally modest imperial metropoles such as London were endowed with monumental architecture signifying national pride and world-power status. By the end of the nineteenth century, similar concerns increasingly shaped the spatial arrangement and built environment of the Western quarters of colonial capitals as well, which were characterized by the separation of place of work and place of residence and the presence of social spaces such as the church, the club, the library, the theater, the race course, and occasion-ally the museum.[7] While in Europe the main beneficiary of such urban renewal schemes was the upper middle class, whose voting power now determined the sort of governments, in the colonies it came down to the considerablly smaller elite of colonial administrators, professional expatri-ates, and the indigenous well-to-do.

The turn-of-the-century modernization of Bangkok had more in common with urban development in colonial than in metropolitan centers. The dynamics of public debate and concerted decision making—involving town councils, professional bodies, and government agencies—that was common in European cities was entirely absent in Bangkok.[8] In spite of being carried out by the Public Works Department, the planning and construction of the Dusit district benefited only the royal elite; public spaces where commoners could congregate and enjoy themselves were notably absent. Instead, the walls and wrought-iron fences of the suburban residences, which even today mark off much of its area, asserted the royalty's continuing control of the land through conspicuous ownership of it. Within those walls and fences lay the playgrounds where the royal elite rehearsed their modern selves in front of the camera's recording eye.[9]

Urban Layout and Palatial Architecture from the First Reign to the Early Fifth

The contrast between the concentric layout of Bangkok's royal citadel, situated in the inner loop of the Chao Phraya River, and the street grid framing the Dusit district, north of it, is immediately obvious by glancing at a map of the city. The walled royal palace stands in the middle of an urban settlement—Rattanakosin City—that encloses within the city walls and a canal an area of little more than four square kilometers (2,589 *rai*).[10] According to Robert Heine-Geldern, the layout and architecture of royal seats were central instruments of statecraft in the Indic polities of Southeast Asia, where the palace replicated in the realm the pivotal place of Mount Meru, the gods' abode, in the Brahmanic cosmology.[11] In other words, the royal palace articulated in the physical space the sovereign's connection to the sacred source of power. Dusit's fenced villas and built-for-cars rectilinear streets, on the other hand, signaled the Bangkok royalty's affiliation to the civilizational sphere of the Victorian ecumene. This suggestion that Western contemporary models of urban layout and architecture constitutive of high status replaced indigenous patterns informed by Indic cosmology is, however, in need of some qualification.

Practical and strategic considerations are invoked to account for the construction of the Chakri's citadel on the eastern bank of the Chao Phraya River—Bangkok—rather than its western bank—Thonburi—where King Taksin (r. 1767–1782) had established his headquarters after the fall of Ayutthaya. The morphology of the Bangkok bank allowed for a more easily defendable artificial island to be created by digging a canal at the river's bend, in imitation of Ayutthaya; moreover, in Thonburi King Taksin had only a timber residence built on a narrow plot of land between two monasteries that hindered further expansion. Although royal demands could justify the removal of a *wat,* relocation of Bangkok's Chinese settlement to furnish a suitable area for the new royal citadel might have been a preferable option.[12] The symbolic significance of building a palace *ex novo* for the newly proclaimed Chakri dynasty must not be discounted either, especially because the stigma of usurpation might have hovered over its founder, who had King Taksin deposed and later executed on grounds of his presumed madness.[13]

Urban layout was deployed in Rattanakosin City as a tool of political legitimation: by articulating spatially the claim to continuity between the Chakri's city and Ayutthaya, Taksin's fifteen-year reign was reduced to a dynastic interlude. In the *Dynastic Chronicles of the First Reign,* the similarity in the layouts of Rattanakosin City and Ayutthaya is evoked in the following terms: "The king wanted the Mahanak canal to be a place where the people of the capital could go boating and singing and reciting poems during the high-water season, just like the custom observed at the former capital."[14] Given that the composition of the *Dynastic Chronicles* actually dates to 1869, what this passage reveals is the new antiquarian sensibility of the Siamese royal elite at that time. In fact, the layout of Rattanakosin City showed an obvious lack of concern for the correct arrangement of the Indic ritual space in which to carry into effect the performative form of government that Clifford Geertz has famously termed (with reference to Bali) the "theater state."[15] In Rattanakosin City the Palace of the Rear, so named because of its ideal location vis-à-vis the royal palace, was actually built on the Thonburi bank. Lack of regard for the implementation of Indic town planning suggests the loss of perceived performative power, or intelligibility, of Indic political semiotics in the traumatic transition from the Ayutthaya to the Bangkok kingdom—a hypothesis supported by the rectification of seemingly unorthodox Brahmanic rites early in the First Reign.[16]

Architectural evidence too suggests that, by the beginning of the Fourth Reign, the Brahmanic notion of interconnectedness of cosmos, realm, and royal authority was on the wane. King Mongkut built conspicuously both in Bangkok and the provinces as he traveled increasingly outside Rattanakosin City to "cast the regal look" (*thot phranet*) upon places other than the closed world of the royal citadel. In Bangkok he had two detached palaces started: one, Saranrom, opposite the Grand Palace; the other in the Sapathum area, east of Rattanakosin City.[17] In Phetchaburi province, stronghold of his political sponsor, the Bunnak family, Rama IV

had a retreat with an observatory built on top of a hill, Phra Nakhon Khiri;
in Nakhon Pathom he had dwellings erected following the restoration of
the local Buddhist shrine; in Ayutthaya he reconstructed the old Palace of
the Front and identified the site of the vanished palace at Bang Pa-in; and
in Lopburi he started the construction of yet another palace, later inter-
rupted because of his dislike of the province's climate.[18]

Commercial expansion was in fact a more decisive factor than royal
initiatives in transforming Bangkok's urban fabric following the establishment of trade relations with Western countries. The traffic of steamers
and the installation of telegraph lines (1861) and gas lighting (1866) pro-
gressively brought Bangkok into the orbit of global modernity.[19] By the
end of the Fourth Reign, three areas had become established west and
southwest of Rattanakosin City: the commercial hub, housing the ethnic
segments of the populace (mainly Chinese but also Indians and Malays);
the port area, on the lower course of the Chao Phraya River; and the
downtown district, where European consulates and factories were located.[20]
Bangkok's first thoroughfare, significantly named Thanon Charoen Krung
(Road that expands/enriches the city) and more prosaically dubbed New
Road in English, was built in the early 1860s in response to the demands
of the Western community for a road suitable for carriages linking the
consular and commercial districts to the Grand Palace. The *Dynastic Chronicles of the Fourth Reign* record the holding of a festival in 1864 to celebrate
the completion of a number of new roads and bridges.[21] Two years later
D. B. Bradley, the American Presbyterian missionary who started Bangkok's first press, was still pontificating from the pages of his journal, the
Bangkok Recorder, about the need for better roads if the Siamese capital was
to join the ranks of the capitals of the "civilized world."[22] In the 1860s
perpendicular streets flanked by blocks of two-story edifices created a
novel cityscape that was promptly represented in the mural paintings by
the period's leading artist, Khrua In Khong.[23]

The style of palatial architecture, the other signifier of royal authority in the urban landscape, underwent a significant redefinition too in
the period from the First to the Fourth Reign. In Siam, as in the rest of
Southeast Asia, brickwork was a mark of exclusivity since domestic architecture was made of wood (it was not so much size and design but the
extent and refinement of decoration that distinguished commoner and
aristocratic houses).[24] Apart from bricks as building material, traditional
royal and religious buildings shared design features (e.g., the junk-shaped

base of both Wat Na Phra Men's ordination hall and the vanished Sanphet Prasat Throne Hall in Ayutthaya) as well as decorative motifs, such as the carved figures inspired by Indic mythological characters on roofs, lintels, and door and window frames. Even the *prasat,* the soaring structure characteristic of royal buildings as well as royal objects (e.g., the conical crown and the palanquin), was derived from the religious architecture of the Khmer. The affinity of palace and temple extended to the building interiors: both were decorated with mural paintings and furnished sparsely with lacquer cabinets and gilded furniture.

The reliance on Ayutthayan architecture as the model for Rattanakosin City's earliest buildings had a very physical dimension that has been obscured by the overemphasis laid on the Burmese sack of Ayutthaya in Thailand's national historical narrative: its burned-down edifices were in fact cannibalized to provide building materials for the new royal city under construction.[25] With the influx in the Second and especially the Third Reign of masons and decorators as well as building materials from China (part of the overall revival of trading and cultural relations with the Middle Kingdom at that time), the few wooden structures originally built in the Grand Palace were replaced by masonry (*tuk*). Structural and decorative elements typical of Chinese architecture (such as tiled roofs, stone gateways, and rock statues) were incorporated in the buildings in the Grand Palace compound; its inner court (*fainai*), reserved for the female courtiers, was even embellished with the Chinese-style Siwalai Garden.[26]

In the Fourth Reign royal architecture became even more eclectic as Western styles came into prominence. The original Ananta Samakhom Throne Hall, built in 1854–1859 for the reception of the increasingly frequent embassies from Western countries and demolished some fifty years later, featured an external canopy and a central colonnade and crystal chandeliers in the interior. Eclecticism characterizes also the first of the several palaces built in the Fifth Reign, the Chakri Throne Hall (Chakri Maha Prasat), whose foundation stone was laid on 9 May 1876. The throne hall, built to celebrate the centennial of the dynasty, had halls for ceremonial and representational purpose on the ground floor and living quarters on the upper floors. The building was designed by a Singapore-based British architect, John Clunish, in that blend of neoclassical and Italianate styles typical of mid-Victorian colonial architecture—except for the spire roof, which made the Chakri Throne Hall stylistically awkward yet visually unique: the British magazine *The Graphic* published an engraving illustration of it shortly after its completion, in 1880.[27]

According to an unsubstantiated account, the spire roof was imposed by Chaophraya Si Suriyawong (head of the powerful Bunnak family, regent during Rama V's minority, and supervisor of royal building schemes since the Fourth Reign) against Chulalongkorn's wishes. Based on this account, the Chakri Throne Hall is sometimes presented as the material embodiment of the internal power struggle between the king's modernizing party (Young Siam) and the older generation of nobles and court officials.[28] No doubt, the Chakri Throne Hall was intended as a showpiece of the modernizing spirit bandied about by the young Rama V to strengthen his stand vis-à-vis the other factions of the court in the eyes of European observers; but to see its spire roof as an outcome of this internal power struggle is perhaps too far-fetched. Hybrid designs were not uncommon with European architects active in Asia, who followed the nineteenth-century vogue of eclecticism. For example, at the competition held in 1888 for the Imperial Diet's building in Tokyo, Hermann Ende submitted the plan of a German Baroque-style edifice capped by a timber roof.[29] Ende's plan was rejected on the grounds that its hybrid style would compromise the building's symbolic import—the modernization of Japan's political system via the promulgation of a constitution and the creation of the Diet in the years 1889–1890.

Even after the completion of the Chakri Throne Hall, the Grand Palace continued to look very much like a work in progress. Poor building maintenance was underpinned by the belief that only building, not restoring, accrued merit; consequently, buildings often not older than twenty or thirty years were demolished and replaced by new ones.[30] More Western-style buildings were erected in the outer court in the 1880s to house the ministries of the Royal Household, Treasury, Interior, and Foreign Affairs; outside the palatial compound the edifices of the ministries of Justice and War, the Cadet Academy, and the Wachirayan Library were built. The creation of the Western-style title of heir to the throne provided additional cause for the transplant of exotic architectural styles in the Bangkok landscape. A Tudor-revival palace was built in the Sapathum area for Crown Prince Wachirunhit; following his premature death in 1895 and the designation as heir of Vajiravudh, construction of the massive French Renaissance–style Borom Phiman began inside the Grand Palace compound in 1897.

Given the absence of a government agency responsible for public works during the first two decades of the Fifth Reign, foreign contractors carried out large building projects in the 1870s and 1880s. "All these buildings, constructed by German and Italian companies," commented Charles

Buls on a visit to Bangkok in 1900, "are in poor European style, heavy and uniform. They show their bricks and their cement. The joints are traced into the cement and then badly imitate large stones [rustication] under their yellow whitewash."[31] By the turn of the century, Italian and German draughtsmen and architects were instrumental in giving shape, now as government employees, to the royalty's desire for a residential architecture that would adequately reflect as well as project their self-image as civilized individuals.

Building the Modernizing Elite's Bangkok

First established at the end of 1889, the Department of Public Works (*krom yothathikan*) was upgraded into a ministry (*krasuang yothathikan*) at the launching of the cabinet council in April 1892. The Ministry of Public Works initially included five departments: General Affairs, Controller, Post and Telegraph, Railways, and Public Works. Head of the department, and then minister until March 1893, was Prince Naritsara (Narit) Nuwatti-wong (1863–1947),[32] the one brother of Rama V with artistic inclinations. During the following six and a half years the ministry was led by Krommun Sanphasitthi, Kromkhun Phithayaphap, and Phraya Thewerong. In September 1899, Prince Narit (who in the meantime had led the ministries of the Treasury, War, and Justice) returned to head the Ministry of Public Works until 1905, when he moved to the Ministry of the Royal Household.[33] The office was temporarily entrusted to Phraya Suriya, who was replaced, in July 1906, by Phraya Sukhum.

Phraya Sukhum (later Chaophraya Yomarat, 1862–1938) was a major state notable from the Fifth to the Seventh Reigns; his brilliant career in the bureaucracy started with his position as teacher at the Suan Kulap court school and culminated with his term as minister of the interior (1922–1926).[34] He was acting minister of public works until the end of 1907, when he and Prince Naret Worarit, who had been minister of municipal government since 1892, had their positions swapped.[35] Until then, the Ministry of Municipal Government (*krasuang nakhonban*) had administered the Krung Thep province (i.e., Rattanakosin City and surrounding districts); following the appointment of Phraya Sukhum, the Ministry of Municipal Government also came to control the Sanitary Department (*krom sukhaphiban*), which had been established around 1894 under the authority of the Ministry of Agriculture. Under the new arrangement put in place in 1907, the Sanitary Department was responsible for the construction of roads and bridges in Bangkok while the Public Works Department executed royal projects and public works in the provinces. In 1912, the Ministry of Public Works was restructured and its name changed to Ministry of Communications (*krasuang khommakon*).

Like other departments in the Siamese administration, the Ministry of Public Works employed a considerable number of Westerners. The Public Works Department in particular had a sizeable Italian presence, numbering about twenty toward the end of the Fifth Reign. The first to join was engineer Carlo Allegri (1862–1938), a native of Milan, who arrived in Bangkok in 1889 to work for Grassi Brothers, one of the foreign building firms active in Siam. The following year Allegri joined the newly established Public Works Department in the capacity of assistant to the engineer in chief, the Briton E. F. W. Wilkinson, whom Allegri eventually replaced in 1892.[36] In his role of head of the department, Allegri was involved in the realization of all major building projects of the later half of the Fifth Reign. With the transformation of the Ministry of Public Works into the Ministry of Communications, Allegri had his position reduced to adviser to the Ananta Samakhom Throne Hall project, and at its completion in 1916, he was pensioned and returned to Italy.[37] Besides Allegri, the two longest-serving employees of the Public Works Department were Emilio G. Gollo, who joined in 1899 as head of the Engineering Division to become deputy engineer in chief; and Mario Tamagno, who was head of the Architectural Division from 1901 to 1925.[38]

These long-forgotten figures of Italian expatriates in turn-of-the-century Bangkok have recently been brought to attention by an ostensibly celebrative publication.[39] The claim that art-knowledgeable Rama V hired Italian architects and engineers out of admiration for their technical and artistic genius while they, in turn, attempted to transplant their heritage into a tropical kingdom, panders of course to nationalist pride on both sides. In fact, Siam was one of several countries where, because of their professional reputation and ideal descent from the Renaissance masters, Italian artists and architects were employed by modernizing elites with an urgent need for a Westernized public image. Such was the case of the architectural transformation of Moscow and St. Petersburg into "European" capital cities in the late eighteenth and early nineteenth centuries, and the introduction of formal art training in Japan in the early Meiji era.[40]

Yet in the case of Siam, nothing clearly indicates that the decision to hire Italian draughtsmen, painters, and decorators responded to a precise design. With the increase in job opportunities resulting from the several projects launched in the late 1890s, Allegri's position as engineer in chief might well have been crucial for the expansion of the Public Work Department's Italian contingent. There were also some German employees in the department, including Karl S. Döhring (1879–1941), who designed for Rama V Banpun Palace, in Phetchaburi province (built posthumously); for Prince Damrong, Woradit Palace, in Bangkok; and the Thai-style Chulalongkorn University building (later the Faculty of Arts).[41] Cabinet documents show, alas, the Siamese authorities' dissatisfaction with the Public Works Department's activity. Phraya Suriya, in a report written during his short period as acting minister (1905–1906), stigmatized the disparity between the building plans drawn by the foreign draughtsmen and their execution by local workers, the foreigners' lack of practical experience and their reliance on Chinese masons, the meager productivity and widespread malpractice among officers and suppliers, and even Allegri's inadequacy when it came to the finish and decoration of buildings, allegedly far below European standards. Similar complaints were noted in the report drawn by the next minister, Phraya Sukhum;[42] on the other hand, financial grievances by some employees are also documented.[43]

Thai scholars often propound that the sojourn in Europe in 1897 aroused in Chulalongkorn the desire for a suburban palace. His stay in the country residences of European royalty would have made him appreciate a lifestyle in which courtly magnificence was paired with natural surroundings. The ability to accommodate foreign guests in a suitable style is also mentioned as a further motivation. Dissatisfaction with the Grand Palace as a place of residence was also probably increased by the dominant medical theories, which postulated a causal connection between crowded environments and the spread of infections. The sewage and refuse generated in the Grand Palace had to be disposed of manually, and, given that the inner court alone housed some three thousand women toward the end of the nineteenth century,[44] hygienic conditions must have been a major concern.

The clearance of the area destined for the king's new suburban residence began in February 1899, and subsequently temporary dwellings were built. A year later Rama V started spending his evenings at Dusit Park, which he reached from the Grand Palace riding in his landau.[45] In May 1901 it was decided to relocate there a teak building that lay unfinished on Sichang Island, in the Gulf of Siam. The wooden mansion, re-built and enlarged to house the extended royal household under the super-vision of the chief court carpenter, Kon Hongsakun, was also equipped with the latest domestic accoutrements: electricity and running water. Following its inauguration on 27 March 1902, the mansion, named Wimanmek, became the king's residence. But while the water and sewage systems provided Dusit Park's occupants with modern hygienic standards, landscaping, pathways, decorative canals, and bridges were utilized to create the customary spatial arrangement of royal palaces: outer court, middle court, and inner court (to which only the king and the women had access). The inner court was extended in the reign's final years with the addition of a "garden harem" to house Rama V's several daughters and minor wives.[46]

Soon after the Dusit Park area was cleared, construction of a thoroughfare linking the developing royal district to the Grand Palace began. Its outer section, from the city walls to Dusit Park, was started in August 1899. In announcing the construction of the section within the city walls in June 1901, the royal gazette established that the two sections were to be called Ratcha Damnoen Nok and Ratcha Damnoen Klang (Outer and Central Royal Progress, respectively).[47] Reiterating the long-established attention to roads as an index of civilization, Western com-mentators hailed Ratcha Damnoen, with its "three carriage-ways, sepa-rated from one another by double lines of trees and bordered by shady footpaths," as "the finest boulevard in Bangkok."[48] Concrete bridges were built between 1903 and 1907 to span the three canals (Lot, Bang Lamphu, and Phadung Krung Kasem) along Ratcha Damnoen's course. These bridges, with their wrought iron railings (and, in one case, rostrate columns modeled on Roman design), added a further continental element to the Dusit district.[49]

In 1903, the Aphisek Dusit Throne Hall was added to the Dusit Park compound. A one-story edifice enlivened by a projecting porch with fretwork decoration, the throne hall, used for royal audiences and cabinet meetings, was built east of Wimanmek. Henceforth, the Grand Palace's function became predominantly ceremonial. In December 1902, nine months after the inauguration of Wimanmek, Rama V laid the foundation stone of a forty-room mansion. The mansion was planned by a Munich firm and built under the direction of an architect of the Public Works De-partment, C. Sandreczki, who was relocated to the Privy Purse.[50] Along with an irregular plan and uneven elevation, the new royal mansion, named Amphon Sathan, was probably the first Bangkok building with an elevator.[51] Amphon Sathan's unostentatious façade, with stucco reliefs and fretwork window frames in Jugendstil, Art Nouveau's sober German inflection, was offset by the interior decoration, which followed the more flamboyant French and Italian fin-de-siècle style. The heavy drapery, carpets, crystal chandeliers, and paintings in the king's wing created a truly dandified ambience. The mural decoration was the work of Cesare Ferro, a Turinese painter who was employed by the Public Works Department during 1904–1906 to design coins and stamps. Besides decorative panels filled with floral and vegetal motifs, Ferro painted scenes of Bacchanalia and the Indic tale of the *kinnari,* the mythological half-bird and half-female creature;[52] the manifest eroticism of these scenes followed continental fashion, which prized interior decoration for arousing the senses and stimulating "nervous vibration."[53] In Florence Rama V also purchased some nudes by Odoardo Gelli, the painter of *The Royal Family,* to hang in Amphon Sathan. After its inauguration in February 1907,[54] Amphon Sathan became Chulalongkorn's official residence until his death three and a half years later.

As mentioned in chapter 1, royal patronage of monasteries declined sharply in the Fifth Reign. King Chulalongkorn had demonstrated his piety early in his reign by having Wat Ratcha Bophit built right across the canal encircling the Grand Palace. He sponsored no other religious edifice for the next thirty years, except for Wat Niwet in Bang Pa-in. While the building of Dusit Park was under way, a new monastery was planned in accordance with the custom of having a temple adjoining the royal palace and also to make up for the removal of a small temple dating to the Third Reign, Wat Laem, which had been pulled down during road construction in Dusit. The foundation stone of the new Wat Benchama Bophit was laid on 1 March 1900.[55] A year and a half later, work began on the monastery's ordination hall (*ubosot*) based on Prince Narit's design.[56] Wat Benchama Bophit's *ubosot* (which was not completed until the Sixth Reign) is celebrated as a masterpiece of modern Thai architecture, "break-[ing] away from the traditional construction of a Siamese temple."[57] In fact, the eclectic mixture of Thai and Western architectural and decorative motifs—the guardian lions flanking the entry staircase, the multilayered roof covered with glazed tiles, the columned portico and stained glass windows—is reminiscent of the eclectic style of the 1860s–1870s. Archival documents also show that one of the *ubosot*'s most distinctive features, its white marble coating (whence its English name, the Marble Temple), was an idea of the Public Works Department's engineer in chief, Carlo Allegri.[58] Allegri also arranged for Chulalongkorn to choose the stained glass for the *ubosot*'s windows during his brief stay in Milan, in May 1907.[59]

Along the thoroughfares framing Dusit Park nineteen mansions were built for Chulalongkorn's sons and several others for his daughters (many of these mansions were transformed into government offices after the overthrow of the absolute monarchy). Prince Damrong states that, unlike in previous reigns, the construction of the mansions for the royal progeny was concentrated in the reign's later years because Rama V waited until their return from Europe so that they could choose the style.[60] Two among these princely mansions deserve a mention: Bang Khun Phrom Palace, the property of Prince Boriphat (1881–1944), who had studied in Germany (today it is the seat of the National Bank of Thailand); and Suan Parut Sakawan, owned by Prince Chakrabongse (1883–1920), who had been a cadet in the Tsar's army and married a Russian woman, Catherine Desnitsky. The first palace, occupying a large plot of land stretching from the Chao Phraya's bank to Samsen Road (parallel to Ratcha Damnoen), comprises a grand mansion in the German baroque style (built between 1902 and 1906) and a smaller house (built in 1913) noticeable for its Art Nouveau decoration and furniture.[61] Two detached villas stood also in the compound of Suan Parut Sakawan, along Ratcha Damnoen Nok: the main one was built in 1903–1905 for Prince Chakrabongse; the smaller one was to serve as temporary home for Crown Prince Vajiravudh while his princely residence was being built. In the first three years of his reign, Rama VI resided, however, in Dusit Park, while his own royal palace, Chitralada (the incumbent monarch's place of residence), was under construction on a large plot of land opposite Dusit Park.[62]

In his autobiography Prince Chula Chakrabongse, Prince Chakrabongse's son, gives a firsthand account of life at Parut Sakawan in the 1910s. The mansion's ground floor housed a blue drawing room, a sitting room in pale pink for Chakrabongse's Russian wife "to have small tea parties," a dining room decorated in the English style with wood paneling, and a billiard parlor. To the two original floors a third one was later added, in which a room was devoted to a collection of Buddha images, such as those owned by "most Thai families of well-to-do status." There were two kitchens, both situated outside the mansion: the one for the preparation of European food was housed "in a Swiss chalet-like building" and run by Russian chefs with Chinese assistants; the second kitchen, "a long way off," was run, instead, by "a big team of women to prepare Thai food." The smaller villa in the compound was kept open for guests and to hold parties; it had a "white and gold ballroom with hyacinth blue silk panels of Louis XV style" and a banqueting room. Part of the large garden, with ponds, hillocks, and waterfalls, was arranged as Lady Chakrabongse's "private zoo": monkeys, gibbons, deer and gazelle, tiger cubs, and a baby elephant lived there. Finally, there were the servants' quarters, "a little town within a town" housing hundreds of people; the stables with "some eight horses"; and a garage where Prince Chakrabongse "kept several cars of different types for appropriate uses."[63]

Not long before his death, Chulalongkorn bought a forty-acre property along Sanghi Road (today Ratcha Withi), not far from Dusit Park. The property, Phaya Thai, was to be developed into a farm for experimenting with vegetable and rice cultivation and poultry breeding.[64] According to Prince Chula Chakrabongse, Rama V intended to pursue the life of a farmer after his planned abdication at the age of sixty (when he died, he was fifty-seven).[65] At its inauguration in May 1910, only some wooden dwellings stood in the Phaya Thai compound; later it became the residence of Queen Saowapha when she moved out of Dusit Park (queens customarily vacated the palace they had inhabited with the sovereign after his death). Among the several buildings added at this stage were a throne hall that doubled as a theater and cinema hall, a two-story mansion, and a Japanese-style pavilion. After Saowapha's death in October 1919, Rama VI effected a major restyling of the complex. Older edifices were pulled down and new ones erected, including several masonry residences, a cruciform throne hall with fretwork decoration, a teak house by the pond, and even a columned "Roman garden." In the late 1920s, dire times for state finances, Phaya Thai was converted into a hotel under the management of the Railways Department; in 1932 it became a military hospital, a function it has maintained ever since.[66]

What was accomplished in turn-of-the-century Bangkok under the umbrella of municipal improvements was, in essence, the creation of a more comfortable and pleasurable private space for the royal elite. The contribution of the foreign employees of the Public Works Department was to adapt the town-planning and architectural practices then enjoying global currency to their patrons' demand for a residential architecture suitable to express their civilized status and Westernized taste. Scholars with royalist loyalties tend to point out that the costs of land purchase and con-

struction of the palaces in Dusit were borne by the Privy Purse in accordance with the separation between revenues for public expenditures
and revenues destined to the royal household established by Rama V.[67] The
corollary of this argument is that the seizure of princely mansions for housing offices by the constitutional government after 1932 was an illegitimate
move. What this argument ignores is the use that was made of public resources to build the infrastructure (water and electricity supply, sewage
system, and the road network) necessary for residential purposes. Indeed,
the building of such infrastructure considerably increased the value of the
lands acquired by the Privy Purse when the Dusit area had been rice fields.
In his guidebook to Bangkok (1904), photographer and long-time resident J. Antonio noted pointedly, "Immediately the new site was selected a
veritable land 'boom' took place in the surrounding district and the clear-
ing of the jungle and filling in of the swamp took place with astounding
rapidity for Siam. Roads were planned in all directions and buildings
sprung up like mushrooms."[68] The royalty's lead in suburban living was
soon followed by members of the nobility and even the officialdom: San-
pakan Hiranchakit, manager of the Siam Commercial Bank, was said to
own the finest villa in Bangkok aside from the royal villas.[69]

The extent to which the royal household's needs impinged on
"public" interest is fully revealed in the correspondence between Chulalongkorn and Chaophraya Yomarat, who in the last decade of the Fifth
Reign was the minister first of Public Works and then of Municipal Government. The correspondence shows that Chaophraya Yomarat acted as
the king's factotum, coordinating and solving problems arising from the
realization of royal projects; Rama V, on his part, remarkably kept track of
each project's details, from the terms of contract offered to individuals to
be employed to the quality of bitumen for the asphalting of Ratcha Damnoen Avenue.[70] The detrimental effect the building of Dusit Park had over
municipal works is stigmatized by a contemporary witness, the Belgian
Émile Jottrand, according to whom the opening of "Birthday Bridge 48,"
in November 1901, was matched by the installation of three bridges inside
Dusit Park. On a later occasion, Rama V keenly exercised his right of pre-
emption: "The bridge of Pratu Pi has been in a scandalous state for many
years and after a long time they got a bridge from Europe to replace it. But
the king thought it had come just in time for one of the canals in the
Park, where he had it erected. The dimension did not correspond but
they did what they could anyway."[71]

The concentration of materials and manpower for the rapid realization of Dusit Park not only caused the postponement of priority municipal works; it also affected, if Jottrand's testimony is to be believed, the life of the Bangkok residents. Because of the unusually high wages the Privy Purse could afford to pay in competition with the Public Works Department itself, an increase in living costs occurred over the period April 1899–April 1900. It is worth quoting Jottrand at length here, for his is a controversial account of the turn-of-the-century modernization of Bangkok:

> *The fixed rate for a day of work for a coolie at the railways, at public works, and elsewhere is two salungs. . . . The king, eager to see rapid progress on his residence, has decreed that wages for a day of work in the Dusit Park would be one tical [10 salungs]. Thousands of coolies work on the royal park; there are never too many, they are never refused work, and it has become impossible to make progress at the railways and at other important projects. Moreover, it goes without saying that the increase in wages has caused an unavoidable increase in the price of commodities, salaries, and all other expenses. On the other hand, the necessary materials for the construction of Dusit are stocked for a period of six months or more, and in many cases suppliers of the court are forbidden to deliver elsewhere. There is a short supply of bricks and cement for the buildings that are being constructed in the city. I do not exaggerate when I say that the Dusit Park monopolizes a great deal of Bangkok's resources, to the detriment of all those who suffer as a result of this artificial and short-lived activity. . . . As enlightened and Europeanized as he [Rama V] may be, he is anxious to retain the privileges of Louis XIV: that the good pleasure of the king is the law!*[72]

The Suburbanization of Courtly Life

While most obviously prompted by the desire for a hygienically sound, aesthetically pleasing, and distinctively modern living space, the suburbanization of courtly life late in the Fifth Reign carries an ideological implication that is worth considering. The invention of the villa as a site of spiritual solace providing rest from the weariness of city life dates to the times of Imperial Rome. This classical imprint resonated in the modern characterization of the suburban villa that emerged first in Renaissance Italy, where the wealthy urban classes purchased landed estates to transform the family patrimony into a sort of dynastic possession. This form of investment allowed elites whose economic privilege was founded on urban-based trading and banking activities to indulge in what has been called "the dream of the countryside."[73] This active daydreaming was nurtured by nostalgia for rural roots that, in fact, were alien to such an urban class. In the course of the nineteenth century, the villa's ideal and ideology was appropriated first by the haute bourgeoisie and eventually by the middle class, eager to relocate from the decaying old city centers to newly built, rationally planned suburbs. It was the contemplation of this trend that led urban historian Lewis Mumford to contend that the architectural and social institution of the villa "is concerned not with the happiness of the whole community but with the felicity of the governors."[74] The historical trajectory of the villa institution in Southeast Asia follows a similar pattern, from residences for colonial governors and Chinese tycoons to present-day suburban housing projects targeting the new-rich living in congested and polluted megalopolises such as Bangkok, Jakarta, and Manila.

As I argued at length in chapter 1, modes of courtly consumption in the Fifth Reign underscored a novel attitude that placed a premium on self-fulfillment and self-realization over the mere demonstration of status. This attitude was constitutive of a new self-image, clearly expressed in Rama V's description of himself to Queen Saowapha as "someone who has been working since childhood."[75] Chulalongkorn's self-image as a "working monarch" explains his determination to spend the evening hours in relaxation at Dusit Park, in whose natural environment he was able to pursue his dream of the countryside. He pursued this dream to the extent of having a large wooden house, modeled on those of Thailand's Central Plains, built in 1904 just across the pond from Wimanmek—where the refinements of modern life were readily available. In this Ruanton (Country house) Rama V received, according to popular myth, the "rustic friends" (*phuan ton*) he made in his incognito trips to the provinces—supposedly because country folks would find themselves in a familiar environment there. What we know for sure about Ruanton can be inferred from a photograph taken by Oeb, one of Chulalongkorn's young minor wives. In it, he appears sitting in Ruanton's porch with only a *phanung* around his waist while busy cooking a meal in a wok.[76] This private image goes a long way in showing how the "staged authenticity"[77] of this rural corner of Dusit Park enabled Rama V to indulge in an aestheticized version of the good and simple country life—notwithstanding the imported upholstered chair visible in the photograph. Aestheticizing nostalgia of rural life is also apparent in Chulalongkorn's alleged intention to devote himself to farming in the Phaya Thai estate after his planned abdication at the age of sixty.

Daydreaming proved specially congenial to Vajiravudh, who turned his father's rural fantasy into a municipal fantasy by locating in a corner of Phaya Thai a miniature city, called Dusit Thani, of which he is said to have been "the chief planner and chief architect."[78] Dusit Thani had been originally built inside Dusit Park and was relocated in Phaya Thai at the end of 1919, when the complex underwent a redevelopment. Dusit Thani was entirely lost at some point in the developments that affected Phaya Thai after Rama VI's death. Spread over almost one acre of land, the miniature city included models (in 1:12 scale) of both Bangkok's buildings (the Grand Palace, the offices of ministries, and barracks) and modern and exotic edifices such as a factory, a hospital, a cinema, a mosque, a walled castle, a clock tower, and a town hall; there were also shops, restaurants, a hotel, and a lighthouse at the mouth of the stream running through the city, which was electrically lit at night.[79] Royalist mythographers have tried their best to show that Dusit Thani was a testing ground for the trial of constitutional government—an argument subscribed to (if somewhat cautiously) even by Walter Vella in his study of Rama VI's reign.[80]

In fact, Dusit Thani is an example of the passion for miniature (and, conversely, gigantic) objects that spread in the nineteenth century, particularly in England where Vajiravudh was educated. In her study on this mania for miniature and gigantic objects, Susan Stewart points at the dollhouse as a "homemade universe" allowing the child the manipulation of time, space, and activity.[81] Stewart's remarks seem apposite for someone like Vajiravudh, who arguably suffered from "Peter Pan syndrome" and for whom the administration of Dusit Thani's "homemade universe" must have been both easier and more rewarding than the actual exercise of his power in years of growing public disaffection with the absolute monarchy. This psychological condition might perhaps account for the fact that Rama VI pushed his municipal fantasy to the point of having two newspapers and one weekly printed with his articles for "circulation" in Dusit Thani and presiding over such comical acts as the election of a mayor, the granting—and even the amendment—of a constitution, and the creation of two "political parties": the Blue Ribbon and the Red Ribbon.

With Dusit Park and Phaya Thai being the exclusive playgrounds of the kings and the royal harem, it was left to an ostensibly religious site to provide the space for the socialization of the whole elite in the new suburb. From the beginning of its construction, an annual fund-raising fair was held at Wat Benchama Bophit in December. In 1900, its second edition, the fair lasted about ten days; the attractions included a theater, an exhibition of Buddha images and one of porcelains belonging to the royal family, a maze, a European restaurant, and some four hundred stalls made of canvas and paper fixed on wooden frames. Besides typical entertainments such as fireworks and *lakhon* (dance) performances, the royal family turned themselves into an attraction at the fair: princesses baked cakes for sale, and the king himself ran a stall where he auctioned his belongings to raise money for the temple. Entry to the fair was reportedly open to anybody, and security on the grounds was maintained by two hundred sailors who limited themselves to "push[ing] the crowd back by about two meters when the passage of the king or one of the queens is announced."[82] At the 1904 fair, a temporary photo studio was set up; the following year a photographic contest, which drew 140 contestants, both Siamese and foreigners, was organized.[83] In 1907, the first three letters sent by Chulalongkorn to his daughter from Europe were auctioned;[84] and in 1908 some of the paintings purchased by Rama V in Europe the previous year were put on display.

Wat Benchama Bophit's was no ordinary temple fête. Its purpose was to be a forum for the cultural modernization of the elite under the king's aegis, a transient site for the localization of global markers of *siwilai*. It would not be long before the Dusit district would boast a permanent site, too.

Chapter 4

Field of Glory

With Dusit Park and the princely mansions built nearby, the Siamese royal elite acquired a private space at once more comfortable and more suited to their self-image as civilized individuals than the cramped Grand Palace. The palace, however, retained during the early years of the twentieth century its symbolic preeminence as the realm's "exemplary center," and Bangkok continued to be lacking in what David Cannadine calls "sites of consensual pageantry."[1] Traditional Siamese state ceremonies were performed in or around the sacral spaces of the royal palace and the temples and, most characteristically, along the river; this was the case of the *kathin,* the ceremony marking the end of the Buddhist lent, and the *longtha,* the bathing of the king's sons. The riverine setting of the most splendid pageants of the Siamese political theater accorded with the predominantly aquatic environments of Ayutthaya and early Bangkok: in an environment where the majority of the population dwelt along the river banks and the canals, royal processions by waterway were designed to attract the largest possible number of spectators. Yet by magnifying the distance between the sovereign and his subjects, who lay far in the background as uninfluential observers of the epiphany of regal power, this riverine setting also heightened the unpopulist character of Siamese royal pageantry—typical, according to Geertz,[2] of Indic state ritual in general.

While one might argue that differences in the political theater of precolonial Southeast Asia and ancien régime Europe were more a matter of emphasis than content, monarchical rhetoric in the post-Napoleonic period was reinvigorated by "a supplementary 'national' foundation."[3] Ideal proximity between monarch and subjects was emphasized by a new kind of political spectacle, whose choreography prescribed that crowds be visible to the national leader as well as to themselves.[4] The urban renewal schemes undertaken in most European capitals in the second half of the nineteenth century created monumental public spaces as suitable stage sets for the performance of such spectacles. As Carol Breckenridge suggests, these newly built urban spaces and newly invented rituals constituted, along with newly naturalized exotic objects (of both Eastern and Western provenance), the means for the self-identification of the fin-de-siècle transnational elite.[5]

The Westernized pageants staged for King Chulalongkorn's return and jubilee in 1907 and 1908, examined at length in the next chapter, are an important element for the following discussion as well, since their staging revolved around the still inchoate Phra Lan (Sacred field), also called Royal Plaza in Bangkok's Anglicized toponymy: the open space at the end of Ratcha Damnoen Avenue with the equestrian statue of Rama V in the middle and the Ananta Samakhom Throne Hall in the background. The placement of the Phra Lan in the ceremonial topography of Bangkok on the occasion of the jubilee celebrations in November 1908 was further highlighted the following year by the celebrations for Rama V's coronation anniversary; had he lived longer, the Dusit district might have ended up replacing the Grand Palace as the realm's symbolic center.[6] After the death of Chulalongkorn in 1910, the celebratory function of the Phra Lan changed into a commemorative one as its monumental space was turned into the focal point of the Rama V Memorial Day, which was instituted in 1912 as an occasion for merit making as well as for rejoicing and is still observed to this day on 23 October (the date of his death).[7] The aim of this chapter is to disentangle the original intent of the Phra Lan as a "field of glory," an urban tableau celebrating King Chulalongkorn's rule, from its present significance as a "field of memory," to paraphrase Pierre Nora's suggestive expression "*lieu de mémoire*"[8]: a site imbued with rhetorical meanings that functions as a catalyst for the collective remembrance of the Fifth Reign as the founding moment of Thai modernity.

The Absolute Monarchy's Grand Theater Manqué

Early in 1907, Rama V started fancying a project that would suitably mark the forthcoming fortieth anniversary of his reign: a monumental throne hall to adjoin his new suburban residence. The royal edict that announced the building of the Ananta Samakhom Throne Hall was issued on 1 March 1908; it stated that the edifice was built in replacement of the namesake throne hall in the Grand Palace, which had been erected under King Mongkut and was now destined for demolition because of its advanced decay.[9]

Yet in spite of being the wish of a sovereign at the apogee of an exceptionally long reign, the project of a new throne hall met with criticism from the very beginning on two counts: its cost and its style. Chulalongkorn did not live long enough to see the Ananta Samakhom completed and used as the grand ceremonial theater of his reign. The intervening shifts in royal taste and in the system of government perverted the building's original intent, assigning to it functions and representational meanings wildly discordant from those originally intended.

Because of its dimensions, the engineering difficulties involved, and the use of imported materials, the Ananta Samakhom easily became the most costly building erected up to that time in Siam. The sums apportioned in the annual budget reports over the decade 1909–1919 total 5,492,940 baht—a handsome sum equivalent to some 420,000 pounds sterling of the time.[10] Thai secondary sources, however, invariably indicate the much larger figure of 15 million baht (roughly 150–200 million baht in today's value).[11] The question of how this alleged cost of 15 million baht came about and why it has been accepted at face value despite the accessibility of the budget reports (could it be that the costlier the building, the greater the glory of its patron?) would be worth pursuing in itself. The Ananta Samakhom was also the monarchy's first representational building entirely Western in style. Disapproval of this choice was voiced in an anonymous (and seemingly apocryphal) account, according to which King Chulalongkorn wanted a Siamese-style throne hall but the lack of local builders capable of undertaking a suitably grand project forced him to rely on the European employees of the Public Works Department, who came up with their own design. This account of the origins of the Ananta Samakhom, recently restated by art historian Piriya Krairiksh,[12] is traceable back to the poem "King Chulalongkorn's Grief at Imagining Future Blame of the Excess of Western-style Architecture Built in His Reign," which Chaophraya Thammasak Montri, a reformist aristocrat and an early figure of public intellectual, penned sometime after Rama V's death:

> *The transformation in Siam's appearance makes people astonished:*
> *The old field has suddenly changed.*
> *I heard what the King said about the Ananta Palace,*
> *Aware, as he was, of future complaints by the people:*
> *"King Chulalongkorn really had a weakness for Western buildings.*

True, we are in want of Siamese draughtsmen,
but did phraya Ratcha Songkhram need a dozen of them from overseas?
Heavenly engineers had to be employed to realize his plan."
"The Palace had to be finished in time for the celebrations;
This an architect alone could have not achieved."
Yet the king passed away without seeing his wish accomplished.[13]

Although the manifest targets of this poignant composition are the "heavenly engineers" from overseas, it is not too far-fetched to read it as an oblique criticism of the cultural Westernization of the court. It is also likely that the real cause of Chaophraya Thammasak's dissatisfaction with the Ananta Samakhom was, more than its style, its large cost. This was indeed something of an issue even in Rama V's lifetime; his correspondence to Chaophraya Yomarat indicates that the king was aware of silent opposition to the project. That the cost involved in the realization of the building was a matter of concern in some quarters of the administration is revealed in a letter written by Rama V two days before his departure for Europe, in March 1907 (a time when the idea of a new throne hall must have been still under consideration). Chulalongkorn lamented what he felt was the prejudicial opposition to the project by foreign as well as Thai officials, whose arguments he summarized in four points: at an estimated cost of one million baht (eventually, it cost more than five times as much), the new throne hall would be a waste of money; it would also be superfluous, since the recently built Phratinang Aphisek Dusit (in Dusit Park) could be easily enlarged; unprofitable, being a building designed only for ceremonies, which could be neither rented nor inhabited; and far too grand, to the point of being possibly regarded as a misuse of money and labor. On this account, Rama V demanded that Chaophraya Yomarat speak his mind on the matter:

Now, even though nobody openly voices these four objections, I know that this is what they think, and I feel discouraged. If you think that there are only personal benefits, that I don't need [to build] a palace to celebrate the reign's anniversary, that ceremonies can be performed here, and that therefore it would be better to abandon this project, I will not be enraged, but I couldn't help regretting such a decision.[14]

That criticism was not openly voiced falls squarely within the pattern of autocracy. And, predictably enough, the approaching fortieth anniversary of reign cleared the way for the project.

The project of the throne hall building was entrusted to Annibale Rigotti (1870–1968), an architect from Turin who arrived in Bangkok late in 1907 under an initial two-year contract.[15] Rigotti's assistant was Mario Tamagno, head of the Public Works Department's Planning Section; Carlo Allegri, the department's engineer in chief, was the project's responsible; and Chaophraya Yomarat, then minister of municipal government, its supervisor. Before construction could start, the problem of how to estab-lish the foundations of such a massive building in the Dusit district's marshy land had to be solved. The solution was provided by a special drill, the Compressol, made available by a French firm; hundreds of holes (8 to 10 meters deep) were drilled into the ground and then filled with concrete; an iron grid coated with concrete was then laid down to provide a stable base for the building.[16] Eventually, the throne hall's foundation stone was laid in a ceremony staged on the early morning of 11 November 1908, the opening day of the celebrations for the fortieth anniversary of reign.

Following belatedly the dictates of nineteenth-century architec-tural historicism, on its way out by the early 1900s, Tamagno designed a Baroque basilica-style edifice with a Latin cross plan measuring approxi-mately 49.5 meters in width, 112.5 meters in length, and 49.5 meters in height. The central cupola, standing on a high-colonnade tambour and coated with copper, soars at the intersection of the nave and the transept in correspondence to the position of the throne inside. Complementing the central dome are six other spherical surfaces, which might have been intended as a reference to the seven planets of Buddhist cosmology:[17] an elliptical dome, which covers the spiral stairways at the nave's eastern end; three half domes, corresponding to the apses at the nave's western end and at both ends of the transept; and two small cupolas, capping cylindrical staircases at the edifice's sides. Except for this obscure numerical symbolism, the design of the Ananta Samakhom Throne Hall made no particular con-cessions to exoticism, conforming to the ornate classicism of fin-de-siècle Italian architecture, an example of which is the magniloquent King Victor Emmanuel II memorial in Rome (built 1885–1911).[18] The white marble coating, already used for Wat Benchama Bophit, was a favorite feature of such edifices. The external sculptural decoration along the cornice features marble *putti* holding floral garlands, as well as copper-cast friezes and vessels.

The Baroque model is carried out in the interior as well, where seventy-four marble columns on high pedestals and the profusion of sculpted and painted decoration, with a predominance of gold, produces a bombastic effect.

Glimpses of the early stage of construction are found in the king's correspondence to Chaophraya Yomarat (whom Rama V termed "*kongsi*" in his role of supervisor, proof of the lasting import of Chinese masons). In a letter written in April 1909, the king was lavish with praise for the working team: "The foreigners, so different from our master builders who are bossy and do not give any help, deserve praise. They work hard till late at night as they do in Italy. I am very satisfied. I congratulated Allegri on this."[19] The following October, watching the throne hall rising from the gardens of Dusit Park, Rama V wrote that he trusted its structure, dome apart, to be completed in seven months. This time the praises were all for Chaophraya Yomarat ("I have never seen such a capable *kongsi* in my entire life") and his ability to check on both the "malaise" (*rok*) of the local workers (a hint to laziness and petty corruption) and, in contrast to previous statements, the tardiness of the foreign employees: "The foreigners were made to agree on the materials and the work schedule until they could take it no more. The fact is, they do not consider in advance what they will need to use; so, when materials are not there, they use the excuse of waiting for the delivery to take holidays. If not closely controlled, they would stop working altogether." The following day, Chulalongkorn wrote again to Chaophraya Yomarat in a tone both cryptic and facetious: "The construction of the Ananta Samakhom is not an ordinary work. Should it be . . . completed in ten years, I will relinquish the throne and become the grass-gatherer for the elephant crawl."[20]

Once the building's bare structure in reinforced concrete had been erected, the made-to-order components started to be assembled: marble and granite slabs from Genoa, Turin, Milan, and Carrara; bronze and copper casts from Stuttgart; ceramics from Vienna; and finally, curtains, tapestries, and carpets from England.[21] This work of assemblage is an apt metaphor for the incongruity of the Ananta Samakhom in the surrounding landscape—a marble cathedral in the desert of Bangkok's royal suburb.

By October 1909, when Rigotti went back to Italy to coordinate the realization of prefabricated parts, the choice of an interior decorator was already under consideration. The initial choice fell on Cesare Ferro, who had already painted the interiors of the Amphon Sathan mansion but had since returned home. Engineer Allegri submitted Ferro's demands (six months for the preparation of the sketches in Italy and a three-year contract to work in Bangkok at 120 pounds per month plus 160 pounds for a return passage) to Chaophraya Yomarat along with his proposals. Ferro suggested decorating the domes with major events taken from the history of Siam, or the dynasty, and asked "to be provided with an exact history of such events. Out of those I could then select the motives for four grand frescoes." For the decoration of the vaults forming the continuous ceiling, Ferro had in mind "European allegorical paintings representing moral qualities, uses, customs, wealths, commerce, agriculture, etc. etc., of Siam," in the conviction that "panels of living character will not prejudice in any way the classical style of the whole building . . . simply serv[ing] with its vivid colors and its moving lines to give life to the severe magnitude of the Hall."[22] Informed of the ongoing negotiation, Rama V warned Chaophraya Yomarat to "keep very vigilant with Ferro, an idler by nature and made worse by his long stay in the Public Works Department."[23] Eventually, after being presented with a minutely detailed contract, Ferro turned down the offer becoming, instead, associate professor at the Turin school of art, the Accademia Albertina.[24]

The replacement to Ferro was found in Galileo Chini (1873–1956), a Florentine painter and ceramist.[25] Although Chini had exhibited a major work at the Venice Biennale of 1907, visited twice by Chulalongkorn while there,[26] it is unlikely he received the commission because of the king's enthusiasm for his work.[27] Carlo Allegri spent most of 1910 in Italy, following the realization of components for the throne hall.[28] At that time he must have approached Chini, who accepted the offer of 100,000 francs (equivalent to 53,000 baht) for the execution of the throne hall's mural decoration, giving his assurance he would complete the work in thirty months.[29] The choice of Chini was approved by Rama V, who, however, warned Chaophraya Yomarat to draw a contract with strict terms in case Chini's working pace was like Ferro's; for if so, "he will never finish in time."[30] The covenant between Chini and Allegri, on behalf of the Siamese government, was finalized in Florence on 17 October 1910,[31] six days before King Chulalongkorn's sudden death. The following March Chini departed from Genoa on a German steamer bound for Singapore; he reached Bangkok at the end of June. His arrival apparently went unnoticed: three months later he was still waiting for an audience with the king or another court official—a clear indication of Vajiravudh's lack of interest in the Ananta Samakhom.[32] Finally, Allegri requested on Chini's behalf an entry permit to temples and the royal library's manuscript collection so that the artist could study specimens of Siamese painting.[33]

Within the thirty-month deadline set by the contract, Chini painted five large scenes on the interior of the domes and sketched the decoration of the vaulted ceiling, which was brought to completion by his two aides, G. Sguanci and Carlo Rigoli (the latter active throughout the Sixth Reign as executor of Prince Narit's sketches in the Borom Phiman Palace and Wat Ratcha Tiwet). In spite of its Western style, Chini's decoration is the only element in the building that employs indigenous iconographic motifs and even evokes the cluttering of pictorial space typical of Thai mural art. Each bay of the vaulted ceiling is painted with a central halo, inscribed with the initials and the dynastic name of a Chakri monarch, surrounded by an intricate pattern of human and animal figures (Garudas, elephants, birds, deer, *putti,* and youth) interspersed with floral motifs.

In the large frescoes, Chini blended academic naturalism with the decorative quality of Art Nouveau, itself redolent of Orientalist suggestions. Seen in their chronological order of realization,[34] the five fresco scenes represent Rama VI enthroned (this scene, not originally envisaged for the domes but made necessary by the dynastic succession, was accommodated on the lunette above the nave's eastern entrance), Rama I's triumphal return from Cambodia and Chulalongkorn freeing the slaves with the port activity and the rising Ananta Samakhom in the background (on the half domes of the transept), King Mongkut receiving the tribute of priests of different religions and scientists (apse at the nave's west end), Rama II and Rama III inspecting, respectively, Wat Arun and the Grand Palace's southwestern fortification (elliptical dome over the spiral stairways).[35] Chini obviously followed Ferro's suggestion of an iconographic cycle illustrating the dynasty's history, which was well suited to both the throne hall's architectural typology and its intended ceremonial purpose. However, Chini's frescoes do not represent, strictly speaking, historical events; rather, the scenes evoke synthetic views of the accomplishments of each reign. In spite of their didacticism, the scenes were somewhat discordant with the self-image of the modernizing elite. Prince Narit, for instance, found it indecorous that Rama V be surrounded by Michelangelesque figures of partly nude slaves (both males and females),[36] whom he had not only freed but also attempted to clothe in the pursuit of his civilizing mission.

Interior decoration aside, progress toward the completion of the Ananta Samakhom slowed down considerably at the beginning of the Sixth Reign. The situation worsened after the outbreak of World War I, which delayed the shipping of the prefabricated components from overseas. When King Vajiravudh demanded the delivery of the building by March 1916 (the end of the Buddhist year 2458), the use of locally produced parts was considered; but Tamagno guaranteed the delivery of all pending orders by July 1915, and the conclusion of the works by the date set by the king.[37] The Ananta Samakhom was finally inaugurated in January 1917, during the one-week celebrations for Rama VI's thirty-sixth birthday.[38] On that occasion, all those involved in its realization were bestowed honors: Chaophraya Yomarat and his assistant, Phraya Prachakon; Allegri, Gollo, Spigno, Guasco, and Levi of the Public Works Department's Engineering Division; Tamagno, Rigotti, Salvatore, Rigazzi, Tavella, Moreschi, and Tamaglia of the Planning Division; Rigoli and Sguanci for the painted decoration (Chini had been bestowed the Order of the White Elephant before going home in 1914); Tonarelli, Novi, and Innocenti for the sculptural decoration.[39]

The eight years required for the construction of the throne hall compared favorably with similar projects (the Victoria Memorial in Calcutta was four years in the planning and fifteen more in the building, from 1906 to 1921). However, by 1917 the grandeur of the Ananta Samakhom was unsuitable for a monarch who had become an increasing target of public criticism.[40] Moreover, King Vajiravudh was anything but fond of the edifice so strongly wanted by his father. For one, he knew that it would fail to impress Westerners, used to much older and grander buildings.[41] The Ananta Samakhom was very soon featured in picture postcards as Bangkok's latest architectural landmark.[42] But the qualified praise of it ("generally considered to be the finest piece of this style east of Suez"[43]) in the Bangkok guide written by Danish military adviser and amateur archaeologist Erik Seidenfaden proves that Rama VI's reservations were justified. Even more awkward was that the Western-style Ananta Samakhom epitomized that "cult of imitation" increasingly decried by Vajiravudh in his activity as publicist from 1915 onward. While professedly targeting the Westernized lifestyle of a growing segment of the Bangkok populace, Rama VI's sarcasm about the "cult of imitation" betrayed his growing preoccupation with the threat that too extensive a secularization of Siamese society could pose to absolutism.

As growing public criticism and financial constraints determined a dramatic downscaling of royal ceremonies in the 1920s, the Ananta Samakhom was kept shut for most of the decade. Neglected as the monarchy's grand ceremonial theater, the Ananta Samakhom was ironically put to use, the day after the coup that on 22 June 1932, terminated royal absolutism, as the temporary place of detention for Prince Boriphat, the representative in the capital of Rama VII (who was away at the summer residence in Hua Hin), and other high-ranking princes and officials. Six months later, on 10 December 1932, the Ananta Samakhom hosted the ceremony of promulgation of Siam's first constitution, drawn by the promoters of the June coup but officially—if reluctantly—bestowed on the nation by King Prajadiphok, who in 1934 left Siam for England, never to come back (he abdicated the following year). The end of the absolute monarchy marked the beginning of the Ananta Samakhom's new social life as the setting for the National Assembly. The hall's design, akin to the many domed buildings built around the globe in the nineteenth century to extol the virtue of democratic government, was even congenial to its new function; but the Ananta Samakhom failed to acquire a deep symbolic identification with the parliamentary institution, which itself struggled to achieve preeminence in the often tumultuous Thai politics. Thus, in 1974—a time when the process of democratization in Thailand seemed to be at a decisive turning point—a parliament house specifically designed for the purpose was built behind the Ananta Samakhom, on a plot of land bordering Dusit Park. It is still in the Ananta Samakhom, however, that the ceremony of the opening of parliament, instituted by Rama IX, takes place. Exploiting the symbolic linkage between the monarchy and democracy skillfully forged by the incumbent king, royalist mythographers have attempted to rewrite the history of the Ananta Samakhom, which is now presented as a forum presciently built by Rama V for the time when an elected assembly would become suitable for Siam.[44]

The lack of historical foundations for such a claim is all too obvious in Chulalongkorn's written rebuttal to the petition that a number of senior officials had submitted to the throne in 1887 proposing substantial reforms in the line of a parliamentary monarchy:

In fact, it would be impossible for the king to govern the country following a European system because it is hard to find able persons to be members of parliament. Besides, the people would never be pleased with Western institutions. They have more faith in the king than in any member of parliament, because they believe that the king practices justice and loves the people more than anybody else.[45]

Rama V penned this dismissal of the parliamentary system as a viable institute for Siam in 1888. He certainly did not change his mind in the following twenty-two years of his reign; nor did his two sons and successors deem that the intervening evolution of society warranted a change in the system of government. Likewise, there can be no mistake about the Ananta Samakhom's being built as the grand ceremonial theater of a modernizing yet convincingly autocratic monarch, despite the ironic twist given to this original intent by later developments. All in all, the best use of the Ananta Samakhom has been as the imposing background for that considerably more successful example of self-aggrandizement that Rama V's equestrian statue has proven to be.

Larger than Life

By the Fifth Reign's later years, the taboo on the vision and representation of the royal body was arguably a thing of the past, at least for the people in Bangkok. Rama V's effigy had circulated on coins and stamps since early in his reign, and at the beginning of the 1900s illustrated postcards had further expanded the range of the visual representations of the Siamese sovereign in circulation. However, three-dimensional statuary of the king in a public place had yet to be seen. Thus, when the larger-than-life equestrian statue of King Chulalongkorn was unveiled on 11 November 1908 —the opening day of the celebrations marking his fortieth anniversary of reign—the amazement among those present must have been considerable.

Without discounting the larger-than-life size and realism of the bronze statue of Rama V, the very image of the king riding a horse must have been a cause of puzzlement. In Siam, as in other Indic cultures, the animal associated with royal authority and military prowess was not the horse but the elephant, whose pachydermic silhouette on red ground still characterized the Siamese flag at that time. On ceremonial occasions the king was customarily borne by officers on a palanquin; he did not ride in a horse-drawn carriage (such a means of conveyance was used in the progress staged for the king's return from Europe, in November 1907). Because the very idea of an equestrian statue was alien to the iconography of political authority, the Siamese lexicon did not possess a definition for it, and an apposite expression, *phraborom rup songma* (kingly image on horseback), had to be coined. Having bolstered throughout two millennia the glory of Roman emperors, Christian monarchs, and national heroes, there was no reason why such a *topos* of celebrative statuary should prove unsuitable for a benevolent Oriental despot such as Chulalongkorn, even if he was definitely less apt than most of his bronze counterparts at riding horses for marshalling troops on the battlefield or even as a mere means of transport.

Iconographic newness was not the only reason that made the equestrian statue of Rama V a "first" in modern Siamese political symbolics. Perhaps even more important is that the statue was officially paid for by his subjects and the foreign residents in Siam as a token of gratitude. As the minister of the interior at that time, Prince Damrong was personally involved in the statue project; but as the House of Chakri's own historian, he wrote a peculiarly economical account of such an enterprise. Published in a miscellaneous volume of Damrong's writings long since out of print, his piece is translated here in full both because of its conciseness and its historiographical relevance (all renditions of the making of the statue in the secondary literature are based on it, whether this is acknowledged or not).

The king's equestrian statue was occasioned by two circumstances. First, by the time of the king's second trip to Europe in 1907, the Ananta Samakhom project was under way, and because of this, the area around the building site was cemented and linked to Ratcha Damnoen Avenue. Second, it was then more than one year before the fortieth anniversary of reign, and the king had given a mandate to the crown prince to consult with the ministerial council to organize the celebrations. Celebrations had already been held for the Bangkok centenary and the king's return from his first European tour in 1897, but now it was felt that, given the special occasion, something really special had to be done. The king had pursued the development of the country and the welfare of the people; for this, Siamese of all races and languages donated money in grateful reciprocation to the king, who could use it according to his wishes. The Ministry of Municipal Government had the task of promoting the initiative among the people of Bangkok and the Ministry of Interior among those in the provinces, according to two principles: donations, even those of a few satang only, should be voluntary; and everybody must be informed of the initiative and given the opportunity to make merit. From the council of ministries came the proposal of erecting a memorial to the king's fame, but it was agreed to wait until the amount of money collected was known before making any decision.

While contributions were being solicited, the news came from Europe that during his visit to Versailles, in France, Rama V was very impressed by the equestrian statue of Louis XIV in front of the palace, and commented that an equestrian statue of himself in the open space where Ratcha Damnoen Avenue joins the grounds of the Ananta Samakhom Throne Hall would look majestic, as much as those found in many European countries. The cost for such a statue was about 200,000 baht. At the same time, it became clear that people were happy to contribute and a large sum was being collected. The council passed a resolution, and the crown prince informed the king that the equestrian statue would be presented to him as a token of gratitude by the Siamese people on the occasion of the celebrations for the [fortieth] anniversary of reign. Rama V gave his approval, and this is how his equestrian monument came about. After the statue was paid, there was more than one million baht left, so the crown prince in-formed the king, who said that the money should be used for a building of public utility; however, no decision was taken before Rama V's death. After Vajiravudh ascended the throne, he decided to use that money to build Chulalongkorn University. The ceremony of unveiling, including the address of dedication of the statue and the king's reply, was recorded in the Royal Gazette.[46]

Despite its brevity, several inconsistencies can be noted in Prince Damrong's account of the statue's origins. To start with, by the time King Chulalongkorn embarked for Europe (on 27 March 1907), the idea of an equestrian statue was already under consideration. While at sea, the king instructed Chaophraya Yomarat that the money being collected among the officials for the reign anniversary should be used for building a monumental gate to Dusit Park, sketches of which had been drawn by Damrong, Prince Narit, and Phraya Suriya. The latter, who had served as ambassador in Berlin before becoming acting minister in the Ministry of Public Works in 1905, even made the proposal (obviously reminiscent of the Brandenburg Gate) to place an equestrian statue on top of the gate; but then the project was temporarily shelved. "Now seems to be the right time for it," wrote Rama V to Yomarat in April 1907; "send me some suggestions about an artist and the budget for the realization."[47] The gate was given ephemeral shape as part of the pageant decorations at the king's return in November 1907, while the idea of erecting a permanent structure continued to be bandied about for some time.[48]

As soon as Rama V arrived in Paris in mid-June, he headed to the workshop of the Seusse Brothers at 13-15, boulevard de la Madeleine, where work on his cast had already begun on the basis of photographs. Two sculptors, both of whom had won prizes at the Paris Salon, worked on the statue: Georges E. Saulo sculpted the king's figure (portrayed in the dress uniform of a field marshal), and Clovis E. Masson sculpted the horse.[49] Saulo perfected Chulalongkorn's likeness, which he had sketched beforehand on the basis of photographs, in sessions in Paris as well as Munich and Hamburg, during the king's stay in Germany.[50] "I must say," the king wrote to his daughter flaunting the authority of an art connoisseur, "that French sculptors are quicker and more realistic than the Italians."[51] Expeditious the French certainly were; in June 1908 the statue was finished and ready for shipment—an accomplishment the foundry's owners proudly claimed when they later tried, unsuccessfully, to sell Rama V two bronze fountains for Dusit Park.[52] However, the sculptors represented rider and horse in a still pose uncommon in the iconography of equestrian statuary, in which forward postures are favored to signify the ruler's volitive disposition and governing ability. The still pose may even appear to echo visually the fixity of Buddhist icons, although a mischievous observer could interpret it as an allusion to King Chulalongkorn's unfamiliarity with riding.

As for the sight that aroused his desire for an equestrian monument, it is to be noted that in each of the Italian cities Rama V visited at the beginning of his first tour of Europe, in 1897 (Venice, Turin, Rome, and Florence), there were several equestrian monuments, ranging from the antique to the modern. The sight in Rome of the statues of Marcus Aurelius, the genre's oldest extant specimen (second century A.D.), and Giuseppe Garibaldi (unveiled in 1895) was even recorded by a member of the royal suite.[53] Damrong's emphasis on the statue of Louis XIV, seen by Chulalongkorn at the Palace of Versailles only in 1907, seemingly betrays an anxiety about a suitably authoritative source of inspiration for his brother's monument. In writing his account, Damrong might have had in mind the equestrian statue of King Norodom of Cambodia (r. 1860–1890), which stands today in the precinct of the royal palace in Phnom Penh. On

ascending the throne, Norodom, who had grown up as a captive in Bangkok, welcomed France to become Cambodia's "protector" in lieu of Siam.
King Norodom's statue was a gift by the French, who thriftily recycled a
spare statue of Napoleon III, substituted its head, and oddly matched it
with a plaster horse.[54] After all, French generosity had already been ex-
pended on the construction of Norodom's new palace—ironically, a smaller
replica of Bangkok's Grand Palace. Damrong might have altogether ignored
the not-so-flattering French connection of Norodom's statue; but it is intriguing that the genealogy he forged for the statue of Rama V ideally
linked it to the most illustrious of France's monarchs—and the very personification of absolutism: the Sun King.

Concerning the issue of fund-raising, archival documents show
that it was a much more systematic operation than suggested by Prince
Damrong. With its emphasis on voluntary contributions and popular response, Damrong's account evokes what a historian of revolutionary Russia
has termed "the myth of spontaneity."[55] Quite apart from Bolshevik pop-
ulism, "spontaneous" contributions were well known to royal image-makers
to emphasize the bond between rulers and their grateful subjects; in Meiji
Japan, for instance, the crown prince was presented by the people of Tokyo
with the majestic Asaka Palace as a wedding gift in 1909. Among the
records of the Fifth Reign in Bangkok's National Archives, there are three
boxes in which the provenance and amount of thousands of donations are
recorded. Individuals, officials of each ministry, diplomatic personnel and
overseas students, foreign firms and banks, even the Apostolic Secretariat
contributed to the equestrian statue of Rama V.[56] Souvenirs were distributed in return in proportion to the sum disbursed. Bronze, silver, and gold
medals went to the donors of sums in the range of tens, hundreds, and
thousand baht, respectively. Donors of less than 10 baht received an image
of the king in one of the following three sizes: 4 cm by 6 cm, 25 to 99
satang; 9 cm by 12 cm, 1 to 4.99 baht; 13 cm by 18 cm, 5–9 baht. As
evinced by the documents, the recording of contributions and the conse-
quent distribution of souvenirs were arguably more laborious than the
fund-raising itself, going on for years well into the Sixth Reign.

What seems unquestionable in Damrong's account is the reference to Chulalongkorn's desire for a monumental urban tableau "as majestic
as those found in many European countries." By the time the king left for
Europe in March 1907 the project of a Western-style throne hall was being

finalized; an equestrian statue must have appeared the perfect complement for it. Still, Bangkok escaped the spread of "statuemania," the turn-of-the-century mushrooming of monuments of state notables in public spaces.[57] Only in 1932 was a second statue, representing Rama I enthroned, unveiled at the feet of the Memorial Bridge, the first to span the Chao Phraya, which was built to celebrate the one hundred fiftieth anniversary of the Chakri dynasty. And it was really only during the two Phibun Songkhram governments (1938–1944 and 1948–1957) that statuary was deployed as a vehicle of political propaganda, thanks to the services of the Italian sculptor Corrado Feroci (naturalized Thai with the name Silpa Bhirasri).[58]

Because of the lack of artisans capable of casting lifelike bronze statues locally, one might think of statuemania as above all technically unviable in Fifth Reign Siam. But as Maurice Agulhon reminds us, "a political power expresses itself with the historical characters it chooses to honor. The old French monarchy erected statues of kings and saints almost exclusively. The idea of bestowing this honor on other 'great men'—on servants of the state or on national heroes—came only with the Enlightenment."[59] However different the criteria underlying the selection of "great men" deserving commemoration were in the countries where the phenomenon took root, turn-of-the-century statuemania promoted the institutionalized remembrance and commemoration of a pantheon of founding fathers (on rare occasions mothers) as rituals of nationhood. Standing alone in the Bangkok cityscape for almost a quarter of a century, the Rama V statue proclaimed, on the other hand, the absolutist ideal whereby he was the only *pater patriae* deserving honor and, eventually, commemoration.

Finally, Prince Damrong's preposterous claim about the statue of the Sun King being the catalyst of Chulalongkorn's emulative drive reveals its ideological motivation. Louis XIV's famous maxim, *"l'état c'est moi,"* was not only a suitably witty expression of self-aggrandizement; it also articulated with remarkable conciseness the notion that his subjects, divided into orders by birth, were united as one people only in the person of the sovereign.[60] Similarly, the concept of *chat* that entered Thai official political discourse in the final years of the Fifth Reign conflated the Indo-Buddhist notion of righteous kingship (*dharmaraja*) with that of European absolutism into an idea of nation as the unity of the Siamese of all classes and races in the king's person. As such, the concept of *chat* signifies an intrinsically different political idea from nationalism, with which it has

been mistakenly paralleled by historians. Intriguingly, the Chakri absolutist ideology was articulated in the very speeches given by Crown Prince
Vajiravudh and King Chulalongkorn at the ceremony of unveiling of his
equestrian monument. These speeches are analyzed in the next chapter
within the larger examination of the role played by pageantry, along with
monuments, in the project of inscribing Rama V's achievements onto the
Siamese public memory.

Part III
SPECTACLES

Chapter 5

Refashioning the Theater of Power

The splendor of traditional Siamese state ceremonies had been a cause of amazement to foreign observers since the seventeenth century. Yet the final years of the Fifth Reign witnessed a series of public spectacles unprecedented in scale. In November 1907, a majestic pageant was staged for King Chulalongkorn's return from Europe. The following month, a three-day fête took place among the ruins of Ayutthaya. This celebratory crescendo reached its climax in November 1908 with the week-long festivities for Rama V's "record reign." His cremation, in March 1911, sounded on a mournful note the Fifth Reign's commemorative coda.

These carefully orchestrated spectacles, which are subjected here to "thick description," served a rather different purpose from the liturgy of court ritual that Chulalongkorn himself rearranged systematically in his manual *Praratchaphiti sipsong duan* (Royal ceremonies of the twelve months) and that H. G. Quaritch Wales was still able to record in the late 1920s.[1] Their rationale lay not in the cyclical time frame of Indic statecraft but in modern monarchical ideology, which bound the sovereign's achievements —and even his death—to the state he personified. The cluster of spectacles of 1907–1908 invoked the Fifth Reign's apogee by celebrating history in the making in the presence of masses not familiar with the Positivist idea of progress, which was part and parcel of the modernizing elite's identity.[2] Aimed at impressing the populace as much as foreign observers through the display of Siam's wealth and progress, Rama V's jubilee celebrations were akin to the "great new rituals of self-congratulation" that had flourished in Europe in the second half of the nineteenth century.[3] By performing a narrative of the modernizing elite's accomplishments in the public domain, these spectacles revealed the final intent of shaping the public memory of Chulalongkorn's reign.

This performative narrative unfolded in the three acts and finale of the political drama that is detailed in this chapter: first, the welcoming pageant, which glorified the monarchy's ability to effect progress; next, the antiquarian fête in Ayutthaya, which framed Rama V's achievements in historical perspective; then, his consecration as the undisputed—and un-disputable—pillar of the modern state and "father" of his people by the "record reign" celebrations; last, his posthumous apotheosis as *pater patriae*. The modernizing elite's self-congratulatory image was literally spelled out in the public addresses delivered on these occasions. In these speeches Rama V, separating his historical roles of actor and witness, proffered an appraisal of his reign and his epoch, candidly exposing his faith in the in-herently progressive character of the modern age. Also significant is the part played by Crown Prince Vajiravudh in the organization of the cele-brations, lending support to the argument that the three catchwords of Sixth Reign state ideology—nation, religion, and monarchy (*chat, sasana, phramakasat*)—had in fact been bandied about since the final years of the Fifth Reign.[4] Finally, it is in relation to the refashioning of the theater of power that the Dusit district's ceremonial space is best appreciated as an element of the overall celebratory project within which it was conceived.

First Act

On 17 November 1907, King Chulalongkorn returned to Bangkok after an absence of almost eight months. Although welcoming celebrations had also been held on his return from the first European tour, ten years earlier (16 December 1897), they hardly compared with the 1907 pageant. The core event was a progress along Ratcha Damnoen Avenue, which had been decked out with nine ephemeral triumphal arches representing as many ministries (Map 1). Other attractions included the renovation and decora-tion of buildings and the massive use of electric lighting (some thirty thou-sand lamps were set up by the Siam Electricity Company). Photographs were taken at each stage of the king's approach to Bangkok and progress there; an album containing some 150 photographs was presented to the king in April 1908.[5] These photographs, reproduced even on picture post-cards, are among the sources documenting the event, along with an account by Prince Damrong and the *Bangkok Times* report.[6]

On his way to Bangkok, Rama V was met in the island of Penang by Prince Damrong and two of his daughters, Chumponkhet and Wuthi-chai. On the way to the Gulf of Siam the royal party stopped at Trat (penin-sular Siam), Chang Island, and Chantaburi, where brief ceremonies were

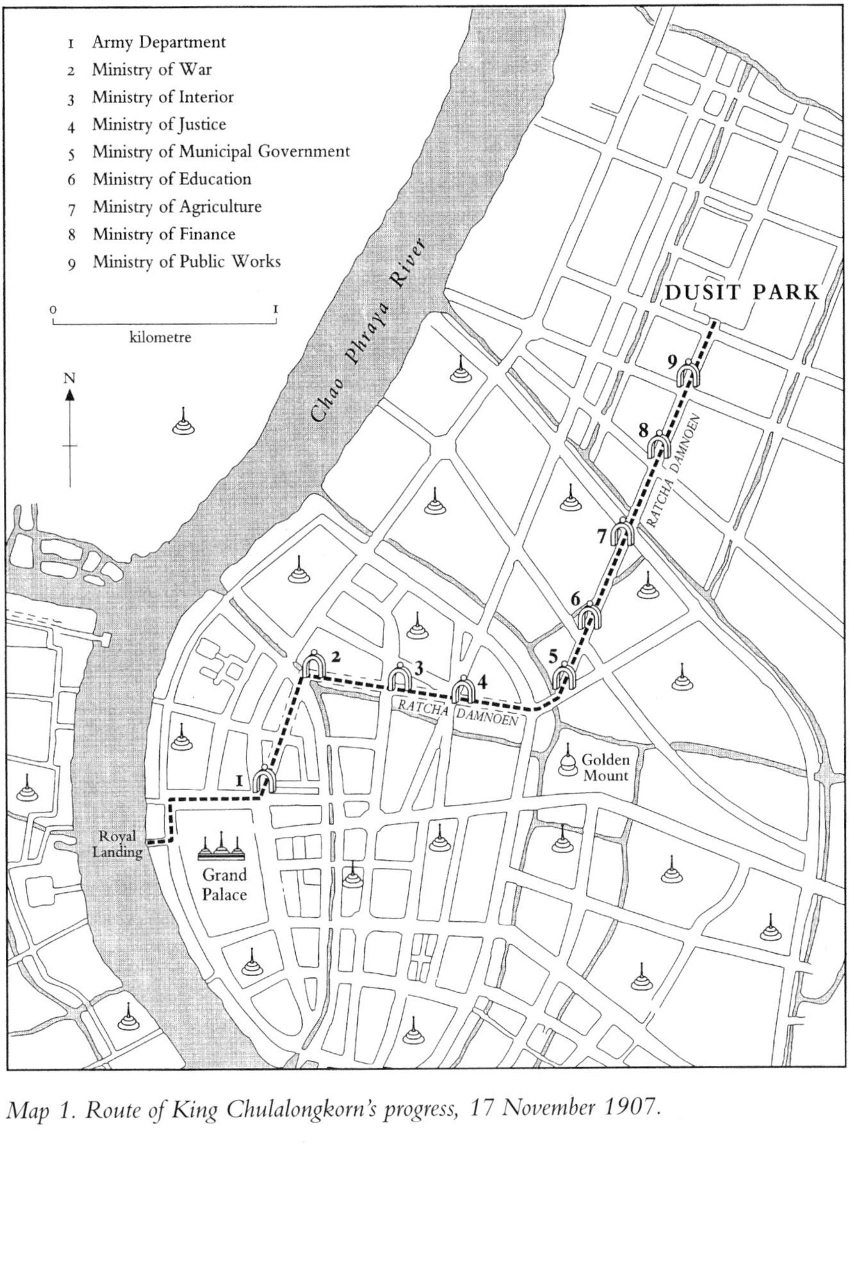

1 Army Department
2 Ministry of War
3 Ministry of Interior
4 Ministry of Justice
5 Ministry of Municipal Government
6 Ministry of Education
7 Ministry of Agriculture
8 Ministry of Finance
9 Ministry of Public Works
0
1
kilometre
N
Chao Phraya River
DUSIT PARK
RATCHA DAMNOEN
RATCHA DAMNOEN
Golden Mount
Royal Landing
Grand Palace

Map 1. Route of King Chulalongkorn's progress, 17 November 1907.

organized.[7] In the early hours of 17 November, a flotilla of private launches, steamers, and boats welcomed the royal yacht *Maha Chakri* at Paknam, the mouth of the Chao Phraya River. To allow the Bangkok population to witness the yacht's arrival, a special train was set up; it reached Paknam at 6:15 A.M. and returned to the capital at eight, in time for the king's disembarkation.[8] Around 10:30 A.M. the royal yacht moored at the Bangkok landing stage, where Vajiravudh, the princes of the royal house, monks and high-ranking officials, and representatives of the diplomatic corps had gathered inside a pavilion. Amid the firing of a salute by the gunboats, the whistling of the assembled flotilla, and the royal hymn played by the navy band, Rama V stepped ashore at the auspicious time of 10:48 A.M. The first words of welcome were those of the crown prince, who read an address on behalf of the princes, officials, and foreign dignitaries. Restating the absolutist principle of the oneness of the nation's body politic and the sovereign's mortal body, Vajiravudh remarked,

> *Among the many benefits of this travel that can be enumerated, the most important are the recovery of Your Majesty's health and the relaxation from the great worries of royal duty. In Siam every government activity is accomplished by the sovereign alone; for this reason, his well-being is strictly related to the welfare of the populace. . . . Besides, the knowledge and experience acquired from the keen examination of foreign matters will be conducive to the advancement of Siam itself. . . . Therefore, We may humbly conclude that this travel has benefited not only Your Majesty but the country as a whole.[9]*

From the landing pavilion the king was borne on a palanquin into the Grand Palace preceded by a band playing indigenous tunes. "To the foreigner at least," the *Bangkok Times* remarked, "this procession, a real bit of old Siam, was not the least interesting spectacle of the day." After the performance of rites and the address by the monkhood in Wat Phra Keo,[10] Rama V and the crown prince left the royal palace in an open carriage for Sanam Luang, the open field opposite the Grand Palace. There, the minister of municipal government, Prince Naret Worarit, presented the king with the longest and most significant of the day's addresses, disclosing the nature of the progress as a preview of the forthcoming "record reign" celebrations.

Prince Naret reviewed the achievements of the reign for the people at large: individual freedom, material contentment, the spread of education, and increasing prosperity, which together had resulted in a peaceful climate. As hallmarks of the reign, Prince Naret mentioned in particular the patronage of faiths; the abolition of bondage; the administrative, judiciary, and military reforms; the establishment of schools; the development of agricultural and commercial infrastructure, of communications, and of health services; the care for the people in the provinces; and the ascent of Siam's status in the international arena. The warm welcome the people were giving the king manifested their gratitude for those blessings, the minister concluded, praising also the crown prince's regency.[11] In his reply, Rama V proudly claimed the achievements of his reign but also framed them, significantly, in a global perspective:

> *The time elapsed since Our enthronement has been a memorable epoch in the history of mankind, an epoch characterized by rapid progress in many fields. Our effort has been directed to give Siam a place in the movement toward progress, which is the distinctive trend of our age. One generation represents a very short time span in the history of a country; still, there are many differences between the Siam of today and that of a generation ago.*[12]

At the beginning of Ratcha Damnoen Avenue stood the first triumphal arch, the Army Department's ("perhaps the most successful of all," according to the *Bangkok Times*): a pair of huge papier-mâché elephants decked for warfare with their trunks auspiciously raised and a giant crown resting on their tusks (figure 11). The section of road between this arch and the bridge over the Lot Canal was decorated with masts surmounted by royal umbrellas and ropes of flowers. Just past the corner of Ratcha Damnoen and Ratchani Road stood the arch of the Ministry of War: two dragons leaning on the sticks of seven-tiered umbrellas supporting the emblem of the dynasty—the *chakr-tri* (Wheel of the Dharma intertwined with Siva's trident)—and a huge crown (figure 12). Beyond this arch stood the pavilions of the Foreign Office and the Western banking and mercantile community, the latter a forerunner in conceiving the welcoming pageant.[13] There the royal carriage halted to allow the foreign entrepreneurs to present their homage to the king: a carved silver basket containing a written address.[14] Rama V handed to their representative a message emphasizing the friendly relations between the Western business community and the government and the linkage between the success of foreign enterprises and Siam's prosperity.[15]

The progress then resumed, passing through the arches of the Ministry of the Interior and the Ministry of Justice. The first arch was made of four latticework towers linked by gangways at the top; the second had a gilded design and Buddhist imagery (figure 13). Ropes of lotus flowers and lanterns hanging across the road complemented the decoration of this section of Ratcha Damnoen leading to a new bridge, which was inaugurated in the course of the progress. Across the bridge stood the arch of the Ministry of Municipal Government, a three-door Chinese gateway (figure 14). The street decoration along that stretch also featured Chinese motifs (yellow flags inscribed with ideograms, lanterns, and silk strips). After passing the arch, the royal carriage stopped to let the representatives of the Chinese and the Indian Muslim communities pay homage. As had happened with the Western merchants, the presentation of gifts was followed by an exchange of written messages; that of the Chinese community contained a salient passage on the possibility of Chinese residents visiting their homeland in the future without compromising their loyalty to Siam; the king replied by stressing his beneficial policies toward the Chinese immigrants in spite of his country's lack of diplomatic relations with the Midde Kingdom.[16] Rama V's reply to the Indian merchants similarly emphasized his commitment to equal treatment of all the ethnic and religious groups within the kingdom.

The progress resumed, reaching the arch of the Ministry of Education, which was decorated with cutout figures from mythology. Flags inscribed with "Long live the king" in Thai, Pali, and English hung over the roadway; and the small arch of the Royal Military College and tableaux put up by schools stood nearby. Some three thousand primary school pupils had been assembled to sing the royal hymn as Rama V passed by, "evidently highly pleased with the efforts of young Siam," according to the *Bangkok Times*. Next was the Ministry of Agriculture's Moresque arch. There, the progress made its last stop to allow the local entrepreneurs to pay their homage. Their written address praised the privileges that had been granted to foster home industry and commerce as well as the growing international interest about Siam resulting from the royal tours.[17] The lampposts they presented to the king were on display on the sides of the road. In the final stretch of Ratcha Damnoen stood the last two arches: that of the Ministry of Finance featured a circular passageway with two large coin models hanging up (figure 15); that of the Ministry of Public Works, a colossal Indo-Saracenic gate (21 meters long and 40 meters high), surmounted by flags and enveloped in electric lights.[18] In front of it stood, on a tall pedestal, the plaster statue of the Hindu deity presiding over Chulalongkorn's day of birth, Phra Hatsabodi (figure 16). After the firing of a salvo signaled the king's arrival in Dusit Park, commemorative medals were handed out along the route at the arch.

The entertainment was to continue in the evening with a fireworks show offered by the Western business community; the show was, however, ruined by a heavy burst of rain.[19] The arches as well as the public buildings, private premises, and even tramcars, all of which were electrically lit, nevertheless provided a nocturnal spectacle. The next day there was a review of troops on Sanam Luang and a dinner for the royal princes followed by a reception for the foreign dignitaries in the Grand Palace. Ordinary people—reportedly so many of them that "along by the palace wall it was almost impossible to walk for the crowds of sightseers"—congregated in the open to watch *lakhon* performances.[20] Bangkok's two tram companies did indeed register an absolute record of earnings: some 12,000 baht on the day of the progress, and some 10,000 on the next.[21]

Royal progresses were a well-known spectacle in the Southeast Asian theater of power. Clifford Geertz says of one of the most famous literary texts of the region, the *Negarakertagama* (a political treatise in verses composed in the fourteenth century at the height of the Javanese empire of Majapahit), that it "is not only centered around a royal progress but is in fact part of it."[22] In Siam, the king customarily performed a procession by land on the occasion of his coronation (a tour around the city that, starting in the Fourth Reign, also included a visit to temples), and by water in the annual *kathin* ceremony. It was the fluvial procession of barges staged on that occasion that bedazzled seventeenth-century European visitors of Ayutthaya such as Schouten, Tachard, Kaempfer, and van Vliet; Carl Bock found it still splendid in 1883.[23] Yet it was the royal entry staged in European cities in the period from the fifteenth century to the seventeenth, itself modeled on the Roman triumph, that provided the model for Chulalongkorn's progress in November 1907. Its mise-en-scène—the ride in a carriage, the triumphal arches, the welcoming addresses by the clergy, officials, and merchants—came straight from the royal entry.

Figure 11. *Arch of the Army Department (National Archives).*

Figure 12. *Arch of the Ministry of War (National Archives).*

Figure 13. Arch of the Ministry of Justice (National Archives).

Figure 14. Arch of the Ministry of Municipal Government (National Archives).

Figure 15. Arch of the Ministry of Finance (National Archives).

Figure 16. Arch of the Ministry of Public Works (National Archives).

Figure 17. Fortieth anniversary of reign celebrations in Ayutthaya, 30 November 1907 (National Archives).

Figure 18. Ceremony of the laying of the foundation stone of the Ananta Samakhom
Throne Hall, 11 November 1908. Second from the right is Chaophraya
Yomarat; third from the right is Carlo Allegri, engineer in chief of the Public
Works Department (National Archives).

Figure 19. Unveiling of the equestrian monument, 11 November 1908 (National Archives).

Figure 20. Siamese pavilion at the Paris Universal Exposition of 1899 (L'exposition universelle de 1889), *p. 65.*

Figure 21. Siamese pavilion at the Turin International Exhibition of 1911. Watercolor by Cesare Ferro (frontispiece, Catalogo descrittivo della Mostra Siamese all'Esposizione Universale delle Industrie e del Lavoro in Torino, 1911*).*

According to an authority on Renaissance pageantry, "A royal entry reflected the achievements of the present and reviewed those of the past while turning an optimistic eye to the future."[24] The symbolism of the royal entry thus fit the occasion well: returning to Bangkok after several months of absence, King Chulalongkorn retook possession of the city —and metonymically of the whole realm—while celebrating the triumphs of his European tour and his reign's exceptional duration. The very route of the progress, moving from the "exemplary center" (the Grand Palace) to the king's new residence (Dusit Park) along the recently built boulevard, traced onto the cityscape the transformation of the monarchy's image. The twin themes of progress and prosperity, emphasized in the vocal and written addresses, connect to the image of Rama V as champion of the people's well-being that was central to his self-representation as much as to the Indo-Buddhist *dharmaraja* ideal. As for Vajiravudh, who had been regent during King Chulalongkorn's absence, his presence next to his father throughout the progress amounted to a public investiture.

One can push the comparison between the mise-en-scène of the European royal entry and the Bangkok progress beyond superficial similarities in order to better understand the latter's symbolism. Triumphal arches, both architectural and ephemeral, were a central element of the choreography of royal entries. Particularly important for conveying political messages in allegorical form were the statues, emblems, and inscriptions that decorated the arches and exploited the imagery of mythological heroes and Roman emperors. Explanatory books were even published to expound this allegoric idiom to those lacking a classical education because "absolute monarchies did not leave the understanding of visual symbols to the imagination."[25] Royal and religious emblems (e.g., conical crowns, tiered umbrellas, the *chakr-tri*) featured prominently in the arches and street decoration of Chulalongkorn's progress too, and one may assume most of the onlookers to have been familiar with such symbols. They might have been less familiar with the function and activities of the modern governing apparatus. If, therefore, the purpose of the ephemeral arches was to visualize the institutions of the Siamese state, whose achievements the pageant celebrated, they probably were only partly successful.

Only two of the nine arches along Ratcha Damnoen made an obvious visual connection to the ministry they stood for: the Army Department's arch, with its traditional warfare tableau, and the Ministry of Finance's, with its giant coins. An indirect reference was that of the Ministry of Justice's arch, whose Buddhist imagery signified the link of moral law (*tham;* Pali, *dhamma*) to judicial law (*yutthitham*), and the Ministry of Education's arch, whose mythical imagery and inscriptions in Pali (like Latin, a clerical language) came the closest to reproducing the iconography of Renaissance and Baroque triumphal arches. Their main function, however, would appear to be the creation of an otherworldly landscape along a triumphal avenue, Ratcha Damnoen, then running for most of its length through Bangkok's rural outskirts. The three "Oriental" arches in particular (those of the ministries of Municipal Government, Agriculture, and Public Works) and the massive use of electric lighting point to international exhibitions as a major source of inspiration.[26]

Like visitors to exhibitions in Europe and America, the people of Bangkok must have been truly amazed by the grand and exotic spectacle offered by Chulalongkorn's progress. In reviving the grandest pageant of Western absolutist monarchies and adapting it to the Bangkok stage, its organizers produced a celebration of Rama V's autocratic rule as much as of his self- and public image as a modernizer. But the eulogies of the king's civilizing role were intended for the edification of the elite audience only; loudspeakers (not yet invented) would have been no use since the panegyrics were couched in the court idiom unintelligible to most spectators. It was the extravagant triumphal arches, the uniformed soldiers lining the street, and the dazzling night illumination that conveyed to the masses the sense of "movement toward progress that is the distinctive trend of our age," as King Chulalongkorn himself put it.

Second Act

In contrast to the cosmopolitan spectacle seen in Bangkok, the pageant staged two weeks later in Ayutthaya, known to Thais as "the old capital" (*krung kao*), had a distinct antiquarian flavor. The attractions included a wooden throne hall built specifically for the event, a fireworks show, and of course the local ruins. The pageant's underlying conception was aptly expounded by the *Bangkok Times:* "The idea of the festivities was to recall that past and set it before the eyes of the people of today, associating it with the rejoicings that are naturally taking place in recognition of the blessings of the present age."[27]

The reason for locating the fête in Ayutthaya lay in a historical analogy: in 1907, Chulalongkorn's reign had equaled in duration Rama-thibodi II's (1491–1529)—a record that Rama V was to outdo the following year. The event was planned long in advance. Already in December 1906 Prince Damrong, the minister of interior, informed the king that he had instructed the province's high commissioner to use convict labor to uncover the site of the razed royal palace and clear the pathway to it; he had requested 20,000 baht for the organization of the pageant.[28] Following the desertion of Ayutthaya caused by the Burmese sack in 1767, the jungle had reclaimed the area; new settlements (the core of the modern town) had sprung up in a different area since the 1830s. By the early years of the twentieth century, as reported by a British former employee of the Royal Survey Department, the province's high commissioner had the vegetation regularly cleared and paths laid out in the ruin area for the local elite and the Westerners who came to visit.[29] The high commissioner, who bore the apt title of Phraya Boran Buranurak (preserver of antiquities), was himself an amateur archaeologist who had identified the sites of the palaces mentioned in the chronicles of Ayutthaya;[30] he took charge of most of the pageant. The design of the wooden throne hall was allegedly based upon the descriptions by M. de la Loubère and other seventeenth-century European visitors to Ayutthaya, and so were the other temporary buildings (including a special pavilion for the Western guests) and the festive decorations. Likewise, the entertainments—*khon* and *lakhon* performances, and even the fireworks—were all touted as "traditional."[31] Although no attendance figures are available, the 64,000 metal alloy pendants (*sema*) produced in Paris as mementos for the occasion provide an indication of how many people were expected to turn up.[32] Special rewards were reserved for those holding ranks in the administration.[33] Well attended by the Siamese, the celebrations attracted few Westerners, reportedly kept away by "the uncertainty attending one's abode for the night, and the difficulty of obtaining food."[34]

The celebrations began on 30 November and lasted until 2 December. After the customary performance of court rituals, King Chulalongkorn took his seat in the throne hall's terrace facing an open space where people had gathered (figure 17).[35] Phraya Boran Buranurak read an address on behalf of the officials and the people of the province in which he sketched the achievements of Ayutthaya's greatest kings and praised Rama V as the inheritor of their power and virtue.[36] Chulalongkorn, in his reply, pointed out that while Ayutthaya's kings had established their sovereignty over the territory and preserved its integrity, he had faced the task of giving the country prosperity, stability, and freedom. He also reminded the officials in the audience that the pursuit of those aims and the securing of the people's loyalty depended upon the fulfillment of their duty.[37] In the evening, Chulalongkorn watched the *lakhon* and fireworks shows from the throne hall's terrace. There were more entertainments over the next two days, including dances, bullock races, kick-boxing, and more fireworks. An exoteric ceremony was also performed, in which the thirty-two kings of Ayutthaya and King Taksin were commemorated in effigy by as many Buddha images (in the Indic cabbala, thirty-three stands for Indra and the other thirty-two lesser gods inhabiting Mount Meru). But it was the conclusive event, on the evening of 2 December, that imbued with meaning the whole festivities: the official launch of the Antiquarian—or Archaeological—Society (*borankhadi samosom*).[38]

King Chulalongkorn began his speech, given in the presence of nobles and high officials, by pointing out that while most countries possessed evidence of their past dating back a thousand years, and some even three times as much, Siam had lost most of its historical records in war. The fragmentary nature of the surviving evidence, he went on, documented no more than the past four or five centuries, not enough to make Siamese history notable; moreover, knowledge of the past was derived largely from court chronicles that were themselves in need of verification. To advance knowledge of the past thousand years of Siamese history one must start, Chulalongkorn proposed, by studying the several regional polities that had been powerful at one time or another; and while hoping for a history of Siam to be compiled as soon as possible, he emphasized the need for the careful examination of sources and documents. Whatever the result of the scrutiny of evidence, he concluded, it should cause no embarrassment but be welcomed as a contribution to a better understanding of Siamese history.[39] The king's exhortation was put into practice the following day, which was devoted to a sightseeing tour of Ayutthaya's ruins.

With their contrasting mise-en-scène, the Bangkok and Ayutthaya pageants articulated the modernizing monarchy's self-congratulatory narrative from two distinct yet complementary viewpoints: the attainment of progress and civilization, and its taking place in a historical continuum of royal achievements. These celebratory representations of the king's agency constituted two sides of the same ideological project: the symbolic empowerment of the royal elite in political as well as cultural terms. A shared notion of the past is crucial to establishing bonds among members of the same community or social group. Shared notions of the past come, however, in different forms: a spontaneous one, a collective memory that, as French sociologist Maurice Halbwachs proposed in the 1930s, is propelled by continuous attachment to an ancestral territory and direct witness to an event;[40] and history, a narrative of past events extending beyond living memory that is instilled primarily through schooling and is a distinctive feature of the cultural stock of the citizens of modern nations.

Rama V, still fresh from the conferral of the doctorate by the University of Cambridge for his patronage of Orientalist scholarship, understood that it was not only material wealth and military strength that made a nation modern, but also a documented—and possibly far-reaching—history. As he repeatedly stressed in his speech at the launch of the Antiquarian Society, it was time for a history of Siam based on empirical evidence to be written. In fact, the first initiative in this sense resulted from the activity of a group of European government employees, who in 1904 had formed the Siam Society.[41] What is especially noteworthy about Chulalongkorn's vision of the Siamese past is that, unlike the historical narrative that became hegemonic in later years, the central Thai kingdoms of Sukhothai, Ayutthaya, and Bangkok did not have a pivotal place in it; in the picture of premodern Siam he sketched out, several regional polities coexisted within the geographical space that by the early 1900s had been bounded as Siam's national territory. By anticipating the orientations of much later historiography, Rama V's speech at the founding of the Antiquarian Society can be regarded as "a landmark of historical scholarship in Siam."[42] But the establishment of the Antiquarian Society was not simply a further step in the cultural modernization of the elite; its aim was to increase the cohesion of the newly established bureaucracy by complementing their uniform dress with a uniform historical memory.

Third Act

The celebrative crescendo set in motion in November 1907 culminated one year later with the festivities for Chulalongkorn's fortieth anniversary of reign (*ratchamangkhla phisek*), the "record reign" in the history of the Siamese monarchy.[43] The public celebration of anniversaries of reign is a conspicuous example of invented tradition. Launched by the Golden Jubilee of Queen Victoria in 1887, when her fiftieth year on the throne was publicly celebrated, the fashion of a ceremonial anniversary was immediately imitated by other European monarchs.[44] The organization of Rama V's "record reign" celebrations was entrusted to a committee made up of the cabinet's ministries and the chief commanders of the navy and the army under the crown prince's presidency. When a student in Britain, Vajiravudh had taken part in the pageant for Queen Victoria's Diamond Jubilee in 1897. The jubilee started with Victoria's entry into London on 21 June (the day after the anniversary of her accession); on 22 June, the queen rode in an open carriage drawn by eight horses for six miles, from Buckingham Palace to St. Paul's Cathedral and back, in a procession headed by five hundred representatives of the colonial troops followed by British and foreign princesses and princes; among them was Vajiravudh, who rode with the Duke of York and Prince Waldemar of Denmark.[45] King Chulalongkorn, who was touring Europe at that time, deferred his visit to Britain until the end of July because the jubilee's program contemplated the attendance of the offspring of foreign royalty only.

Vajiravudh's experience probably came in handy when he was put in charge of the celebration's organizing committee. Initially, the program for the celebrations extended over four days (10 to 13 November) and was budgeted at 200,000 baht.[46] Although hardly exorbitant (the cost of Vajiravudh's second coronation, in 1911, approximated 5 million baht),[47] the Office of the Royal Treasury did not have such a budget, so funds had to be drawn from alternative sources.[48] Eventually, the celebrations lasted twice the number of days originally planned: eight days, starting on 11 November, and preceded, on 10 November, by Brahmanic ceremonies in the Grand Palace and Wat Phra Keo. Kicking off the celebrations was the unveiling of the equestrian statue of the king. The events staged over the next four days included a motorcar parade, a procession of floats, and the king's visit to the Chinese district. There were also banquets for officials and foreign representatives, and a military review on 18 November marked the end of the celebrations. A precise estimate of popular participation is not possible; the total revenues of Bangkok's two tram companies in the days of 11 to 15 November—some 36,000 baht (a daily average in excess of 7,000 baht)—were, however, somewhat lower than in the two days of festivities following Rama V's return from Europe a year earlier.[49]

The jubilee's opening ceremony was the laying of the foundation stone of the Ananta Samakhom Throne Hall, on the early morning of 11 November. At the auspicious time set by the court astrologers (7:29:8 A.M.), Rama V laid down a number of bricks covered with gold, silver, and bronze and containing inside medals, stamps, king's letters concerning the building, and a copy of its plan. Among those present at the ceremony were the minister of municipal government, Phraya Sukhum (who on the jubilee's occasion was granted the title of Chaophraya Yomarat), the Italian architects of the Public Works Department (Allegri, Tamagno, and Rigotti), and the representative of the French firm that had provided the machinery to sink the building's foundations (figure 18). The ceremony ended with the distribution of medals to the officials, offerings to the monks, and the firing of a salute.[50] In spite of the morning rain, a sunny afternoon graced the unveiling of the king's equestrian statue. The open space at the end of Ratcha Damnoen Avenue, the Phra Lan, presented a remarkable scene of pomp. Royal symbols (the wheel, flags, and tiered umbrellas) were to be seen everywhere. In the middle, next to the statue concealed by a yellow silk cloth, stood a canopied platform. Around it, the princes of the royal household, high-ranking officials, foreign representatives, provincial lords from the north, and even dignitaries from the Malay sultanates (then in the process of becoming British protectorates) had gathered. In addition, the Phra Lan accommodated a standing crowd who had come to witness the ceremony (figure 19).

At four o'clock Rama V, wearing the full-dress uniform of army field marshal, made his appearance in the royal pavilion, on the far end of the Phra Lan, and from there walked, flanked by two rows of officials, to the central platform. The crown prince then began his dedication, which highlighted, more than the king's accomplishments, the special relationship he had established with his subjects. First Vajiravudh congratulated his father for attaining an absolute record in the "history of the Thai nation" (*tamnan haengchat thai*)—a record, he remarked, that was even more significant given the degree of welfare the people had come to enjoy. At a difficult time in Siam's history, when the country was pursuing the path toward progress, Vajiravudh continued, Rama V had made his appearance as an avatar to lead Siam to its present prosperity. The king's action had been inspired by compassion (*metta,* a Buddhist virtue), which had won him the heart of his subjects and even the admiration of foreigners; like a merciful father, Rama V had promoted the well-being of his subjects and offered them an example of probity. The ensuing feelings of loyalty and devotion,

Vajiravudh concluded, had prompted the realization of the statue, which would stand as a testimony to future generations.[51]

In his much longer reply, Chulalongkorn developed in historical perspective the theme, already outlined in the speeches he had given the year before, of his reign as one of momentous change. His fortieth anniversary of reign, Rama V said after the opening thanks, should not induce too much pride; foreign sovereigns, after all, had equaled and even exceeded such a record (an allusion to Queen Victoria); the real merit of so long a reign was that it had allowed the implementation of a series of reforms whose results were now apparent. The key to a ruler's success, he continued, lies in his ability to engage his own times. In the past, the country's defense and agricultural development had been the primary concerns; the establishment of diplomatic relations in the Fourth Reign had opened the way to international trade that benefited the people but also demanded changes in the way of government that King Mongkut had not time to pursue. In his own reign, Chulalongkorn continued, the necessity for major reforms had become pressing, but these had to be pursued with thoughtfulness so that changes would not upset the traditional customs and habits of the people. A generation was needed for that, particularly because domestic reforms had a slow start while the pace of change outside Siam was dramatic. Still, the achievements of the last forty years, Rama V proudly claimed, surpassed those of the previous five centuries. International relations, he then noted in a crucial passage, had effaced the time when small things were considered important and near places remote, and when aims and desires reflected this narrow worldview. But dealing with the foreign powers required a stable government capable of maintaining the country's independence and fostering its development. Critical to this end was the solidarity (*samakkhi*) between nobility and populace, which would create a sense of national unity (*chat annung andiao*) regardless of ethnic and religious differences among the country's inhabitants. External as well as internal factors had hindered modernization, but its results, the king concluded, were now evident, and the statue erected by public subscription should serve both to encourage efforts toward a brighter future and to be a reminder of social harmony in Siam.[52]

Chulalongkorn then pulled the cord holding the silk cover, which got caught in one of the bronze horse's ears. When the statue was finally disclosed, the inscription on the bronze plate on its marble base was also revealed.[53] After the firing of a salute the king returned to his pavilion.

From there he presented new colors to twelve army companies, which then performed the ceremony of trooping the color, thus characterizing the whole afternoon as a display (as far as the situation allowed it) of state pomp and martial pride. In contrast, the progress of motorcars organized by Prince Damrong on the following day was probably the oddest spectacle of the jubilee. Some 112 cars, largely from the royal garage, were all painstakingly decorated; the king's in particular, with its papier-mâché sculptures of Garuda and the hero Narai, resembled a movable artwork. Thus decked, and after a heavy afternoon downpour, the cars were driven around the city by princes, officials, and members of the diplomatic corps.[54] From Dusit Park the motorized procession headed, through the recently opened Prachechin Road, for the Pathumwan area to inaugurate a "birthday bridge," Chelim Lok 55. The minister of municipal government gave a speech emphasizing the contribution of the king's Privy Purse to public welfare.[55] Meanwhile, crowds had gathered along New Road to watch, in the *Bangkok Times*' comment, "a somewhat ragged procession."[56]

The *Bangkok Times* was considerably more appreciative of the carnival procession staged along Ratcha Damnoen on the thirteenth, "the great popular event of the whole celebrations."[57] Taking part in the procession, which lasted from the early afternoon to the evening, were some twenty thousand people and seventy-seven floats carrying tableaux vivants that represented government undertakings and economic activities, as well as the provinces' geographical features and agricultural and manufactured products. The country and its inhabitants were thus made into a spectacle for the people of Bangkok and, at the same time, synoptically surveyed by the royal gaze. Opening the procession was the crown prince's float, representing the abolition of bondage, followed by those of ministries and departments. Worthy of a mention as the most fanciful and ingenious floats were the Health Department's, with a cardboard hospital and impersonators of doctors and patients preceded by carriers of giant models of medicine bottles, surgical instruments, and medicinal herbs; the Inland Revenue Department's, with porters of goods liable to taxation and graphics showing revenue increase during the reign; the floats of the Railways and the Post and Telegraph Departments, with cardboard models of locomotives, telephone and telegraph sets, and giant stamps and postcards; and the Irrigation Department's float, which was surrounded by a hundred men walking close to each other holding bunches of paddy on their heads to represent a rice field. In between the ministerial floats those of sixteen provinces, displaying costumes, agricultural products, and other distinctive features, were paraded. Closing the procession were twenty-four floats marshaled by private firms and entrepreneurs.

The next day the floats were put on display along the Grand Palace walls and further inspected by the king, while the people from the country-side wandered around Bangkok. That night they might have had, together with the city dwellers, a glimpse of the cinematographic show held for the royalty and their guests on the Phra Lan. Four days later (18 November), several thousand people again congregated at Sanam Luang, the open space opposite the Grand Palace, for the review of the troops that closed the jubilee. A recent addition to state ceremonial, the general military review had been first performed for the coronation anniversary in 1906. Troops were indeed a common sight at all the jubilee ceremonies, evidence of the modernization of the state as well as of its new powers of coercion and repression.

As anticipated by the welcoming pageant in November 1907, the jubilee's leitmotif was the progress Siam had achieved in Chulalongkorn's reign of forty years. Yet while the 1907 pageant had been played out as an ephemeral event, the memory of which was retained only in photographs, the record reign celebrations were heightened by the production of mne-monic sites that hallmarked its momentousness and allowed for its later recollection. The realization of the foremost among these mnemonic sites, the king's equestrian statue, was detailed in the previous chapter. Com-memorative medals and—a first for Siam—celebrative stamps (not to men-tion the mementos distributed to contributors to the statue) also served this purpose. The mise-en-scène of contemporary European political the-atrics was appropriated almost wholesale by the planners of Chulalong-korn's jubilee. Because the event celebrated his civilizing rule, there was little attempt at original inventions—except for the quaint procession of bedecked motorcars, hard to imagine at a royal jubilee elsewhere but a feature that modernized the procession of decorated barges performed for the *kathin*.

Given the globalized style of the pageantry, one needs to look at the speeches delivered by the king and the crown prince to detect the specific political ideology underpinning the celebrations. These speeches presented Rama V both as the embodiment of the Buddhist benevolent monarch and a national leader standing as his country's unifying symbol in accordance with post-Napoleonic monarchical rhetoric. Language provides, in this case, a useful indicator. Whereas the Thai vocabulary of power in which the speeches were couched blended these distinct conceptions of royal authority, the English translations and the commentary that appeared in the *Bangkok Times* spoke the unmistakable language of late-nineteenth-century nationalism: "The spirit of unity, inspiring mutual confidence and help among all, from Prince to peasant, is the ideal His Majesty sets before the nation. It never has been realized anywhere but it is the end that every good ruler and patriot strives for."[58]

In fact, it is in the articulation of concepts such as *samakkhi* and *chat* that, as Eiji Murashima has pointed out, the distinctive character of modern Siamese state ideology unravels itself.[59] *Chat* expressed the idea of a community unified by loyalty to a leader acting according to the *tham,* or moral law. *Chat* carried thus more affinity with the absolutist doctrine of the sovereign's immortal "political body" (complementing his mortal "natural body") than with the nineteenth-century political idea of nation to which it is often, and mistakenly, likened. As for "*samakkhi,*" translatable as "unity" as well as "solidarity," it had been invoked by Chulalongkorn since a speech in 1903 in which he noted that even if conflicting factions were to emerge within the ruling elite, the king's leadership was primary and was the pillar of the state in accordance with the idea of *chat.*[60] The reiteration of the need for *samakkhi* in his speech at the statue's unveiling, a speech addressed above all to the officials, might be taken as betraying concern over growing dissatisfaction with the autocratic government at a time otherwise regarded as the apogee of the absolute monarchy. Discontent was on the rise among officers of commoner background because of the restrictions introduced in the entry requirements to the military academy between 1906 and 1909.[61] And, indeed, in 1912 a coup planned by military and naval officers with the intention of deposing King Vajiravudh was discovered and suppressed. Rama V, however, had not had to face a challenge to his authority; until the very end of his reign when his time came, he could regard himself as a harbinger, not an opponent, of change.

Finale

The last public spectacle associated with Rama V took place posthumously, on 16 March 1911, the day of his cremation. King Chulalongkorn had died of uremia (a kidney dysfunction) at 00:45 A.M. on 23 October 1910. The next day the corpse was moved from Dusit Park to the Grand Palace in a procession in which the royal urn, borne on a catafalque, was escorted by Vajiravudh, the male members of the royal family, high-rank officials, and regiments of the army, the royal guard, and the navy.[62] Chulalongkorn's death was the first of a Siamese monarch to elicit a worldwide response. The next day telegrams of condolence were sent from several of the European sovereigns and heads of state Rama V had met in the course of his trips: King Edward and Queen Alexandra, Tsar Nicholas II, the Austrian and German emperors, the royals of Italy, Spain, the Netherlands, Norway, the presidents of France and the Swiss Confederation, the khedive of Egypt, and even the Japanese emperor. Bangkok's firms and banks were closed on the day after the king's death, and foreign residents too expressed their sorrow, often accompanied by the request of an appointment to pay homage to the king's corpse.[63] Even in French Indochina flags were reportedly flown at half mast on 25 October.[64]

Interposed with the public mourning for Chulalongkorn's death were Vajiravudh's accession ceremonies, which culminated with his coronation on 11 November. The anniversary of Chulalongkorn's coronation was also celebrated with memorial services and the inauguration of the last but one of his birthday bridges, Chelimdet 57, completing Phraya Thai Road, which linked the Dusit district to the new railway station at Hua Lamphong.[65] A few weeks later, Rama VI issued an edict thanking the populace for "the touching demonstration of affection and respect to the memory of His Majesty's late royal father" and wishing that it could result "in prosperity and happiness for everyone."[66] The next February (1911), as the date of the cremation approached, dispositions were issued for those wishing to participate in it, thus officially transforming the king's cremation ceremony into a public event. On 13, 14, and 15 March, all "without distinction of class, race, or language, men as well as women," were allowed to attend the services performed at the lying in state in the Grand Palace's Dusit Throne Hall. The services included the reading of chapters from the Buddhist scriptures, the chanting of prayers, meditation, and the collection of donations for the repair of temples, construction of new buildings, educational purposes, and nursing. Those who intended to witness the funeral procession were asked to bring offerings of flowers and joss sticks and to assemble on both sides of Sanam Chai Road and in the upper section of Sanam Luang (the Pramane Ground). At the end of the procession, spectators could join in, bringing their offerings. From the seventeenth to the twentieth of March, King Chulalongkorn's ashes lay in state in the Dusit Maha Prasat for the last public homage. Mourners were told to dress in white, but exceptions were allowed in accordance with individual customs.[67]

Because of the reduction in the scale of cremations during the Fifth Reign,[68] Chulalongkorn's funeral pyre was considerably smaller than that erected for King Mongkut, and the same applied to the temporary buildings and the area occupied on Sanam Luang.[69] The pyre, a central tower with four smaller structures at the corners, was raised on a platform measuring eleven and a half square meters; the Public Works Department also built pavilions for the royalty and for state officials and the diplomatic corps.[70] Because of the abolition at funerals of sideshows such as fireworks and plays, which Chulalongkorn saw as diminishing the solemnity of the ritual,[71] the only other structures present on Sanam Luang were refreshment tents (water tanks were also placed along the route of the funeral procession). The cremation ceremony's mise-en-scène was a traditional one but for the parade of modern military uniforms—a choice made more significant by the presence of the representatives of Western countries. The initial idea of using a carriage pulled by horses to convey the urn was abandoned in favor of the royal funeral car pulled manually (the same used for Mongkut's funeral but with a few technical improvements).[72] A volume of religious sermons was also printed for distribution at the cremation.[73]

The setting of the ceremony was Bangkok's historic core—Rattanakosin City. The funeral procession's route followed the perimeter of the Grand Palace counterclockwise, from the western to the northern gate. Shortly after 1 p.m. the urn was removed from the Dusit Throne Hall and borne on a palanquin to Wat Chethupon (Wat Pho), where the urn was placed on the funeral car while ministers, officers, and consular representatives assembled. Meanwhile the troops heading the procession (the royal guard and regiments of the cavalry, artillery, engineers, infantry, plus five musical bands) began marching past Sanam Chai Road, which runs along the royal palace's eastern walls. Preceded by the bearers of royal insignia, the funeral car drawn by 220 pullers made its appearance; it was followed by the king and the royal princes; the top military officers; the special representatives of Belgium, Denmark, Germany, Great Britain, Italy, the Netherlands, Russia, the United States of America, and Japan; high-ranking officials; the diplomatic corps; ministerial personnel; and, finally, the navy band and the marines. When the funeral car reached the building of the Ministry of Justice, the procession halted briefly to allow the mourners to take their seats in the pavilions; then, at a given signal, the procession moved again into the open space of Sanam Luang toward the pyre. Prince Patriarch Wachirayan, carried on a palanquin, was followed by Prince Atsadang, who, garbed in courtly robes, distributed roasted rice, and Prince Chakrabongse, who held the long strip of silk connected to the urn. Behind it walked King Vajiravudh with the other princes. At 6:33 P.M., Rama VI lit the funeral pyre; as soon as this was done, the troops volleyed and the band played the royal hymn. The next day Rama V's ashes were enshrined in the Dusit Throne Hall.[74]

According to the estimate of the *Bangkok Times,* Chulalongkorn's cremation ceremony was attended by ten thousand to twelve thousand people. The day after the ceremony the newspaper wrote, "This is said to be the first time in history on which members of the *ratsadorn* [populace] as such have been allowed to take part in the cremation of a king, and the same was also true for their being freely admitted to the lying in state."[75] The participation of ordinary people to the king's cremation marked a significant change in the aloof character of Indic state theatrics that was consonant with the populist image of the monarchy projected in the Fifth Reign's later years. At the same time, the staging of Chulalongkorn's cremation adhered in large measure to Bhramanic custom, the only exceptions being the military honors and the musical tunes (Chopin's Funeral March and the death march from Handel's *Saul,* which had already entered the funeral liturgy[76]).

This traditionalism foreshadowed the funeral ceremony on 13 September 1912 of the other great Asian modernizer, Emperor Meiji, in which the ox-drawn hearse, the costumes and paraphernalia, the musical accompaniment by gongs and drums, and the coffin's journey from Tokyo to Kyoto, the old imperial capital, produced an even more impressive spectacle of Oriental pomp than Bangkok's.[77] Fujitani contends that the emperor's funeral was antiquarian in style because the government saw the ongoing revival of old customs by the dynasties of Austria, Prussia, and Russia (indeed, Europe's most conservative) as suitable for expressing the majesty of Japan's imperial household as well.[78] The Japanese delegate who participated at Rama V's cremation (a presence ignored by Fujitani) could have only furthered such an orientation.

In more general terms, the revival of vernacular ritual signaled a reaction against cultural Westernization, which started in Japan in the latter half of the Meiji era and in Siam only in the Sixth Reign. In Europe, the study and reelaboration of vernacular cultures played a significant part in the awakening of nationalist sentiments, an awakening that culminated in the efflorescence in the last quarter of the nineteenth century of newly invented traditions that invoked publicly the nation's primordial past. However, the initial institutionalization of a national cultural heritage in Siam, as well as in Japan, made its own the dichotomy posited by Orientalist scholarship between traditional cultural expressions, whose authenticity was construed in spatial and temporal opposition to modernity, and modern ones, which were discounted as a mimicry of Western civilization.[79] Also, the staging of vernacular culture as a signifier of the nation's uniqueness did not start with the antiquarian spectacles of Chulalongkorn's cremation and Emperor Meiji's funeral; both Siam and Japan had been representing themselves by means of "traditional" artifacts at international exhibitions in Europe and America since the 1870s. It is to these spectacles that we shall turn our attention in the next chapter.

Chapter 6

On the World Stage

At the same time that the Siamese modernizing elite appropriated Western objects to refashion their self- and public images, they were also engaged in representing Siam by means of its material culture for the European and American audiences of international exhibitions—one of the prominent invented traditions of the second half of the nineteenth century.[1] What the promoters of these events concocted by blending the profit-making rationale of trade fairs, the classificatory approach of museums, and the entertainment of itinerant shows was an eminently modern kind of spectacle centered on the display of commodities. A crucial ingredient of their success was also the synergy with the printed media, which amplified the resonance of exhibitions by allowing those who could not physically pay a visit to do it vicariously via guidebooks, catalogs, illustrated periodicals, and ephemera. Even though in a reverse dynamic to that examined thus far, things produced and circulated—physically as well as symbolically—within the global capitalist marketplace at the turn of the nineteenth and twentieth centuries made it possible for the Siamese elite to represent their rule as civilizing, both to themselves and to the wider Victorian ecumene.

The vogue for international exhibitions started in 1851, with the Great Exhibition of the Work of Industry of all Nations, held in London. The Crystal Palace, the demountable glass and iron building erected on that occasion to house the universe of modern consumer goods, set the pattern for the ephemeral grandeur of subsequent events, which took place at regular intervals of a few years until the eve of World War II. Particularly in the relatively peaceful period 1870–1914, international exhibitions were a sublimated expression of rivalry between world powers, especially Britain and France. Seen first in London, exhibitions became closely identified with Paris, whose bustling image at that time earned the French capital the appellation of *ville lumière*. Meanwhile, on the opposite side of the Atlantic the ascendancy of the United States as a major world power was foreshadowed by the ever-increasing dimensions of world's fairs, as international exhibitions came to be popularly known there.

Promoted as ecumenical events, international exhibitions were, in fact, prime sites of nationalist representation by virtue of an exhibiting strategy of juxtaposition that "othered" all participating countries while situating them within the hierarchical order of (Western) civilization. Euro-American nations, culturally "other" among themselves, were represented by industrial products that demonstrated their level of progress and, conversely, artworks said to embody their distinctively "national" genius. Placed at various stages on the evolutionary yardstick of progress were the ethnically "other," represented by artifacts and even "living exhibits." The political reality and ideology of imperialism were as central to the idea of international exhibitions as nationalism and global capitalism. The governments of Britain and France spared no expenses to extol the importance of their imperial possessions in the eyes of metropolitan audiences, who were able to marvel at the Indian cultural artifacts and the replicas of Khmer monuments and even taste the dishes and smell the fragrances of their overseas colonies without ever setting foot there. International exhibitions also helped promote diplomatic ties, as with the Franco-British Exposition of 1908, which cemented the new friendly climate in the relations between the two countries following the Entente Cordiale of 1904.

Siam's participation at some of the grandest international exhibitions of the period is examined in this chapter: the *expositions universelles* held in Paris in 1878, 1889, and 1900; the World's Columbian Exposition in Chicago, in 1893; the Louisiana Purchase Exposition in St. Louis, in 1904; the Esposizione Internazionale in Turin, in 1911. In attempting to project a distinctive national profile by means of material culture, the Siamese authorities faced the dilemma, shared by a handful of non-Western sovereign states (including Japan, China, the Ottoman Empire, Persia, and a few others), of pandering to Western curiosity for the exotic and, at the same time, producing evidence of their accomplishments on the way to progress. Even Orientalistic representational styles could be appropriated and put to use by the exhibiting country. The case of Meiji Japan is most instructive in this regard. At Chicago in 1893, besides making a huge impression with their wooden pavilion, the Japanese were invited to attend the concomitant World's Parliament of Religions where they promoted, as Japan's national faith, a rationalistic form of Buddhism, which was the product of the Meiji religious revival. At the St. Louis fair of 1904, the year of the Russo-Japanese War, Japan hosted a Red Cross stand within its pavilion to signify its commitment to the international conventions in time of peace as well as war. In 1910, the Japan-British Exhibition contributed to legitimate the former's occupation of Formosa and Korea by representing Japanese rule in the same light as British rule in India and Africa.[2]

Siam's self-representation on the exhibitions' global stage was ultimately bound to the nature of its economy as well as to the financial constraints faced by the organizers. But despite Siam's initial placement among Europe's colonies, participation at such venues eventually contributed to project its image as one in the family of modern nations. Indeed, taking part in an exhibition involved a formal procedure (invitation by the local ambassador, acceptance, dispatch of representatives to the host country) that mirrored modern diplomatic relations. Another notable aspect was the localization of the world's fair format on a domestic scale as early as 1882, when an exhibition was held for the centennial of the Chakri dynasty on Sanam Luang, the field facing the Grand Palace; on display were natural and manufactured products and arts and crafts, among which stood out the king's jewelry.[3] The Annual Exhibition of Agriculture and Commerce was also held in April 1910 and April 1911 at the Agricultural College in the Sapathum Palace, and reports of it published.[4] Rama VI even planned a Siamese kingdom exhibition to be held in January 1926 in conjunction with his fifteenth anniversary of reign; the project was canceled following his death in November 1925, yet publication of the accompanying souvenir volume went ahead.[5] Above all, the technological innovations and scenic inventions first presented at world's fairs were exploited to great effect in the pageants staged for Rama V's jubilee celebrations.

At the Bazaar of Exoticism

If in its diplomatic maneuvring with France and Great Britain the Siamese government tended to lean toward the latter, a look at diplomatic relations as entertained through international exhibitions reveals a different picture. Over the period 1851–1911 Siam participated at none of the exhibitions held in England,[6] but regularly attended exhibitions in Paris—right in the "crocodile's mouth," to use King Mongkut's Aesopian allegory of French imperialism. Siam's semiofficial debut at Paris' second *exposition universelle,* held in 1867 and visited by eight million people, was due to the initiative of the consul for Siam in France, Amedee de Gréhan, with the endorsement of Rama IV. De Gréhan also authored a book whose subsequent editions include details on Siam's participation at subsequent Parisian exhibitions.[7] In 1867 Siam was awarded a gold medal for its exhibits of cotton, tobacco, cereals, and fishing implements; three *mentions honorables* for clothes, fans, and swallows' nests; and a special medal for the nine-meter-long models of the royal barges.

Eight years after defeat in the war with Prussia, which had caused the collapse of the Second Empire, France marked its comeback in the international arena with an exhibition that attracted twelve million visitors. The main portion of the *exposition universelle* of 1878 was in the area of the Champ de Mars where lay the Rue des Nations, a street front several hundred meters long flanked by pavilions epitomizing the architectural styles of the exhibiting countries.[8] The Siamese exhibit, however, was housed with those of Persia and the French colonies of Tunisia, Morocco, and Annam in a single pavilion that, in the elegiac words of an observer, "brotherly united [them] in a 10-meter façade" by dividing it into five segments—one for each country.[9] A small Siamese kiosk, whose purpose was to showcase the models of three royal barges that were never delivered, was situated at the Trocadero, the site of the exposition on the opposite bank of the Seine.

The effort that went into arranging the Siamese exhibit for this exhibition was considerably bigger than it had been in 1867. An English-language catalog of the exhibit was even printed at the Bangkok press of Reverend Bradley and made available at the venue in a French version.[10] The Siamese exhibit included 460 items for sale, to which commissioner de Gréhan added some objects from his personal collection. In the end, Siam was awarded two grands prix (for silk fabrics and apparel), a gold medal (hunting and fishing implements), a silver medal (musical instruments), three bronze medals (agricultural products, painting and drawing materials, and samples of their application), and two *mentions honorables* (furniture and saddlery). At this stage the king still figured as the only exhibitor, so the exhibits highlighted Siam's agricultural and manufacturing sectors as a whole rather than individual entrepreneurs, as was later the case.

A book published for the occasion, *Le royaume de Siam au Champ de Mars en 1878,* pointed out that "the first and principal clients of His Majesty the King of Siam" were high-society figures, including aristocrats and stage diva Sarah Bernhardt, all of them "guarantors of understanding and good taste" (*intelligence et bon goût*).[11] The irony underlying the circulation of luxury objects at the turn of the century was such that while the Siamese exotica on display at the *expositions universelles* enjoyed the aesthetic legitimation of these cosmopolitan tastemakers, the mass-produced Western kitsch exhibited there ended up furnishing the residences of the Bangok elite. *Le royaume de Siam* also reviewed the history of diplomatic relations between Siam and France, particularly in the reigns of Louis XIV and his contemporary, Narai. Still, the author did not refrain from proffering advice for the present, as when he compared the three prizes awarded to Siam for educational exhibits (musical instruments, painting materials, and drawings) to the three gold medals won in the same category by Japan, "an eminent model to follow in the vital sphere of teaching." This piece of advice was followed by the praise of the activity of the French (and, secondarily, American) missionaries in Bangkok, "humble and ardent pioneers of Christian civilization who work not only for the conversion of the souls but also for the development of the minds."[12]

In 1889 Paris hosted its fourth *exposition universelle,* which between May and October attracted twenty-five million visitors. It was on that occasion that Gustave Eiffel's iron tower was built despite strong criticism; never dismantled, it became Paris' foremost architectural symbol and tourist attraction (Rama V too ascended it on both his visits to the French capital). Because the exposition celebrated the centennial of the revolution that had ousted the Bourbon dynasty in 1789, several monarchies refused to participate; Queen Victoria went as far as recalling the ambassador in Paris so that no British official representative would be present at the opening. The Siamese authorities, however, after some initial hesitation, accepted the invitation. Siam's exhibit was housed in the Palais des Industries Diverses, on a 250-square-meter area sandwiched between the Japanese and Egyptian displays. Exhibits included apparel, silk and linen clothes, embroidery, jewelry, copper and ivory enamelware, musical instruments, fermented rice, and a gilded furniture set that included a canopied bed, armchairs, and sofas.[13]

The workmanship of the Siamese enamelware in particular was praised by an Italian journalist reviewing the exhibition for the readers back home as "lacking the mechanical finish of European jewelry but presenting those small imperfections that reveal individual labor, man's creative hand—in a word, the artist." The reviewer commented favorably also on the 64-square-meter kiosk, sent in sections from Bangkok, that stood along the extension of the Rue du Cairo, the exposition's exotic promenade (see figure 20). The kiosk's fretwork pattern, the glass mosaics of its roof, the floor's marquetry, its red upholstery, and the gilded and carved decorations showed a "pomp neither jarring nor heavy . . . the Asian sensibility that sustains this miracle should be studied by our artists whose creations are so often out of place."[14] According to Sylviane Leprun, who has examined colonial displays at French exhibitions, a stereotypical view of exotic artifacts as small, ornamental, and charming yet not beautiful became established following the London exhibition of 1867.[15] The comments quoted above indicate, however, that handcrafted items such as the Siamese enamelware evoked in Europeans nostalgia for artisan workmanship that also animated contemporary art and social critics such as John Ruskin and William Morris. Similar to the representation of landscapes and ways of life, the Orient's material culture stood in late-nineteenth-century Europe as a mirror image whereby to mourn the loss of individual genius caused by the Industrial Revolution. The irony, again, shows itself in the fact that European appreciation of the intrinsic aesthetic value of Siamese arts and crafts was contrasted by the Siamese elite's thirst for Western luxury objects through which they fashioned their new self-image.

The Parisian exposition of 1889 was the first that devoted a considerable space to France's *mission civilisatrice* in Indochina. A forty-meter-tall model of a Khmer sanctuary tower stood at the center of a 6,000-square-meter walled enclosure, in which agricultural products, cloth, jewels, weapons, musical instruments, and miniature dwellings were exhibited. The model was said to be a reproduction of an archway of Angkor Wat, which French explorer Henri Mouhot had brought to world fame in the early 1860s when the Cambodian province of Siemreap, where the monumental complex of Angkor lies, was still subject to Bangkok's suzerainty; as a result, control over this province became a major cause of dispute. When, in 1907, control over Siemreap was ceded to the king of Cambodia, the French and their Phnom Penh protégé were not alone in rejoicing; reflecting the "cordial" climate recently established between Paris and London, the *Daily Telegraph* commented, "It is well that its [Angkor's] future is to be cared for by so appreciative a people as our neighbours across the Channel."[16]

As a result of France's annexation of Laos in 1893 and the conse-
quent confrontation at the mouth of the Chao Phraya River in July that
year, Franco-Siamese relations grew increasingly tense in the mid-1890s.
Thus, when in 1895 the French minister-resident in Bangkok presented
Minister of Foreign Affairs Devawongse with the invitation to participate
in the *exposition* planned for 1900, Siamese acceptance did not immediately follow. The decision to participate was taken only in 1898, after
Chulalongkorn's visit to France the year before.[17] An apposite commission
was formed with Prince Phanurang as president, Prince Norathip as secretary, and Phraya Suriya Nuwat as commissioner-general; the consul for
Siam in Paris, de Gréhan, commissioner-general at the previous exhibitions, was demoted to the office of vice commissioner. Moreover, in the
exhibition's original plan the Siamese display was to be placed in the colonial section; it was only after strong protestations that the organizers agreed
upon relocation.[18] Siam thus ended up for the first time with a pavilion of
its own. Designed by architect E. Chastel (who happened to be de Gréhan's
son-in-law), the pavilion featured two separate halls linked by a gangway;
the main hall had an octagonal shape and was topped by a thirty-meter
spire. According to the threefold typology of colonial pavilions proposed
by Leprun,[19] that of Siam would qualify as a "stylized interpretation" of
Siamese architecture, which was evoked by characteristic elements such as
the spire and the gilded ornamentation. In any case, the final result must
have been far from impressive; there is no mention of the pavilion in the
general publications about the exposition, and its only description is found
in the booklet accompanying the Siamese display.[20]

As the event symbolizing the start of the twentieth century, the
Paris *exposition* of 1900 was designed to outclass all previous such events. It
was open for seven months, from 14 April to 12 November; thirty-six
countries mounted exhibits, and fifty-one million people visited. Three
permanent structures were built for the occasion: the Grand Palais, the
Petit Palais, and the Alexandre III Bridge, which linked the two sites of
the exhibition across the Seine. French colonies too were highlighted as
never before. France's few strongholds in India were evoked on a grand
manner by the model of a Hindu temple, stalls, workshops, and a restaurant,
the whole spreading over a 3,000-square-meter area. But the main effort
went into the Indochinese display, which occupied a 20,000-square-meter
site with architectural models and even a make-believe village where Cambodian and Laotian people were stationed. The largest building was the

replica of a Khmer temple with a monumental staircase built atop an artificial hillock; the interior of the temple replica was shaped like a grotto for
worship. A large stupa stood behind the temple and two smaller stupas in
front of it, on both sides. Unlike most of the attractions at the exhibition,
the Indochinese village was free of charge.[21] Author Maurice Talmeyr,
among the few critics of this exhibition, wrote disparagingly in the prestigious *Revue des deux mondes* of "Hindu temples, savage huts, pagodas, souks,
Algerian alleys, Chinese, Japanese, Sudanese, Senegalese, Siamese, Cambodian quarters . . . a bazaar of climates, architectural styles, colors, cui-
sine, music."[22]

Siamese exhibits encompassed the usual range of natural and manufactured products but for one item: a five-by-twelve-meter map of the
kingdom (1:760,320 scale). The map was an exhibit of the Royal Survey
Department, which had been officially established in 1885 as an agency
of the Ministry of Agriculture under the direction of the Briton James
McCarthy.[23] Although mentioned only in passing in Thongchai's *Siam
Mapped*,[24] this map, based on the charting carried out in the previous two
decades by both the French and the British, is emblematic of the production of Siam's "geo-body" at the turn of the nineteenth century. In 1900,
this map was still a work in progress. The only border marked on it was
that between Siam and British Burma after the surveying carried out by
the British in 1890–1891; its toponymy too was borrowed from the Royal
Geographical Society. The eastern portion of the map was based on the
charting of the Indochinese region by the Mission Pavie in 1881–1885;
but the map showed no border, since in 1900 the boundary line was still
the object of negotiations between Siam and France (the treaty that settled
the question was ratified only seven years later). However, the map's social
life had started before its exhibition in Paris in 1900. The original sheets,
drawn by the Royal Survey Department, were zincographed by the British
Survey Office in Calcutta and then lithographed in a twelve-sheet format
by a firm in Edinburgh; one hundred printed copies of the map had been
put on sale in Bangkok at the price of 24 baht already in the early months
of 1898.[25] The Pavie map, on the other hand, became available in printed
form only in 1902.

Despite having been already mapped, Siam's geo-body still lacked
an eastern frontier in 1900. The display of this map in progress at the Parisian *exposition* that boasted as never before of France's colonial power in

Indochina emphasized the incongruity of this absent border in the eyes of the French hosts as well as the rest of the world's. The gold medal unsurprisingly awarded to the Siamese map was like a seal stamped on the colonial pacification of Southeast Asia.[26]

"The Most Despotic Country in the Civilized World"

Whereas the Paris exhibitions were above all designed to promote France's self-image as "the queen of civilization" irrespective of commercial profit, at American world's fairs the political rhetoric of republicanism and democracy went hand in hand with an unapologetic concern for trade and business.[27] Asia in particular came soon to be perceived as "an almost unlimited field for the disposal of American manufacture" and a region where "American enterprise is wanted."[28]

It is generally assumed that China and Japan influenced most perceptions of Asia in the initial stage of America's engagement with that continent. Baptist and Presbyterian missionaries from the United States had, however, been active in Siam since 1828; and official relations between the United States and Siam were established in 1856, only two years after Commodore Perry's landing in Japan. Immediately after signing the treaty, King Mongkut addressed a missive to the U.S. president, Franklin Pierce, and sent him gifts in return for those that had been presented by the American envoy. These gifts, which included ceremonial weapons, gold boxes, a silverware set, sets of clothes, and the oldest extant daguerreotype portrait of Mongkut with his queen consort, were put on display for some time at the National Institute in Washington, D.C., the first Siamese artifacts ever to be publicly exhibited in the United States. In his letter of thanks, President Buchanan (Pierce's successor) stated that the objects had "elicited the admiration of thousands of visitors."[29] The Siamese artifacts were eventually stored at the Smithsonian Institution, which was to have a prominent role in setting up scientific and ethnological exhibits at world's fairs.

The first international exhibition on American soil was held at Philadelphia in 1876 to celebrate the centenary of the Declaration of Independence. The Centennial Exposition, as it was officially designated, attracted some ten million people—that is, nearly one-fifth of the U.S. population at that time. Similar to the one at the Paris exhibition of 1867, the Siamese display at Philadelphia was a small affair, which had been arranged by the U.S. consul in Bangkok. At the end of 1874 the consul, acting on instructions from the State Department, presented King Chulalongkorn with a formal invitation to the forthcoming event. But the appointment of the former American consul (and Baptist missionary) J. H. Chandler, then secretary of the Siamese Foreign Office, as commissioner for Siam to the exhibition provoked a dispute over matters of personal prestige with the incumbent consul, F. W. Partridge. The conflict resulted in a considerable delay of the shipment of the exhibits, which reached Philadelphia five months after the exhibition's opening.

Probably because of the delay, the Siamese exhibition was curiously located inside the U.S. Government Building, in the Navy Department's section.[30] A label specified that the exhibits were "presented by His Majesty to the United States of America as a souvenir from the Kingdom of Siam," while the thirty-four-page printed catalog described them as "articles generally used in the country and samples of trade of Siamese origin."[31] These exhibits included native species of wood, rice, and other plants; farming utensils; theatrical masks and musical instruments; models of country houses, temples, and royal barges; a bust of Mongkut; and a photograph of Chulalongkorn in full regalia taken at his coronation in 1873. The display's showpiece was an enamelled silverware set that earned the appreciation of a reporter writing for an Italian magazine:

> *Isn't it strange that a sovereign from an old lineage in the remote and relaxed Asia takes an interest in the fate of a new republic? But then, the king of Siam has been among the first to open the doors to European civilization. The Siamese king has remarkably improved the living conditions in his country, and has signed treaties with the principal European states, entertaining good relationships with all of them. His gifts, enamelled silver cups and lamps, show a simple but original style, different from our taste yet beautiful.*[32]

While the reporter obviously mistook the recently enthroned Chulalongkorn for his father, his comments indicate how even a small exhibit could draw attention to what, for the great majority of Americans and Europeans at that time, was a remote place in Asia, and could even promote an image of the Siamese monarchs as outward-looking and civilizing.

Seventeen years later, and by then a regular guest at the Parisian venues, Siam took part in the Chicago World's Columbian Exposition. Following the fair's proclamation on Christmas Eve of 1890, at the end of January 1891 the U.S. minister-resident in Bangkok presented the minister of foreign affairs with the invitation to the exhibition to be held in 1893. Siam accepted the invitation four months later. The Siamese authorities took a much deeper interest in arranging their display for the Chicago world's fair than they had for previous exhibitions. The office of commissioner-general was entrusted to Phraya Suriya Nuwat, secretary of the Siamese legation in Berlin, who was temporarily transferred to Chicago; the consul-general for Siam in New York, I. T. Smith, who had hoped to get the job, had to content himself with being Suriya's assistant.[33] The minister of foreign affairs, Prince Devawongse, had even to turn down an offer to act as commissioner by author Jacob Child, who had just published *Pearl of Asia* and probably sought the office for publicity.[34] The selection of the exhibits was entrusted to the minister of agriculture and trade (Phraya Phakharawong, who in 1892 was replaced by Chaophraya Surasakdi Montri), a decision that indicates the appreciation of the commercial opportunities afforded by such an exhibition.

A landmark in the history of exhibitions, the Chicago World's Columbian Exposition welcomed from 1 May to 30 October more than twenty-seven million visitors. Its centerpiece was the majestic Court of Honor, the so-called White City, whose five massive neoclassical buildings encircled a large artificial basin. Besides the White City, the fair spread over two more locations: the Midway Pleasance, where ethnological displays and amusement rides were situated; and the secluded Wooded Island, where Japan's pavilion, modeled on an eleventh-century temple, had been erected by specially sent Japanese craftsmen.[35] The Siamese exhibits were housed in the Agriculture, Forestry, Transportation, Ethnological, Manufactures, and Women's Buildings. The author of the sixteen-page guide to the Siamese exhibits, who was also one of the judges, after remarking patronizingly on Siam as "the largest and richest piece of the earth's surface remaining in the possession of a race not strong enough to defend it but sufficiently civilized and willing to develop it," proceeded to explain:

*Under the enlightened policy of the actual ruler mighty changes in the
condition of the people of Siam have taken place. The innovations which
have been wrought within the last few years are indicative of the rate of
progress likely in the future. The post and telegraph system throughout
the country has been extended; telephone service is in active use; the pas-
senger and postal services are being effected by large and new steamers;
tram-car lines and electric cars have been extended; new roads built, bridges
erected, and . . . there is every indication of prosperity and happiness for
the great kingdom.*[36]

In the white and gold Siamese pavilion in the Agricultural Building were exhibited crops, several species of fish, local implements (ploughs,
hoes, rakes, shovels), cooking utensils, and "a very good display of the national military instruments." The exhibits in the Forestry Building, particularly teak, were said to indicate "what a wonderful opening there un-
doubtedly exists for the importation of all ornamental woods from the
southeast corner of Asia into this country." In the Transportation Building,
Siam exhibited joss chairs used to "convey statues and sacred relics," a
wooden cart, and "a quantity of Siamese boats of different shapes and sizes."
Costumes and toys figured prominently in the Siamese display in the Ethnological Building. The exhibits more likely to testify to the country's
progress were found in the Manufactures Building, in a pavilion "inlaid
with variegated glass, and [that] has an artistic and at the same time a very
rich appearance." There, among the ivory handicrafts, enamelware, silverware, lacquerware, tapestries, coins, and models of floating houses, stood
out "the model of a letter-box used in the country from 1883 to 1887;
the improved model in use from 1887 to 1892; and the latest one in actual
use" together with the plan of Bangkok's General Post Office and plaster
models representing post delivery by land and water. The visitor would
thus realize that "postal arrangements in Siam are as perfect as the most
fastidious citizen could desire."[37]

A distinctive feature of the Chicago World's Columbian Exposition was the Women's Building. The building itself, which comprised
parlors, committee rooms, a library, and a congress hall, was based on a
project chosen in a competition among women architects.[38] In the inten-
tions of the organizers it was to serve as a forum for women's clubs and
organizations from various countries to meet and exchange ideas. With a
view to this outcome, in April 1892 the president of the Board of Lady

Managers, Mrs. Bertha Potter Palmer (wife of the fair commission's president), addressed a letter to Queen Saowapha soliciting the appointment of a commission of women to select exhibits that could "most fully and fitly illustrate the progress and achievements of the women of Siam." The request was accompanied by the declaration of "the profound and universal esteem and admiration in which Your Majesty is held by the women of America."[39]

In fact, the task of selecting the exhibits for the display in the Women's Building was entrusted solely to Linchi Suriya, wife of the commissioner-general to the fair, Phraya Suriya; as one of the few Siamese women then living overseas (Suriya was the Siamese ambassador in Berlin), her ability to act as a cultural broker must have appeared unparalleled. The zealous Board of Lady Managers asked Lady Suriya to submit a survey covering ten subjects: physical and aesthetic characteristics of Siamese women; female education and religious belief; maiden life; wives' rights and duties; polygamy; women's general position in society; industrial pursuits, including assistance to their husbands' work; charitable activities managed by and designed for women, including those carried out by the royal family and public institutions; and women of races other than the Siamese living in the kingdom's dependencies. The information required would contribute to a major project planned by the Board of Lady Managers: the compilation of an encyclopedia documenting women's lives all over the world. The task must have proved overwhelming for Lady Suriya; her husband, the commissioner-general, wrote from Berlin to the minister of foreign affairs pleading for help.[40]

The Siamese section in the Women's Building was a hundred-square-foot affair (about 9 square meters). On display were gold- and silverware, silk embroidery, a prince's full state costume and the royal robe used in the ordination ceremony, and a collection of antique jewelry "loaned by the queen," which was particularly admired not only for its intrinsic value ("about $58,000") but also its design, which predated the advent of a Westernized taste ("Nowadays," the catalog remarked, "the Siamese wear European jewelry").[41] These objects from the closed universe of the court conformed to the tendency of most exhibits in the Women's Building to, ironically, reinforce notions of domesticity that underplayed the growing tensions in the demand for women's suffrage in the United States.[42] Even though proto-feminism was not immediately relevant in Siam, there is a chronological coincidence worth pointing out: in

1893, thanks to Queen Saowapha's initiative, Bangkok's first two educational institutes for women were established—Sunanthalai School, open to the daughters of the nobility, and Ratchakumari School, for royal princesses only.[43] Because of her promotion of female education, which continued in the following years, Queen Saowapha is celebrated by some Thai historians as an early champion of women's rights, a worthy counterpart to her late-Victorian contemporaries.[44] On the contrary, Rama V was never a strong supporter of female education; he also upheld polygamy as firmly as autocracy. Yet his polygamous lifestyle attracted much less foreign attention than that of his father, who in 1856, at the time of the negotiation of the commercial treaty with the United States, had gone as far as suggesting an article that would bind the Siamese king to monogamy in order to appease the Puritanism of the Americans.[45]

What captured the American imagination in the 1890s and helped bridge the perceived gap between Siamese absolutism and U.S. republicanism was the abolition of bondage,[46] on which the still fresh memory of the Civil War conferred a special resonance irrespective of the enormous differences in the practice and ideology of slavery in the two countries. At a banquet thrown in Chicago by Phraya Suriya in honor of Rama V's fortieth birthday in September 1893, Major Townsend Harris, who had headed the American mission to Siam in 1856, referred to Siam as "probably the most despotic country in the civilized world. Everything and everybody belongs to the king . . . yet it is the present king who has issued the first edict that no one shall henceforth be born a slave in his dominion." By then, news of the July confrontation with the French had reached the venue, and the American hosts, loyal to their boldly proclaimed principle of self-determination, came out to support (verbally at least) Siam. Another guest at the banquet, I. T. Smith, the consul-general for Siam in the United States, after stating that "Americans dip as naturally in politics as a duck takes to water," voiced his support for the kingdom, at risk, like the other "smaller nationalities of the Oriental world [of being] shaped out, obliterated, or absorbed by the great powers of the Western world." Siam's commissioner-general took a more diplomatic stance and, avoiding any reference to the armed confrontation with France, focused instead on business prospects. He foreshadowed new trading opportunities arising from the construction of the country's first railway line, the Bangkok-Nakhon Ratchasima, which had been initiated the year before (its first section, the Bangkok-Ayutthaya, was opened in March 1897). Phraya Suriya also reportedly described Rama V as "particularly interested in America, and especially in American methods of business" and "desirous to see more American people and to welcome more American enterprise to his hospitable shore." [47]

After rejecting the invitations to the Tennessee Centennial Exposition (1897), the Trans-Mississippi Exposition (1898), and that held in conjunction with the Philadelphia International Commercial Congress (1899),[48] the Siamese authorities agreed to take part in the Louisiana Purchase Exposition, which celebrated the centennial of the purchase of Louisiana from France in 1803 during Thomas Jefferson's presidency. The American legation in Bangkok informed the Siamese minister of foreign affairs of the forthcoming exhibition first in October 1901.[49] Exactly one year later, Crown Prince Vajiravudh visited the United States in the course of the world tour he undertook at the conclusion of his education in England; there he stopped in St. Louis as the guest of the forthcoming fair's promoters. Upon returning home he took a keen interest in the fair and ended up presiding over the royal commission formed for organizing Siam's display at the Louisiana Exposition. The commission included the ministers of foreign affairs, finance, and agriculture as vice-presidents; thirteen other members from the ranks of princes and officers; the American A. C. Carter, an adviser to the Education Department, as secretary-general; and, as commissioner-general in charge of the arrangements in situ, Professor J. H. Gore of Columbia University, whom Vajiravudh had met during his tour.

Eventually postponed to 1904, the Louisiana Purchase Exposition opened on 30 April and lasted until 1 December. The aim of its promoters of establishing a record as the largest exhibition ever was achieved with an exhibition area of more than 445,000 square meters and a total area of some five million square meters. It was eventually realized that such grandiose dimensions could be inhibiting to visitors after the dean of the local Barnes Medical College warned his colleagues to dissuade neurasthenics from visiting the fair because its vastness could make them collapse. Described indeed as "a succession of mental shocks, cumulative and educative," the fair nonetheless attracted more than nineteen million visitors.[50] The site allocated to Siam for its display measured, however, only 3,193 square feet (about 296 square meters). The Siamese pavilion, which was modeled on the recently built ordination hall of Wat Benchama Bophit (guardian lions at the entrance included), marked in any case a definite improvement on the pavilion at Paris in 1900. Designed by the Public Works Department in Bangkok, the pavilion was realized by American carpenters—not in St. Louis, however, but in far-away Washington, D.C., since commissioner-general Gore found them to be cheaper. The pavilion opened a month and a half after the exposition had begun; according to Gore, it (and China's pavilion) aroused the greatest curiosity among visitors.

Professor Gore proved to be an inventive and dedicated commissioner. He had leaflets about the pavilion printed for distribution as well as statistical information for the press and souvenir postcards carrying an elephant's silhouette. On 4 July, Independence Day, Gore tied a Siamese decoration around the pole of the American flag, a gesture he himself described as "widely and favourably commented on. No other foreign commissioner thought of it."[51] The final sum spent for the participation (247,523 baht, some 11,000 baht less than originally budgeted)[52] included the cost of publication (U.S.$2,000) of *The Kingdom of Siam,* of which four thousand copies were printed (three thousand for official distribution and the rest for sale).[53] Unlike previous publications occasioned by Siam's participation at international exhibitions, this was a 280-page volume with thematic chapters written by some of the foreign officials in the Siamese public service, such as Dr. Frankfurter (chapters on history, language, religion) and Colonel Gerini (archaeology). More than as a guide for visitors to the fair (the Louisiana Exposition is mentioned only on the front page), *The Kingdom of Siam* was seemingly designed as a reference for businessmen and politicians. The need for such a reference lay in America's growing interests in the kingdom since the beginning of the twentieth century: in 1904, the very year of the St. Louis fair, an American, E. H. Strobel, was entrusted with the office of general adviser to the Siamese government, a post that had previously been held by the Belgian Rolyn-Jaequemyns (at Strobel's death, in 1908, another American, J. O. Westengard, took his place).

Eventually, the Siamese display at St. Louis was awarded the largest number of prizes thus far given to a Siamese display at an international exhibition: 116 awards (4 grand prizes, 31 gold medals, 34 silver medals, and 47 bronze medals).[54] But some of the exhibits were apparently regarded more as ethnographic curios than commodities: at the end of the fair, the pottery was sold to the Metropolitan Museum of New York while manufacture, agriculture, mining, and fish and game exhibits were acquired by the Smithsonian Institution and the National Museum in Washington, D.C.[55] The rationale underlying this decision was indirectly expressed in the review of the Siamese display written for *The World's Fair Bulletin* by H. E. Hamilton King, the U.S. consul in Bangkok. In it, King reiterated the dichotomy posited by most Western observers of Asian societies between the manifestations (material or otherwise) of "national" culture, whose authenticity also betrayed their backwardness, and those exhibits that demonstrated progress but were considered mere imitations of Western civilization:

> *Avoiding the spectacular and the curios the Commission have confined themselves to that which represents the actual conditions of the country at the present time. . . . If the exhibit were to be criticized in any direction indeed it would be in failing to convey a proper impression of Modern Siam. But this failure arises from the thought that as the new ideas in architecture, transportation, industries, etc., are distinctively occidental rather than Siamese, it were better. . . to give emphasis to the more strictly national characteristics.[56]*

Besides the prizes awarded to the exhibits, a grand prize went to Crown Prince Vajiravudh "in consideration of his excellent taste as shown in the choice of articles he selected for display" and a special commemorative diploma to King Chulalongkorn,

> *in consideration of His humane decree abolishing slavery in His kingdom; for his interest in the literature of the East as shown by the collection, arrangement, and publication of the Buddhist Scriptures for gratuitous distribution to the libraries of the World; and for His benevolence as seen in His donating to the peasantry the Crown lands which they have occupied for a certain period and fixing the ownership by the registration of titles in a Bureau established for that purpose.*

After citing the award's official citation, Gore added gladly that, since the king of England, Edward VII, and the German emperor, Wilhelm II, were also awarded commemorative diplomas, "it is quite generally acknowledged here that this places Him [Rama V] in the same category with their Majesties referred to."[57]

There is more than an irony in the fact that monarchs from the Old World and the Far East were memorially brought together and paid a token of deference by the very country whose republican ideology stood in open opposition to despotism and hereditary privilege. In fact, American capitalism had little use for ideology. In the official souvenir postcard of the St. Louis Exposition, sponsored by Singer, the female personification of America is shown sitting behind a sewing machine and sewing an oversized "Louisiana" on a cloth shaped like a U.S. map being held up by a swarm of *putti,* one standing for each participating country; among them, a topknotted *putto* had found his way.[58]

Bangkok on the River Po

As part of its tardy pursuit of world-power status, the government of Italy in 1908 launched a plan for an international exhibition to be held in 1911 in the cities of Rome and Turin to celebrate the fiftieth anniversary of the country's unification, achieved in 1861 by the House of Savoy through the progressive annexation of independent regional states (an enterprise enshrined in the Italian national historical narrative as the Risorgimento). Turin itself, as the Savoy's base, had been the first national capital before this was moved to Florence in 1865 and finally to Rome in 1870, after that city had been taken away from the pope by the army. Half a century later, Turin was Italy's major industrial center (Italy's first automobile industry, FIAT, was established there in 1899) and still its moral and cultural capital. Turin had also hosted a national exhibition in 1884 and the International Exposition of Modern Decorative Art in 1902 (in which Siam, although invited, declined to participate[59]) and was thus the most suitable location for the international exhibition planned for 1911.

At the end of April 1908, shortly after the plan of the Turin exhibition had been launched, the chargé d'affaires for the Kingdom of Italy in Bangkok presented the minister of foreign affairs with an invitation to the forthcoming event.[60] Diplomatic relations between Italy and Siam went back to a treaty signed in October 1868. Informal relations between Bangkok and Turin had also been fostered both via the "tourism diplomacy" of Savoy royalty's visits to Siam in 1881, 1889, and 1895, reciprocated by King Chulalongkorn in 1897 and 1907, and the presence of several Turinese among the Public Works Department's personnel. One of them was Annibale Rigotti, the architect of the Ananta Samakhom Throne Hall, who with Mario Tamagno designed the Siamese pavilion for the Turin exposition and supervised its construction in situ. Another Turinese was Cesare Ferro, who had spent three years (1904–1907) in Bangkok as painter and decorator and was to return in 1923; his is the watercolor sketch of the pavilion in the catalog of the Siamese exhibit (see figure 21).

Entrusted with the office of commissioner-general for Siam at Turin was Colonel Gerolamo Emilio Gerini (1860–1912), who had arrived in Bangkok in 1880 as a military instructor and ended up becoming a scholar of Siamese culture and one of the founding members of the Siam Society.[61] Gerini's knowledge of and deep sympathy for the country he had lived in for several years led him to assemble an extensive catalog (of which an English-language edition was published in 1912), enriched by a historical introduction on the relations between Siam and Italy.[62] Although rich in background information, the catalog was largely devoted to the exhibits themselves, differing in this respect from the handbook published in conjunction with the Louisiana exposition. As for the Siamese side of the organization, Vajiravudh, who by the time the exposition opened had succeeded his father on the throne, remained the president of the commission created for the St. Louis fair; vice-president was Prince Ratchani; and secretary-general, A. C. Carter, later replaced by A. H. Duke. The sum of 125,000 baht was allocated for Siam's participation in the exhibition at Turin;[63] this was half the money spent at St. Louis, even though the Siamese pavilion there was only one-third the size of the pavilion in Turin. On 23 December 1910, the recently enthroned Rama VI personally inspected the exhibits destined for Turin, on display in the Royal Museum.[64]

The International Exposition of Turin lasted from 29 April to 20 November 1911. The Siamese representative at the opening was Luang Montri, the ambassador in Paris, who had also attended the official celebrations for the anniversary of Italy's unification held in Rome the previous March. The day after the opening Luang Montri met at Siam's pavilion with commissioner-general Gerini and the Italian prime minister, Giovanni Giolitti; but it was another month before the pavilion opened to the public, on 27 May. The local newspaper *La Stampa,* in an article on the exposition's opening, praised the Siamese pavilion as being one of the most interesting and noted that its golden spire was visible from almost every point of the exposition.[65] The site covered a total area of one million square meters, one-quarter of which was indoor exhibition space on both banks of the River Po, which runs through Turin. The Siamese pavilion was placed between those of Serbia and the United States on the right bank, along with those of Germany, France, Belgium, Brazil, Argentina, and one reuniting six other Latin American countries; on the left bank stood the pavilions of Hungary, the French colonies of Algeria and Tunisia, Switzerland, Russia, Turkey, and Great Britain. With an area of a thousand square-meters, the Siamese pavilion was sensibly smaller than those of other countries but nevertheless marked a record of visibility for the kingdom;[66] moreover, its exotic design had no match since the exhibits of China and Japan were inside the Arts and Industries Building.

Siam's white pavilion had a cruciform plan; it rested on triple terraces that descended toward the embankment along the river; and had a polychrome roof with a forty-five-meter-high spire. On both sides stood flagstaffs on which were hoisted the white elephant on the red ground. While it was not a reproduction of any specific building, the pavilion typified the architecture of the early Bangkok period, for example, the Dusit Throne Hall in the Grand Palace. In the catalog, Gerini described it as exemplifying "that genuine Siamese style which still survives in temples and monuments of the past, more than in those which have to a large extent been modernized. When viewed from the opposite bank of the River Po," he emphatically added, "it gives one the momentary illusion of actually finding himself on the shores of the Menam, before one of those sumptuous buildings that embellish the Siamese capital."[67] Gerini also pointed out that "the door-posts and corners of the building are not plumb, but slightly inclined toward one another," an architectural feature that resulted from the necessity to stabilize wooden buildings in lands subject to periodical inundations, and explained the roof structure in the light of Indic iconography, interpreting its decorative motifs as figurations of mythical beings, such as Garuda and the Naga.

Internally, the pavilion was divided into three halls that extended on both sides into wing galleries. On display in the left gallery were animal skins, horns, tanning barks, and mats. The first hall was mostly devoted to the exhibit of the Ministry of Education, which had even printed a separate six-page catalog in English.[68] This exhibit documented the activity of primary and secondary students in both government and foreign missions schools through samples of drawing, embroidery, and knitting; photographs of school edifices, classrooms, and classes at work; abstracts of courses, timetables, and textbooks. Another government agency at the forefront of modernization, the Railways Department, also exhibited in this hall. Photographs of railway lines, stations, bridges, and trains were displayed along with the 1910 report on railway traffic. The remaining exhibits in the hall represented the textile industry. The richly decorated central hall, also accessible from the embankment along the river, was replete with religious and regal insignia probably arranged by Gerini himself: golden images of the Buddha (placed in niches up on the walls) and emblems of the dynasty, including the *chakr-tri;* flags, the Chakri's coat of arms, and two seven-tiered umbrellas; a life-size photograph of Rama V surrounded by festoons and garlands; and life-size portraits of Rama VI and the Queen Mother, Saowapha. At the center of this hall stood a showcase with the masks used in the *Ramakian* performance and chased and enamelled silverware; there were also fans, wicker specimens, and samples of minerals and gems. The third hall was mostly devoted to agricultural and manufactured products: samples of paddy and other cereals, fishing implements, trunks of various trees, resins, essences, perfumery oils, drugs, tobacco, and of course silk fabrics. "Here," the catalogue recited, "men of business will be especially interested." Several photographs illustrated the activity of the Survey, Public Works, and Post Departments. On display in the right gallery were earthenware and models of boats.[69]

The jury at Turin awarded eighty-nine prizes to Siam. The highest prizes (five grands prix) went to the exhibits of the Public Works Department, the Railways Department, and the Post and Telegraph Department, which showed advancements in infrastructure and communication; to the Royal Agricultural College, for its mining exhibits; and to the Royal Commission, for the theater masks.[70] A special diploma was conferred on Rama VI, and there were plenty of awards for ministers and officials, too.[71] Throughout the duration of the exhibition the Siamese pavilion was visited by seven and a half million patrons—"exactly the population of Siam," Gerini remarked—including the king of Italy, Victor Emmanuel III, and Vajiravudh's half brother, Prince Mahidol. One of the organizers pointed out that at this exhibition Siam had "successfully put in evidence the high standard of civilization she has reached, which is such as to place her abreast of the most progressive countries of our Old Europe."[72] A remark, this, that could have hardly displeased King Chulalongkorn.

Epilogue

Monarchy and Memory

This book has shown how and why things Western became, along with cultural and social practices, crucial to the self-representation of the Siamese royal elite in the latter half of the nineteenth century. Before that time, the elite's social identity was grounded in a cosmological, cultural, and trading space in which an Indic civilizational sphere, informing religion, state theatrics, and the arts, overlapped with a Sinic civilizational sphere, whereby imperial recognition and material wealth were bestowed upon the Siamese court. Western material culture, although familiar, was deemed lacking social and symbolic meaning in the local context. But as a result of the hegemonic shift that occurred in Southeast Asia around the mid-nineteenth century, the ritual empowerment of the elite and especially the objects constitutive of high social status that emanated from the preexisting civilizational centers lost their perceivable value as markers of civilization. Connection to and recognition by the new civilizational center, from which *siwilai* spread, had to be secured if the royal elite's prestige and self-esteem were to be revalidated in the globalizing imperial system of which they were now effectively part.

The refashioning of the Siamese royalty's image was thus prompted by the desire to see themselves, and to be seen, as belonging to the civilizational vanguard that effected progress throughout the Victorian ecumene. By representing their rule as a civilizing factor, the elite not only achieved the revalidation of their social identity in the new global arena but also bolstered their domestic claim to sovereignty and entrenched their privileges. While, on the one hand, the monarchy's newly adopted rhetoric of self-representation seemingly accorded with contemporary images of "bourgeois sovereigns," on the other the holding on to absolute power, which European monarchies had long relinquished, was not only maintained but actually strengthened. The objective of this cultural modernization, whereby foreign cultural practices and materials were ultimately localized in the Thai cultural landscape thanks to the royalty's mediation, was therefore antithetical to nation-building.

It comes hardly as a surprise, then, that even Western-educated monarchs such as Vajiravudh and Prajadhipok proved incapable of engaging in the collective project of imagining the modern Siamese nation. Beginning in the 1920s, the diffusion of printed media and public forums in Bangkok made increasingly clear that the royal elite's path to modernity did not correspond to the vision that educated commoners had for modern Siam.[1] In the early 1940s, following the abdication of King Prajadhipok in 1935 and the rise to power of the ultranationalist field marshal Phibun Songkhram, the monarchy came very close to obliteration.[2] Indeed, when eighteen-year-old Bhumibol became heir to the throne in 1946 following the still unexplained death of his brother Ananda Mahidol, who had been made king at the age of ten to fill the dynastic vacuum created by his uncle's abdication, the monarchical institution was on most counts nothing more than a façade.

Had this situation stayed unchanged in the intervening years, the transformation examined in this study would probably appear historically inconsequential. Yet the fact that, fifty years later, the throne holds a pre-eminent position in Thailand's political arena inevitably invites the question of how important the refashioning of its image in the Fifth Reign was for the remarkable monarchical revival accomplished in the present reign. Kevin Hewison's recent appraisal of King Bhumibol as "responsible for defining the modern monarchy"[3] reflects his accomplishment as Thailand's first sovereign who has effectively adjusted his role to the constitutional system of government. Yet an appraisal not limited to the institutional realm will have to take into consideration the historical background of the making of the modern monarchy. To start with, the cosmopolitanism of the turn-of-the-century royal elite marked the very birth and upbringing of Rama IX. Born in Cambridge, Massachusetts, in 1927 to Sangwalya Chukramol (a commoner) and Prince Mahidol Aduladej (a son of Chulalongkorn and Queen Sawang then studying at Harvard Medical School), Bhumibol was raised and educated in Switzerland. He has been a continuous resident of Thailand only since 1951, following his coronation ceremony and wedding to Queen Sirikit the year before.

One of the earliest acts undertaken to refurbish the public image of the monarchy after an eclipse of almost two decades was the royal couple's seven-month state visit to Europe and the United States in 1960 which, in fact, had been engineered by strongman Marshal Sarit Thanarat with the intention of exploiting the royals' attractiveness to boost his international legitimacy.[4] Although the world's population of royals had considerably decreased since the time of Rama V's tours, the visit provided an important occasion to spotlight Thailand's young royal couple as they rekindled relations with Western royalty and heads of state. Particularly during its American stage, the visit made special concessions to the media's thirst for celebrity: King Bhumibol, a keen saxophone player, took the opportunity to join Benny Goodman in a jam session. Jazz and yachting, both deeply associated with Bhumibol's country of birth, defined his public persona as a man of leisure in the early years of his reign. But as the throne sought increasingly from the late 1960s to regain a place in the domestic political arena by taking up the role of advocate of Thailand's underprivileged rural population, such a hedonistic lifestyle became unsuitable.

While concern for the plight of the peasantry has in no way diminished the royal household's considerable wealth,[5] King Bhumibol refashioned his public persona by making himself conspicuous for sobriety and intensifying his spiritual aura. Recoiling from the open display of opulence may be a trait common to most surviving dynasties, bent on effacing their massive financial assets and estates—part and parcel of their lineage—as a symbolic tribute to modern democratic ethos. Yet many would argue that the huge popularity Bhumibol enjoys today has been carefully built during the past quarter of a century upon the accumulation of "moral capital." In fact, one might go even further and propose that the monarchical revival effected by Rama IX has produced a resacralization of the king's person, which seemingly runs contrary to the demotic refashioning of the monarchy in the latter part of the Fifth Reign. Possibly the most eloquent example of this resacralization was the television broadcast on 20 May 1992, in which the contenders behind the bloody political incidents of the previous days, generals Suchinda Kraprayun and Chamlong Simuang, lay literally at King Bhumibol's feet and let him defuse a threatening confrontation as a veritable deus ex machina. A by-product of this resacralization of the king's body is the reiconicization undergone by royal images, which possess today a sacral status that they probably never had in the past. Indeed, while political cartoons that caricatured Rama VI and Rama VII were common in the 1920s, offending a picture of the king or other member of the royal family is today an act tantamount to lèse-majesté.[6]

The Golden Jubilee in 1996 and Bhumibol's seventieth birthday the next year marked the climax of monarchical celebrations that had started with the Chakri Bicentennial in 1982 and had progressed with the Year of the Longest-Reigning Monarch in 1988, when King Bhumibol exceeded Rama V's reign record of forty-two years. Throughout 1996, ephemeral arches framed the flow of motorcars along Ratcha Damnoen Avenue as an explicit reference to the pageant held on the return of Chulalongkorn from Europe in 1907—even though the arches then looked, in photographs at least, somewhat more imposing and accomplished than those put up in 1996. In recent years royal mythmakers have been avidly promoting the parallel between Rama V and the incumbent sovereign, the only ones who have been applauded as *maharat* (great kings) in their own lifetimes.[7] Needless to say, the parallel overshadows some crucial differences. First, and foremost, is that whereas Rama V was an apologetic autocrat, Rama IX is a constitutional monarch whose personal authority, while considerable, derives largely from his moral capital. Self-presentation too, as already mentioned, sets them apart. The bourgeoisified, affable image of King Chulalongkorn stands in obvious contrast to the Olympian and aristocratically démodé persona adopted by Rama IX in his maturity. A most telling particular is the transformation undergone by the camera, from erstwhile gadget of the modernizing elite to constitutive element of Rama IX's iconic self—almost a prosthetic extension of the royal gaze surveying Thailand's countryside and its inhabitants.

Still, it would be difficult to separate the throne's present moral authority from the assiduously cultivated public memory of this institution, which invokes royal figures as major agents of civilization. This is true of as remote a king as Ramkhamhaeng of Sukhothai (ca. 1275–1317), honored as the inventor of the Thai script by a bronze statue in the middle of Sukhothai Historical Park, opened in 1988 to mark Bhumibol's record reign; and it is of course true of Rama V, whose publicly displayed portraits in dress uniform and Western suits in Thailand today act as signifiers of the country's self-image as a modern nation. As virtually the first Siamese to have lived in a wrought-iron-fenced suburban villa, spent holidays overseas, drunk wine, and owned motorcars (not to mention his cookbook of Western recipes ranging from soups to sandwiches), Chulalongkorn's figure holds a special meaning for the nouveaux riches who were brought into prominence by the economic boom of the 1980s. During that and the following decade the Thai culture industry has celebrated in books and magazines the lifestyle of the modernizing elite as an antecedent and model for the affluent urbanite in quest of material sophistication and social distinction.[8] For the edification of this new middle class, antiquarian historians such as the prolific Anake Nawigamune have articulated a secular representation of Rama V as a big spender and bon vivant that complements the official memory of him as the father of modern Thailand.

Royalist mythology, *nouveau riche* aspirations, and historical nostalgia come literally under one roof at Wimanmek, Chulalongkorn's teak mansion in Dusit Park, which in the early 1980s was rescued from dilapidation by Queen Sirikit's good offices and transformed into a museum of Fifth Reign courtly life. Retrofitted with the latest (for the early 1900s) domestic accoutrements, such as a bathtub, and furnished with an array of Victoriana kitsch (including a few upholstered thrones), Wimanmek celebrates the royalty's mastery of *siwilai* exclusively in terms of material culture. The museumification of royal palaces and their transformation into tourist attractions pandering to nostalgia for aristocratic privilege may well be a phenomenon common to many of the countries once ruled by dynasties.[9] But sightseeing at Wimanmek is probably unique in that visitors, on entering the room where Carolus-Duran's full-length portrait of King Chulalongkorn hangs on the wall, are requested by the museum guides to crouch on the floor as a sign of respect to his memory and, indeed, of submission to royal authority.

There are good reasons to argue that, as King Bhumibol restored to the sovereign's figure some of the supernatural aura that Chulalongkorn had curtailed in his push for a modern image, representations of the latter in the public domain have also undergone reiconicization at the same time that media representations of his taste and lifestyle have acted as a model for the new middle class. In fact, collective fascination with Rama V has taken a peculiar devotional form that testifies to the idiosyncrasies of Thai late modernity. Since the early 1990s his equestrian monument has become the gathering point of worshippers who, initially on Thursday and then also Tuesday evening (days linked to Chulalongkorn's horoscope), propitiate the benevolence of the Great King's spirit with offerings of luxury consumer items par excellence (French cognac, Cuban cigars) along with more orthodox candles and incense sticks.[10] This urban cult, which originated among the Bangkok middle class during the economic boom and has now spread to the working class and even the rural population, would appear connected to the twin trends of the resacralization and reiconiciza-tion of the royal body that the palace does not officially endorse yet does not actively discourage either. As the monarchy's moral authority is fur-ther validated by such devotional practices, Peter Jackson's suggestion that the cult of Rama V has been paving the way for what may be regarded as a proto-cult of Rama IX is hard to dismiss.[11]

The public memorialization of King Chulalongkorn thus reveals itself as a pluralistic, even discordant, practice whereby he is remembered as both a statesman and an arbiter of taste and celebrated both by official commemoration (on 23 October) and popular devotion. And if public memory of Rama V shines brighter as a result of the reflection of the almost sacral aura projected by the incumbent sovereign, it also continues to inspire the royal family and their advisers. Consider Princess Maha Chakri Sirindhorn, whom many in Thailand regard as King Bhumibol's moral heir. Following in her great-grandfather's footsteps, Princess Sirind-horn has proved herself a tireless "diplomatic tourist" and had, like him, her travel diaries published (more than twenty titles to date) to finance one of the foundations sponsored by the royal house.[12] Princess Sirindhorn's public role is most closely associated with the preservation of the country's cultural heritage, a role to which she brings not only her considerable per-sonal charisma but also the scholarly qualifications of two master's degrees (in Oriental epigraphy and in Pali and Sanskrit) and a doctorate in develop-mental education. Here too, one can easily see the legacy of the promo-tion by Rama V and his associates of cultural institutions, such as the Bang-kok Royal Museum and the Wachirayan City Library (today the National Museum and the National Library), as well as archaeological research.

Yet King Chulalongkorn's most evident legacy to Princess Sirind-horn is probably a natural talent as a communicator, by virtue of which she is the royal family member enjoying the most visibility in the national media. Her interest in the art and culture of early Thailand has not com-promised the princess' ability to appreciate information technology as a medium to project the monarchy's image onto the ultimate representa-tional space: the Internet. In December 1996, to celebrate her father's fif-tieth anniversary of reign, Princess Sirindhorn initiated the Golden Jubilee Network (*khrukhai kanchanaphisek*) Web site, "an online mass-education project" that provides information about Rama IX and Princess Sirind-horn herself with a more intimate style than the official Thai Monarchy

Web page run by the Thai government's Public Relations Department.[13] The Golden Jubilee Network Web site boasts such technically advanced features as downloadable video files of royal ceremonies and audio files of King Bhumibol's musical compositions (at no charge, needless to say). But even the photographs, selected from the royal household's private albums, effectively project an image of the incumbent monarch and the royal family that is both humane and austere.

Princess Sirindhorn's Golden Jubilee Network Web site is thus both a medium of self-representation (and self-aggrandizement) and a memory site invoking the monarchy's heritage through an archival procedure that, to paraphrase P. Nora, "relies entirely on the materiality of the trace, the immediacy of the recording, the visibility of the image"[14]—only that, as befitting the digital age, it is a *virtual* memory site, not bound to a physical place but floating in cyberspace. Anyone surfing the Internet can pause there to glance at the present and the past of the Thai monarchy and realize that, over the time span from the end of the nineteenth century to the end of the twentieth, it has lacked neither the ability to reinvent itself nor a resiliency that other such institutions failed to harness. Whether anyone can also foresee its future is, of course, a different question.

Notes

Introduction

1. On this anachronism of the Thai political and legal system see David Streckfuss, "Kings in the Age of Nations: The Paradox of Lèse-Majesté as Political Crime in Thailand," *Comparative Studies in Society and History* 37 (1995): 445–475.

2. *Bangkok Times*, 6 September 1897.

3. Quoted in the *Bangkok Times*, 11 September 1897.

4. The making of the documentary is narrated by its scriptwriter and director, Amphon Chirattikon, in her *Tamsadet klaiban* [On the footsteps of *Klaiban*] (Bangkok: Matichon, 1998). The magazine of Thailand's Fine Arts Department too devoted a whole issue to Rama V's tour (*Sinlapakorn* 40, 2 [1997]).

5. The semantic range of the word "civilization" (French, "civilisation"; Italian, "civilizzazione"; German, "Zivilisation") in the later nineteenth-century Euro-American world was akin to that of the later term "modernization," which came into use in the post–World War II period. For the lexical fortune of "*siwilai*" in nineteenth-century Siam, see Charnvit Kasetsiri, "Siam/Civilization–Thailand/Globalization: Things to Come," paper presented at the conference of the International Association of Historians of Asia (Bangkok, May 1996), esp. pp. 6–7.

6. Fred W. Riggs, *Thailand* (Honolulu: East-West Center Press, 1966).

7. See "Prince Charles: Branded for Life," *The Economist* (14 November 1998): 64–65.

8. Stanley J. Tambiah, *World Conqueror and World Renouncer* (Cambridge: Cambridge University Press, 1976), pp. 227–228.

9. Alfred N. Battye, "The Military, Government, and Society in Siam, 1868–1910" (Ph.D. diss., Cornell University, 1974); Tej Bunnang, *The Provincial Administration of Siam, 1892–1915* (Kuala Lumpur: Oxford University Press, 1976); Craig J. Reynolds, "The Buddhist Monkhood in Nineteenth-Century Thailand" (Ph.D. diss., Cornell University, 1973); David K. Wyatt, *The Politics of Reform in Thailand* (New Haven: Yale University Press, 1969). Works on the Chakri Reformation were written also by political and social scientists: David B. Adams, "Monarchy and Political Change: Thailand under Chulalongkorn (1868–1885)" (Ph.D. diss., University of Chicago, 1977); William J. Siffin, *The Thai Bureaucracy* (Honolulu: East-West Center Press, 1966), and Riggs' already cited *Thailand*.

10. David K. Wyatt, "Interpreting the History of the Fifth Reign," repr. in his *Studies in Thai History* (Chiangmai: Silkworm Books, 1994), p. 275.

11. Lucian W. Pye, *Asian Power and Politics* (Cambridge: The Belknap Press of Harvard University Press, 1985), p. 3.

12. On Damrong in English, see Kennon Breazeale, "A Transition in Historical Writing: The Work of Prince Damrong Rachanuphap," *Journal of the Siam Society* 59, 2 (1971): 25–49.

13. Prince Damrong Rajanubhap, *Phraratcha phongsawadan krung rattana-*

kosin ratchakan thi 5 [Chronicles of the Fifth Reign], Cremation volume (Bangkok, 1979); and *Khwamsongcham* [Recollections] (Bangkok: Phrae Phitthaya, 1971).

14. See Benedict Anderson, "Studies of the Thai State: The State of Thai Studies," in *The Study of Thailand*, ed. E. B. Ayal (Athens: Ohio University Papers in International Studies, 1978), pp. 193–247. Anderson (pp. 197–198) questioned the "set of axioms about modern Siam" (noncolonization; first independent modern nation-state in Southeast Asia; Chakri dynasty's role as a "modernizing" and "national" elite; "stability" of society and "flexibility" of its leaders), arguing that evidence pointed in fact to "a semi-colonial, indirectly-ruled condition wholly incompatible with the 'national'—not to say 'nationalist'—terminology typically applied in most Western scholarship on Siam" (p. 210). In spite of reviewing a substantial amount of "counterinsurgency" studies that are by now nothing more than bibliographic curios, Anderson's critique of Thai studies still makes for extremely stimulating reading.

15. Hong Lysa, "Warasan Setthasat Kanmuang: Critical Scholarship in Post-1976 Thailand," in *Thai Constructions of Knowledge*, ed. Andrew Turton and Manas Chitakasem (London: School of Oriental and African Studies, University of London, 1991), pp. 99–118; Craig J. Reynolds and Hong Lysa, "Marxism in Thai Historical Studies," *Journal of Asian Studies* 43, 1 (1983): 77–104; Thongchai Winichakul, "The Changing Landscape of the Past: New Histories in Thailand since 1973," *Journal of Southeast Asian Studies* 26, 1 (1995): 99–120.

16. Chatthip Nartsupha and Suthy Prasartset, eds., *Socio-Economic Institutions and Cultural Change in Siam, 1851–1910* (Singapore: Institute of South-East Asian Studies, 1977); idem, *The Political Economy of Siam, 1851–1910* (Bangkok: The Social Sciences Association of Thailand, 1981).

17. Chaiyan Rajchagool, *The Rise and Fall of the Thai Absolute Monarchy* (Bangkok: White Lotus, 1994).

18. Thongchai Winichakul, *Siam Mapped* (Honolulu: University of Hawai'i Press, 1994).

19. Eric Hobsbawm and Terence Ranger, eds., *The Invention of Tradition* (Cambridge: Cambridge University Press, 1983).

20. Eric Hobsbawm, "Mass Producing Traditions: Europe, 1870–1914," in *Invention of Tradition*, ed. Hobsbawm and Ranger, p. 282.

21. Ibid., pp. 267–268.

22. Ibid., p. 266.

23. Takashi Fujitani, *Splendid Monarchy* (Berkeley: University of California Press, 1996), pp. 19–20.

24. Ibid., p. 20. Fujitani, however, declares himself to be "critical of the monarchy and the nation-state in Japan" (p. 27).

25. Carol Gluck, *Japan's Modern Myths* (Princeton, N.J.: Princeton University Press, 1985), p. 49.

26. Salim Deringil, "The Invention of Tradition as Public Image in the Late Ottoman Empire, 1808–1908," *Comparative Studies in Society and History* 35, 1 (1993): 3–29 (quote from p. 12).

27. Tambiah, *World Conqueror*, p. 198.

28. Ibid., p. 525.

29. Fujitani, *Splendid Monarchy*, p. 19.

30. Eugene Weber, *Peasants into Frenchmen* (Stanford, Calif.: Stanford University Press, 1976).

31. See the considerations by John Girling, *Thailand* (Ithaca, N.Y.: Cornell University Press, 1981), pp. 47–52, which constitute also a response to some of Anderson's claims about "Western scholarly axioms" (see above, note 14).

32. Hobsbawm, "Mass-Producing Traditions," p. 282.

33. Ibid., pp. 263–264.

34. See Matthew Copeland, "Contested Nationalism and the 1932 Overthrow of the Absolute Monarchy in Siam" (Ph.D. diss., Australian National University, 1993).

35. For a detailed discussion of the social trends and public debates under way in Siam in the years immediately before and after the overthrow of the absolute monarchy, see Scot Barmé, "Towards a Social History of Bangkok: Gender, Class and Popular Culture in the Siamese Capital, 1905–1940" (Ph.D. diss., Australian National University, 1997), esp. chaps. 1–5.

36. Craig J. Reynolds, "Thailand," in *Australia in Asia,* ed. Anthony Milner and Mary Quilty (Melbourne: Oxford University Press, 1996), pp. 103–104.

37. Edward Said*, Orientalism* (New York: Pantheon, 1978).

38. Jonathan Friedman, "Global System, Globalization, and the Parameters of Modernity," repr. in his *Cultural Identity and Global Process* (London: Sage, 1994), pp. 199–202.

39. Craig J. Reynolds, "Globalization and Cultural Nationalism in Modern Thailand," in *Southeast Asian Identities*, ed. Joel S. Kahn (Singapore: Institute of South-East Asian Studies, 1998), pp. 127–128.

40. Prince Damrong Rajanubhap, *Monuments of the Buddha in Siam*, trans. Sulak Sivaraksa and A. B. Griswold, rev. ed. (Bangkok: Siam Society, 1973), p. 4.

41. "Indic materials tended to be fractured and restated and therefore drained of their original significance in the process which I shall refer to as 'localization.' " O. W. Wolters, *History, Culture, and Region in Southeast Asian Perspectives,* rev. ed. (Ithaca, N.Y.: Southeast Asia Program Publications in cooperation with the Institute of South-East Asian Studies, Singapore, 1999), p. 55.

42. George Cœdès, *The Indianized States of Southeast Asia*, trans. Susan Brown Cowing (Honolulu: East-West Center Press, 1968).

43. On the Indian Ocean as a global system before the age of colonialism, see K. N. Chaudhuri, *Asia before Europe* (New York: Cambridge University Press, 1990).

44. Friedman, "Global System," p. 201.

45. O. W. Wolters, "Southeast Asia as a Southeast Asian Field of Study," *Indonesia* 58 (October 1994): 1–17 (quotations from pp. 3, 4, 17).

46. Carol A. Breckenridge, "The Aesthetics and Politics of Colonial Collecting: India at World Fairs," *Comparative Studies in Society and History* 31, 2 (1989): 195–216 (quotation from p. 196). The term "ecumene," derived from the Greek *oikoumen* ("the inhabited world"), traditionally defined the community of believers in the Christian faith, a transnational "imagined community" par excellence.

47. Ibid., p. 214. See also Frederick Cooper and Ann Laura Stoler, eds.,

Tensions of Empire (Berkeley: University of California Press, 1997), esp. the editors' introduction, "Between Metropole and Colony: Rethinking a Research Agenda," pp. 1–56.

48. M. R. Seni Pramoj and M. R. Kukrit Pramoj, eds., *A King of Siam Speaks* (Bangkok: Siam Society, 1987), p. 143.

49. Karl Marx, *Capital*, trans. Eden and Cedar Paul (New York: E. P. Dutton, 1951), bk. 1, chap. 4.

50. Thomas Richards, *The Commodity Culture of Victorian Britain* (Stanford, Calif.: Stanford University Press, 1990), pp. 55–56.

51. Clifford Geertz, "Centres, Kings, and Charisma: Reflections on the Symbolics of Power," repr. in *Rites of Power*, ed. Sean Wilentz (Philadelphia: University of Philadelphia Press, 1985), pp. 13–38. Geertz theorizes the following (p. 15): "At the political centre of any complexly organized societies . . . there is both a governing elite and a set of symbolic forms expressing the fact that it is in truth governing. . . . [Governing elites] justify their existence and order their actions in terms of a collection of stories, ceremonies, insignia, formalities, and appurtenances that they have either inherited or, in more revolutionary situations, invented." The reprint of Geertz's essay (originally published in 1977) at the beginning of a collection of essays largely by historians testifies to the influence of his ideas among them. For a description of Southeast Asia's precolonial theater of power based on contemporary European sources, see Anthony Reid, *Southeast Asia in the Age of Commerce*, vol. 1 (New Haven, Conn.: Yale University Press, 1988), chap. 3.

52. See Peter Burke, *The Fabrication of Louis XVI* (New Haven, Conn.: Yale University Press, 1992).

53. See Colin Campbell, *The Romantic Ethic and the Spirit of Modern Consumerism* (Oxford: Basil Blackwell, 1987).

54. Martin Jay, "Scopic Regimes of Modernity," in *Modernity and Identity*, ed. Scott Lash and Jonathan Friedman (Oxford: Blackwell, 1992), pp. 178–195.

55. Dome Sukwong, *Prawat phapayon thai* [A history of Thai cinema], p. 8; cit. in Barmé, "Social History of Bangkok," p. 45. The prince in question, a younger brother of Rama V, was Prince Sanphasat Suphakit.

56. See Anake Nawigamune, *Pramwan phap phrapiya maharat/Chulalongkorn the Great* (Bangkok: Sangdaet, 1989); and *Samut phap ratchakan thi 5/A Pictorial Record of the Fifth Reign* (Bangkok: River Books, 1992).

57. Susan Sontag, *On Photography* (Harmondsworth: Penguin, 1979), p. 153.

Chapter 1   Consumption Modes, Tastes, and Identity of Siam's Modernizing Elite

1. Florence Caddy, *To Siam and Malaya* (repr. Singapore: Oxford University Press, 1992), p. 114.

2. William N. Armstrong, *Around the World with a King* (repr. Honolulu: Mutual Publishing, 1995), p. 132.

3. Malcolm Smith, *A Physician at the Court of Siam* (repr. Kuala Lumpur: Oxford University Press, 1982), p. 81.

4. Malcolm Smith (*Physician*, p. 80) notes that the first time women of the court attended a banquet was in 1908 at Bang Pa-in Palace, on the occasion of the visit of the Duke and Duchesse of Mecklenburg. Indeed, in the description of the dinner in Bangkok quoted above, Florence Caddy remarked on the fact that the elderly nobles looked "as if spellbound with astonishment that women should be able to talk intelligently, sit at table, and eat their dinner properly. The Siamese men and women do not take their meals together" (Caddy, *To Siam*, pp. 113–114).

5. Prince Chula Chakrabongse, *The Twain Have Met* (London: G. T. Foulis, 1956), p. 88.

6. The point is made but not developed by Chaiyan, *Thai Absolute Monarchy*, pp. 134–135.

7. E.g., Arjun Appadurai, ed., *The Social Life of Things* (Cambridge: Cambridge University Press, 1986); Pierre Bourdieu, *Distinction*, trans. Richard Nice (Cambridge: Harvard University Press, 1984); Grant McCracken, *Culture and Consumption* (Bloomington: Indiana University Press, 1988); Daniel Miller, *Material Culture and Mass Consumption* (Oxford: Basil Blackwell, 1987).

8. Bourdieu, *Distinction*, p. 483 (orig. emphasis).

9. See John Crawfurd, *Journal of an Embassy from the Governor-General of India to the Courts of Siam and Cochin-China* (repr. Kuala Lumpur: Oxford University Press, 1967); and George Finlayson, *The Mission to Siam and Hué the Capital of Cochin-China in the Years 1821–1822* (repr. Singapore: Oxford University Press, 1988). Finlayson was a doctor and naturalist who took part in the Crawfurd mission, whose objective was to negotiate a commercial treaty with Bangkok.

10. Richard O'Connor, "Urbanism and Religion" (Ph.D. diss., Cornell University, 1978), p. 176.

11. " . . . of such a splendor which would be not thought of in Europe." Mgr. Jean-Baptiste Pallegoix, *Description du royaume Thai ou Siam* (repr. Westmead: Gregg International Publishing, 1969), p. 64.

12. James C. Ingram, *Economic Change in Thailand 1850–1970* (Stanford, Calif.: Stanford University Press, 1971), p. 29.

13. William Warren (photographs by Luca Invernizzi Tettoni), *Arts and Crafts of Thailand* (London: Thames and Hudson, 1994), pp. 9–24.

14. On the pattern of imports see George V. Smith, *The Dutch in Seventeenth-Century Thailand,* Special Report, no. 16 (DeKalb: Northern Illinois University, Center for Southeast Asian Studies, 1977), pp. 252–263.

15. On both occasions engravings and commemorative medals were produced and presumably presented to the Siamese ambassadors as mementos. Apinan Poshyananda, "Modern Art in Thailand" (Ph.D. diss., Cornell University, 1990) pp. 29–32.

16. Nidhi Aeusriwongse, *Pakkai lae bairua* [Quill and sail] (Bangkok: Amarin, 1984), chap. 1.

17. Charles S. Leckie, "The Commerce of Siam in Relation to the Trade

of the British Empire," *Journal of the Royal Society of Arts* 42 (June 1894): 649–660, repr. in Chatthip and Suthy, *Political Economy of Siam 1851–1910*, pp. 115–152 (quotation from p. 116). Leckie added, "Hunter's cups and saucers are prominent today, as he was able to sell them all for the odd purpose of adorning the famous Wat Cheang pagoda, which is noe [*sic*] of the most handsome of the many beautiful temples of Bangkok."

18. George W. Skinner, *Chinese Society in Thailand* (Ithaca, N.Y.: Cornell University Press, 1957), p. 25. On the pattern of commercial relations between Siam and China, see Sarasin Viraphol, *Tribute and Profit* (Cambridge: Harvard University Press, 1977).

19. See Jennifer W. Cushman, "Siamese State Trade and the Chinese Go-between, 1767–1855," *Journal of Southeast Asian Studies* 12, 1 (1981): 46–61; idem, *Fields from the Sea* (Ithaca, N.Y.: Cornell Southeast Asia Program, 1993).

20. Chaophraya Thipakorawong, *The Dynastic Chronicles of the Bangkok Era: The Fourth Reign*, trans. and ed. Thadeus and Chadin Flood, 5 vols. (Tokyo: Center for East Asian Studies, 1965–1974), 5:14–15.

21. John Bowring, *The Kingdom and People of Siam*, 2 vols. (repr. Kuala Lumpur: Oxford University Press, 1969), 1:410–411 (in which Bowring refers to a building within the Grand Palace carrying the inscription "Royal Pleasure" in both Thai and English); 2:279.

22. Ibid., p. 324.

23. *Les annales du commerce exterieur*, quoted in Henri Mouhot, *Travels in the Central Part of Indo-China (Siam), Cambodia and Laos* (repr. Singapore: Oxford University Press, 1992), 2:100.

24. Manich Jumsai, M. L., *King Mongkut and Queen Victoria* (Bangkok: Chalermnit, 1972), pp. 31–32.

25. Carl Bock, *Temples and Elephants* (repr. Singapore: Oxford University Press, 1986), p. 10.

26. Ibid. On the construction of the Chakri Throne Hall see below, chap. 3.

27. Ingram, *Economic Change*, p. 192. In the same period 1892 to 1910, the percentage of total expenditure devoted to defense decreased from 26 percent to 24 percent, while that of education remained stable at 2 percent. Only after 1932 was the budget for the royal household drastically reduced to less than 1 percent of the total expenditure (ibid., p. 177).

28. When calculated in pounds sterling (at the exchange rate of 1 pound to 13 baht then in place), the cost of Vajiravudh's coronation ceremonies amount to 376,000 pounds against George V's 185,000 pounds (for this figure, see David Cannadine, "The Context, Performance and Meaning of Ritual: The British Monarchy and the 'Invention of Tradition,' " in *Invention of Tradition*, ed. Hobsbawm and Ranger, p. 163, table 1). For a description of Rama VI's coronation ceremonies, see Walter F. Vella, *Chaiyo!* (Honolulu: University of Hawai'i Press, 1978), pp. 16–23.

29. Chaiyan, *Thai Absolute Monarchy*, p. 158.

30. O'Connor, "Urbanism and Religion," pp. 168–169, 178.

31. For comments on the retrenchment of royal cremations in the Fifth Reign, see Horace G. Quaritch Wales, *Siamese State Ceremonies* (London: Bernard

Quaritch, 1931), pp. 138, 145. For the cost of Chulalongkorn's cremation (precisely 968,389 baht), National Archives (NA), Office of the Financial Adviser, Budget Report, Rattanakosin era (R.E.) 131 (1912/13), p. 14.

32. Fine Arts Department (FAD), comp., *Samnao raignan phrachao borom-wongthe khromphraya naretworarit sadet prathet amerika pho.so. 2427* [Itinerary of Prince Naret Worarit's tour of America in 1884], Cremation volume (Bangkok, 1926).

33. FAD, comp., *Somdet phrachao boromwongthe khromphraya damrong ratcha-nuphap sadet tawip yurop pho.so. 2434* [Prince Damrong Rajanubhap's journey to Europe in 1891], Cremation volume (Bangkok, 1968).

34. King Chulalongkorn, *Phraratchahatthalekha . . . mua sadet phraratcha damnoen praphat yurop pho.so. 2440* [The king's correspondence . . . from the 1897 journey to Europe], 2 vols. (Bangkok: Khurusapha, 1962); and *Phraratchaniphon klai ban* [The king's writings from overseas, or, Far from home], 2 vols. (Bangkok: Khurusapha, 1955).

35. Dozens of letters personally addressed to King Chulalongkorn by European firms and shops advertising their goods have been conserved in NA, Records of the Fifth Reign (RV), Miscellany 8.3.

36. Malcolm Smith, *Physician,* pp. 139, 60.

37. Barmé, "Social History of Bangkok," p. 203, quoting as source an editorial published in the newspaper *Ying thai* [Thai woman], 18 October 1932.

38. Chula Chakrabongse, *Twain Have Met,* p. 64.

39. David K. Wyatt, *Thailand* (New Haven, Conn.: Yale University Press, 1984), p. 224.

40. Akin Rabibhadana, *The Organization of Thai Society in the Early Bang-kok Period, 1782–1873,* Data paper, no. 74 (Ithaca, N.Y.: Southeast Asia Program, Cornell University, 1969), pp. 44–45.

41. Craig J. Reynolds, "Tycoons and Warlords," in *Sojourners and Settlers,* ed. Anthony Reid (St. Leonard: Asian Studies Association of Australia in associa-tion with Allen and Unwin, 1996), pp. 119–121.

42. Ibid., p. 122.

43. Douglas R. Howland, *Borders of Chinese Civilization* (Durham, N.C.: Duke University Press, 1996), pp. 13–14. "*Wenming*" literally means "achieving an enlightened status (*ming*) through the knowledge of literature (*wen*)"—that is, the Confucian texts.

44. Skinner, *Chinese Society,* pp. 24–26.

45. See Likhit Dhiravegin, *Siam and Colonialism, 1855–1909* (Bangkok: Thai Watthana Panich, 1975), p. 13; Wyatt, *Thailand,* chap. 7.

46. Atthachak Sattayanurak, *Kanpliangplaeng lokathat khong chonchan phunam thai tangtae ratchakan thi 4-pho.so. 2475* [Transformation of the Thai elite's world-view from the Fourth Reign to 1932] (Bangkok: Chulalongkorn University, 1995), esp. chap. 2; Thongchai, *Siam Mapped,* chap. 2. See also Craig J. Reynolds' seminal article, "Buddhist Cosmography in Thai History, with Special Reference to Nine-teenth-Century Cultural Change," *Journal of Asian Studies* 35, 2 (1976): 203–220.

47. Yoneo Ishii, *Sangha, State, and Society,* trans. Peter Hawkes (Honolulu: University of Hawai'i Press), p. 148.

48. King Mongkut died as a result of the malaria he contracted during the trip to Sam Roi Yot, on the west coast of the Gulf of Siam, to witness a solar eclipse of which he had calculated the timing and sky coordinates.

49. Symbolic capital refers to "degree of accumulated prestige, celebrity, consecration or honour," and cultural capital to "forms of cultural knowledge, competences or dispositions." Pierre Bourdieu, *The Field of Cultural Production*, ed. and intr. Randal Johnson (New York: Columbia University Press, 1993), p. 7.

50. Damrong, *Khwamsongcham*, chap. 5; FAD, comp., *Chotmaihet sadet praphat tang prathet nai ratchakan thi 5 sadet muang singkhapo lae muang betawia khrang ae lae sadet praphat prathet india* [Chronicles of the royal journey to Singapore, Batavia, and to India in the Fifth Reign], Cremation volume (Bangkok, 1966). The first royal tour, between March and April 1871, included Singapore, Batavia, and Semarang; and the second, from December 1871 to March 1872, Singapore, Malacca, Penang, Moulmein, Rangoon, Calcutta, Delhi, Agra, Lucknow, Cawnpore, Bombay, and Benares.

51. Cited in Thongthong Changsangsu, *Khong suay khong di khrang phaendin phraputtha chaoluang* [Beautiful and precious objects of King Chulalongkorn's reign] (Bangkok: Akson Samphan, 1988), p. 51.

52. King Chulalongkorn, *Phraratchahatthalekha phrabat somdet phrachulachomklaochaoyuhua phraratchathan somdet phrachao boromwongthe kromphraya damrong ratchanuphap nai wela sadet phraratchadamnoen pratet yurop khrang thi song pho.so. 2450* [King Chulalongkorn's correspondence to Prince Damrong Rajanubhap from his second journey to Europe in 1907], Cremation volume (Bangkok, 1948), p. 30.

53. Cf. Campbell, *Romantic Ethic*, pp. 37, 55.

54. Norbert Elias, *The Civilizing Process*, trans. Edmund Jephcott, rev. ed. (Oxford, and Cambridge, Mass.: Blackwell Publishers, 2000), p. 190.

55. Malcolm Smith, *Physician,* pp. 104–105.

56. Chulalongkorn, *Phraratchahatthalekha . . . praphat yurop pho.so. 2440,* 2:73. This was followed by the remark, "Of course, Chinese porcelain is cheaper, even though here it costs the same [as the Danish]."

57. *Bangkok Times*, 15 February 1907.

58. Prince Damrong Rajanubhap, *Chotmaihet ratchawang ban pa'in lae wat niwet* [Documents on the royal palace of Bang Pa-in and Wat Niwet] (Bangkok: Fine Arts Department, 1994).

59. Charles Buls, *Siamese Sketches,* trans. and intr. Walter E. J. Tips (Bangkok: White Lotus, 1994), p. 142. Buls was mayor of Brussels between 1881 and 1899, and received Chulalongkorn when he visited the city in September 1897. Rama V then invited Buls to Siam, which he visited in the early months of 1900.

60. Ibid.

61. Giles H. R. Tillotson, *The Tradition of Indian Architecture* (New Haven, Conn.: Yale University Press, 1989), pp. 26–27.

62. Prince Esper Esperovitch Ookhtomsky, *Travels in the East of Nicholas II Emperor of Russia when Cesarevitch, 1890–1891,* 2 vols, ed. and trans. Sir George Birdwood (London: Archibald Constable, 1896), 2:240.

63. Ibid., pp. 245–246.

64. Richards, *Commodity Culture,* pp. 90–91.

65. Apinan, "Modern Art," pp. 63–65, 74–107.

66. Apinan Poshyananda, *Modern Art in Thailand* (Singapore: Oxford University Press, 1992), p. 13. Apinan also compiled a catalog of the royal household's art collection, *Western-style Paintings in the Thai Royal Court*, 2 vols. (Bangkok: Bureau of the Royal Household, 1993).

67. Thomas Dacosta Kaufmann, "From Treasury to Museum: The Collections of the Austrian Habsburgs," in *The Cultures of Collecting,* ed. John Elsner and Roger Cardinal (London: Reaktion Books, 1994), pp. 137–154.

68. John Clark, "Yôga in Japan: Model or Exception? Modernity in Japanese Art 1850s–1940s: An International Comparison," *Art History* 18, 2 (1995): 269. Clark's considerations concern also the art collection of Indonesia's President Sukharno.

69. Russell W. Belk, *Collecting in a Consumer Society* (London: Routledge, 1995), p. 66.

70. Oliver Millar, *The Queen's Pictures* (London: Weidenfeld and Nicolson, 1977), p. 14.

71. Apinan, "Modern Art," pp. 86, 90.

72. King Chulalongkorn, letter of 11 May 1907, *Phraratchahatthalekha phrabat somdet phrachulachomklao chaoyuhua phraratchathan chaophraya yomarat (pan sukum)* [The king's correspondence to Chaophraya Yomarat (Pan Sukhum)], Cremation volume (Bangkok, 1986), p. 35.

73. Chulalongkorn, letter of 22 May 1907, *Klai ban*, 1:233–234.

74. NA, RV, Miscellany 8.3/25.

75. *Times* (London), 26 June 1907 (cited in the *Bangkok Times*, 24 July 1907).

76. William W. Skeat and Charles O. Bladgen, *Pagan Races of the Malay Peninsula*, 2 vols. (London: Macmillan, 1906).

77. FAD, comp., *Prawat kanthunklao thawai parinya nitisan dusathibanthit kittimosak* [Report on the conferral of an honorary doctorate in law to the king], Cremation volume (Bangkok, 1976).

78. Damrong, *Monuments of the Buddha,* p. 33.

79. On the reforms that led to the establishment of the Thammayut (Dhammayutika) order in the Fourth Reign, see Thomas A. Kirsch, "Modernizing Implications of Nineteenth-Century Reforms in the Thai Sangha," in *Religion and Legitimation of Power in Thailand, Laos, and Burma,* ed. Bardwell L. Smith (Chambersburg, Penn.: Anima Books, 1978), pp. 52–65. On the Fifth Reign reform of the *sangha*, see Reynolds, "Buddhist Moonkhood"; and Tambiah, *World Conqueror,* chap. 11.

80. Donald S. Lopez, Jr., "Introduction," in *Curators of the Buddha,* ed. Donald S. Lopez (Chicago: University of Chicago Press, 1995), pp. 12–13. On Indology at Oxford, see Richard Symonds, *Oxford and Empire* (Oxford: Clarendon Press, 1991), chap. 6.

81. David Ludden, "Orientalist Empiricism: Transformations of Colonial Knowledge," in *Orientalism and the Postcolonial Predicament,* ed. Carol A. Breckenridge and Peter van der Veer (Philadelphia: University of Pennsylvania Press, 1993), pp. 250–278. During his six-month tour of India in 1875–1876, the

Prince of Wales distributed to the Indian princes in return for their presents the English edition of the Vedas edited and translated by Max Müller. Bernard S. Cohn, "Representing Authority in Victorian India," in *Invention of Tradition,* ed. Hobsbawm and Ranger, p. 182.

82. Tambiah, *World Conqueror,* p. 80; Phra Rajavaramuni, *Thai Buddhism in the Buddhist World* (Bangkok: Amarin, 1984), p. 31.

83. Prince Chula Chakrabongse, *Lords of Life* (New York: Taplinger, 1960), p. 186.

84. *Bangkok Times,* 5 May 1897 (quoting from the *Times of Ceylon*).

85. Chulalongkorn, *Phraratchahatthalekha . . . praphat yurop pho.so. 2440,* 1:52–53.

86. *Bangkok Times,* 5 and 19 May 1897 (quoting from the *Ceylon Observer*).

87. Chulalongkorn, *Phraratchahatthalekha . . . praphat yurop pho.so. 2440,* 1:55.

88. Émile Jottrand, *In Siam,* trans. Walter E. J. Tips (Bangkok: White Lotus, 1996), p. 364.

89. "The Viceroy of India, Lord Curzon, had been to Bangkok and knew King Rama V. As he considered him the only monarch in the modern world who was a true supporter of Buddhism, he presented the relics to him. Buddhists in Japan, Burma, Ceylon, and Siberia then sent missions to Siam asking for a portion of them, so the King made a proper distribution." Prince Damrong, *Monuments of the Buddha,* p. 32. A new stupa was built within the precinct of Wat Saket, in Bangkok, to house the relics.

90. Norbert Elias, *The Court Society,* trans. Edmund Jephcott (Oxford: Blackwell, 1983).

91. For an assessment of Elias work, see Jeroen Duindam, *Myths of Power* (Amsterdam: Amsterdam University Press, 1994).

92. Seksan Prasertakul, "The Transformation of the Thai State and Economic Change" (Ph.D. diss., Cornell University, 1989), p. 460, n. 57.

93. Ibid., pp. 451–452.

94. These factions, complemented by "Young Siam," the court's party, were originally identified and named by an article in the *Siam Weekly Advertiser,* 31 July 1873. Adams, "Monarchy and Political Change," p. 48.

95. The standard works on centralization are those by Battye and Tej Bunnang (already cited) and by Ian Brown (*The Creation of the Modern Ministry of Finance in Siam, 1885–1910* [London: Macmillan, 1992]).

96. Seksan, "Transformation of the Thai State," p. 459.

97. Duindam, *Myths of Power,* p. 24.

98. Richard S. Wortman, *Scenarios of Power* (Princeton, N.J.: Princeton University Press, 1995), pp. 45, 48, 53.

99. Ibid., p. 52.

100. Ibid.

101. Karl Marx and Friedrich Engels, "Manifesto of the Communist Party," in *The Marx-Engels Reader,* ed. Robert C. Tucker (New York: Norton, 1972), p. 338.

Chapter 2: Presentation and Representation of the Royal Self

1. Jottrand, *In Siam,* p. 2.

2. The expression is from Jennifer Craick, *The Face of Fashion* (London: Routledge, 1994), p. 10.

3. Crawfurd, *Journal of an Embassy,* pp. 93–94.

4. On the history of photography in Thailand and its relation with the royalty, see Sakda Siripan, *Kasattri lae klong* [Kings and cameras] (Bangkok: Darn-suttha Press, 1992), illustrated by a large fund of archival photos. See also the collected articles by Anake Nawigamune, *Thairup muang thai samai raek* [Early photography in Thailand] (Bangkok: Saengdaet, 1990); and idem, *Laoruang thairup* [On photography] (Bangkok: Saengdaet, 1995).

5. Daniel Boorstin, *The Image* (London: Weidenfeld and Nicolson, 1961).

6. Mouhot, *Travels in . . . Indo-China;* Anna Leonowens, *The English Governess at the Siamese Court* (repr. Singapore: Oxford University Press, 1988); Frank Vincent, *The Land of the White Elephant* (repr. Singapore: Oxford University Press, 1988]). Bowring's *Kingdom and People of Siam* (1857) had engravings of landscape scenes and color lithographs of Siamese "types" (like Crawfurd's earlier book), including one of King Mongkut wearing a Chinese-style gown and cap, used as the first volume's frontispiece.

7. Michael B. Hooker, *A Concise Legal History of South-East Asia* (Oxford: Clarendon Press, 1978), pp. 54–55.

8. Bowring, *Kingdom and People of Siam,* 1:131, 238. See also Penelope Van Esterik, "Royal Style in Village Context," in *Contributions to Asian Studies,* vol. 15: *Royalty and Commoners,* ed. Constance M. Wilson et al. (Leiden: E. J. Brill, 1980), pp. 108–110, 117, n. 5.

9. Thipakorawong, *The Fourth Reign,* 1:5–6.

10. Reid, *Southeast Asia in the Age of Commerce,* 1:85.

11. See sketches of the envoys originally published in the *Illustrated London News* (5 December 1857) and a daguerreotype taken at the British court by an Italian photographer (one Caldesi) in Sakda, *Kasattri,* pp. 29–30.

12. Damrong, *Khwamsongcham,* pp. 251–252.

13. Bowring, *Kingdom and People of Siam,* 1:407.

14. Sakda, *Kasattri,* p. 24.

15. Ibid., pp. 33, 59–61. The title of Phraya Krasapana Kicchakot was later bestowed on Luang Wisut. Up to 1932, graded titles *(yot)* were bestowed on commoners along with honorific names *(ratchathinnam)* in recognition of their service to the throne. The most common titles, in ascending order of status, were *khun, luang, phra,* and *phraya.* The upgrading of a title was accompanied by a change in the honorific name.

16. Ibid., pp. 35–37.

17. Photographs in Sakda, *Kasattri,* pp. 42, 78 (Mongkut), and p. 50 (Chutamani).

18. Philip Mansel, "Monarchy, Uniform, and the Rise of the *Frac,* 1760–

1830," *Past and Present* 96 (1982): 103–132; Ernst H. Kantorowicz, "Gods in Uniform," repr. in his *Selected Studies* (Locust Valley, N.Y.: J. J. Augustin, 1965).

19. Among the presents for Rama IV entrusted to the Siamese envoys in 1861 were busts of Empress Eugenie and Napoleon III (now in the Chakri Throne Hall), the latter in military uniform. Apinan, "Modern Art," pp. 42–43.

20. Photographs in Anake, *Chulalongkorn,* pp. 35, 38.

21. Ibid, pp. 46–49. Thomson described the session for the taking of King Mongkut's portrait in his travelogue, *The Straits of Malacca, Indo-China and China* (London: Sampson Low, 1875), pp. 94–95. Thomson's photographs of the Bangkok royalty were rendered into engravings (without any acknowledgment) for Anna Leonowens' book, *The English Governess.* A selection of photographs taken by Thomson in Siam are reproduced in Sakda, *Kasattri,* pp. 78–87.

22. Anake, *Chulalongkorn,* pp. 57–60, 77–81.

23. Ibid., pp. 61–69.

24. Wyatt, *Politics of Reform,* p. 41.

25. Anake, *Chulalongkorn,* pp. 89–91.

26. Damrong, *Khwamsongcham,* p. 269.

27. Prince Wachirayan Warorot, *Autobiography,* trans., ed., intr. Craig J. Reynolds (Athens: Ohio University Press, 1979), pp. 22–23.

28. These uniforms cost 2 Spanish dollars each. Seksan, "Transformation of the Thai State," p. 137.

29. Bowring, *Kingdom and People of Siam,* 1:477.

30. Bock, *Temples and Elephants,* p. 22.

31. Jottrand, *In Siam,* p. 199.

32. Ibid., p. 226. For a photograph of Chulalongkorn in ceremonial garb and the conical crown being carried on a litter for the *kathin* ceremony (probably in 1881), see Anake, *Chulalongkorn,* p. 133. This photograph was rendered into an engraving for Bock's *Temples and Elephants.* The latest photograph showing Rama V in traditional ceremonial garb, yet with hose and shoes, was taken on the occasion of Crown Prince Vajiravudh's tonsure ceremony in December 1892. Anake, *Chulalongkorn,* p. 152.

33. Robyn Maxwell, *Textiles of Southeast Asia* (Melbourne: Oxford University Press, 1990), p. 374. Blouses decorated with lace became a main element in the costume of well-to-do women in cities across the whole of Southeast Asia in the latter decades of the nineteenth century.

34. Emma Tarlo, *Clothing Matters* (Chicago: University of Chicago Press, 1996), pp. 50–53 and chap. 3.

35. Walter F. Vella, "Thianwan of Siam: A Man Who Fought Giants," in *Anuson Walter Vella,* ed. Ronald D. Renard (Chiang Mai: W. F. Vella Fund, Payap University; Honolulu: Center for Asian and Pacific Studies, University of Hawai'i at Manoa, 1986), p. 80.

36. Jottrand, *In Siam,* p. 96.

37. Wyatt, *Thailand,* p. 255.

38. Apinan, "Modern Art," pp. 36–38.

39. Alain Corbin, "Backstage," in *A History of Private Life,* gen. ed. Philippe

Aries and Georges Duby, vol. 4: *From the Fires of Revolution to the Great War,* ed. Michelle Perrot, trans. Arthur Goldhammer (Cambridge: Belknap Press of Harvard University Press, 1990), pp. 463–464.

40. Suren Lalvani, *Photography, Vision, and the Production of Modern Bodies* (Albany: State University of New York Press, 1996).

41. Bock, *Temples and Elephants,* p. 73.

42. Jottrand, *In Siam,* p. 311.

43. Anake, *Chulalongkorn,* pp. 172–184.

44. King Chulalongkorn, *Rayathang thiao chawa kwa song duan* [Narrative of a journey to Java of over two months], Cremation volume (Bangkok, 1925), p. 15.

45. Ibid., p. 30.

46. Cited in the *Bangkok Times,* 10 March 1907.

47. *The Graphic,* 10 February 1872 (reproduced in Anake, *Chulalongkorn,* p. 94).

48. Quoted in the *Bangkok Times,* 11 September 1897.

49. Ibid.

50. This is the number of Chulalongkorn's sons appearing with their father in a series of photographs taken at Taplow Court (Maidenhead) on the occasion of the king's visit. Anake, *Chulalongkorn,* pp. 204–208.

51. *Les Annales,* no. 1252 (19 June 1897), p. 11.

52. *Bangkok Times,* 25 October 1897.

53. Anake, *Chulalongkorn,* pp. 156, 193–195. Since these images were rediscovered and printed on the 1989 Toshiba calendar for Thailand, they have become enormously popular through reproduction in books, magazines, and even New Year greeting cards.

54. *La Gazzetta di Venezia,* 15 May 1897; *La Nazione,* 10 June 1897. Queen Sawang was Saowapha's older sister, but it is apparently Saowapha whom the author of this piece referred to.

55. Quoted in the *Bangkok Times,* 21 July 1897. For an account of Rama V's touring of painters' studios in Italy see Apinan, "Modern Art," pp. 73–78.

56. Chulalongkorn, *Phraratchahatthalekha . . . praphat yurop pho.so. 2440,* 1:194–195; Apinan, "Modern Art," pp. 80–84. At the completion of the portrait in 1899, Gelli was conferred the brevet of Grand Officer of the Royal Order of the Crown of Siam (NA, RV, Ministry of Privy Seal 16.2/92).

57. Aaron Scharf, *Art and Photography* (Harmondsworth: Penguin, 1983), pp. 49, 56.

58. Anake, *Chulalongkorn,* pp. 188–89.

59. Sakda, *Kasattri,* pp. 148–177. Following Lenz's retirement in 1907, his business was taken over by his associates, E. Groote and C. Pruss.

60. Vajiravudh and Chakrabongse were studying in England at that time. Gelli also changed the color of the sailor suits worn by the youngest princes from navy blue (the color for daily wear) into white (the color for summer wear).

61. Susan M. Pearce, *On Collecting* (London: Routledge, 1996), p. 299.

62. Chulalongkorn, *Phraratchahatthalekha . . . praphat yurop pho.so. 2440,*

1:195. A full-length portrait of Queen Saowapha wearing the same costume was painted at the same time by another Florentine artist, Edoardo Gordigiani (see *Samut phap ratchakan thi 5/ Pictorial Record,* p. 9).

63. Simon Schama, "The Domestication of Majesty: Royal Family Portraiture, 1500–1850," *Journal of Interdisciplinary History* 17 (1986): 155–183.

64. Ibid., pp. 157–158.

65. Sunantha, Sawang, and Saowapha were sisters. Sunantha (1860–1880), the king's favorite, drowned in a boat accident on the way to Bang Pa-in. Of Sawang (queen with the title Si Sawarin, 1862–1955) and Saowapha (Si Phatcharin, 1864–1919), Malcolm Smith (*Physician,* p. 142) says that they "were on excellent terms with one another. They did not, of course, live together." See also Saengthian Satthathai, *Sam ratchani khu banlang ratchakan thi 5* [The three queens of Rama V] (Bangkok: Mahannop, 1996).

66. Apinan, "Modern Art," pp. 98–101.

67. *Bangkok Times,* 5 August 1907.

68. Anne-Marie Lecoq, "La symbolique de l'État," in *Les lieux de mémoire,* ed. Pierre Nora, vol. 2, pt. 2 (Paris: Gallimard, 1986), p. 147. Lecoq distinguishes the "historic image" of the sovereign from his "symbolic image" evoked by heraldic compositions, emblems, and the like. The latter (conical crowns, *chakra*s) were impressed on the first flat coins minted in Siam in the Fourth Reign.

69. This was a medal struck for the third anniversary of Chulalongkorn's reign in 1871 and was engraved with his left profile, the *mahatthai* hairstyle clearly visible. Anake, *Chulalongkorn,* pp. 87–88.

70. The effigy of Rama V appeared for the first time on the second series of silver coins issued in his reign; probably minted at about the same time was also a gold coin of similar design. In 1887 the king's effigy also made its appearance on the copper coins of low value, which were minted in England. In 1908 a new type of baht coin, bearing on the obverse a lifelike portrait of the king as he appeared at that time, in uniform and with decorations, was issued. Many of these latter coins were coated with platinum for presentation purposes. Reginald Le May, *The Coinage of Siam* (Bangkok: Siam Society, 1932), pp. 105–119.

71. Postage stamps were first issued in Siam on 4 August 1883, concurrently with the establishment of the Post Department (two years later Siam joined the Unione Postale Universelle). Following the pattern of British stamps (the first ever to be issued in 1840), the Siamese stamps featured the king's left profile in an oval frame with the value expressed in Thai numerals only. This first series, designed by the Post Department and printed in London, was intended primarily for domestic use; a second series was issued in April 1887. The stamps (in eight denominations) were designed and printed in London and had a frontal portrait of Rama V in an oval frame and the inscriptions "*praisani lae ngenkhamtra sayam*" and "Siam value postage revenue." The third stamp series, in circulation between September 1899 and January 1904 in thirteen denominations, was designed and printed by a Leipzig firm and carried the king's left-side portrait (as he appeared then) and the value in Thai and Arab numerals. The fourth series, in circulation between December 1905 and January 1908 in fourteen denominations, marked a change

toward a more continental design. Designed by the Italian Cesare Ferro and printed in Leipzig, the stamps featured Wat Arun on the background and two top-knotted children holding up an oval with the king's left portrait on the foreground. A high-value fiscal stamp in three denominations, unusual in that it bore the king's frontal portrait, was issued in April 1907, and a special jubilee stamp with the image of Rama V's equestrian statue in November 1908. This latter stamp was designed by Mario Tamagno, of the Public Works Department, who also designed the Fifth Reign's sixth and final stamp series, issued in May 1910. The stamp featured the mythic bird Garuda holding an oval with the king's left profile. It was in use until October 1912, when the Sixth Reign's first stamp series (also designed by Tamagno) was issued. Sakerm Siriwong, *Thai Stamps 1983* (Bangkok: Siam Stamp Trading Company, 1983); *Centennial of Thai Postage Stamps* (Bangkok: Communication Authority of Thailand, 1983).

72. See Thongthong, *Khong suay khong di*; Anake Nawigamune, *Singphim khlatsik* [Classic prints] (Bangkok: Matichon, 1994).

73. Jottrand, *In Siam*, p. 236.

74. Chula Chakrabongse, *Lords of Life*, p. 229.

75. Jottrand, *In Siam*, pp. 312, 318–320. On the Wat Benchama Bophit fairs see below, chap. 3.

76. John M. MacKenzie, *Propaganda and Empire* (Manchester: Manchester University Press, 1984), pp. 21–23.

77. See Bonnie Davis, *Postcards of Old Siam* (Singapore: Times Press, 1987).

78. Anake Nawigamune, "Poska khlatsik khong sansan phaengsapha" [Sansan Phaengsapha's "classic" postcards], *Sarakkhadi* (December 1988): 145–151.

79. Tambiah, *World Conqueror*, p. 526.

80. For a wide selection of such political cartoons, see Barmé, "Social History of Bangkok," chap. 3.

Chapter 3: Suburban Playgrounds

1. Naengnoi Saksi (with Naphit Krittikakun and Daruni Kaeomuang), *Phraratchawang lae wang nai krungthep pho.so. 2325–2525* [Royal and princely palaces in Bangkok, 1782–1932] (Bangkok: Chulalongkorn University, 1982), pp. 369–373; Nanthiya Sawangwutthitham, "Bothnam" [Introduction], *Chotmaihet kankosang lae somsaem phrathinang wimanmek, pho.so. 2443–2518* [Documents on the construction and restoration of Wimanmek Palace, 1900–1975] (Bangkok: Bureau of the Royal Household, 1990), pp. 1–21. "*Wang*" is a collective noun for a whole palatial compound, individual edifices bearing the prefix *phrathinang*.

2. Naengnoi Saksi (photographs by Michael Freeman), *Palaces of Bangkok* (Bangkok: River Books, 1996), pp. 23–24.

3. The increase in motorcars since the final years of the Fifth Reign prompted the "establishment of an up-to-date and thoroughly equipped garage automobile in Bangkok" under the management of a Belgian company (*Bangkok Times*, 23 March 1907).

4. Sirichai Narumit, *Old Bridges of Bangkok* (Bangkok: Siam Society, 1977).

5. On nineteenth-century city planning and architecture in both metropolitan and colonial contexts see, among others, M. Christine Boyer, *The City of Collective Memory* (Cambridge, Mass.: MIT Press, 1994), pt. 1; Mark Crinson, *Empire Building* (London: Routledge, 1996); Dallas Finn, *Meiji Revisited* (New York: Weatherhill, 1995); Thomas Metcalf, *An Imperial Vision* (Berkeley: University of California Press, 1989); David Van Zanten, *Building Paris* (New York: Cambridge University Press, 1994); Gwendolyn Wright, *The Politics of Design in French Colonial Urbanism* (Chicago: University of Chicago Press, 1991).

6. Boyer, *City of Collective Memory,* pp. 33–34.

7. Anthony D. King, "Colonialism and the Development of the Modern Asian City: Some Theoretical Considerations," in *The City in South Asia,* ed. Kenneth Ballhatchet and John Harrison (London: Curzon Press, 1980), p. 11.

8. Anthony Sutcliffe, "Introduction: The Debate on Nineteenth-Century Planning," in *The Rise of Modern Urban Planning, 1800–1914,* ed. A. Sutcliffe (London: Mansell, 1980), pp. 1–10.

9. For a photographic selection of places and people in Dusit Park see *Pictorial Record,* pp. 154–159.

10. Kamthon Kunchan and Songsan Nilakamhaeng, "Wiwatthanakan thangkai phap khong krung rattanakosin fang tawanook: tangtae kon remsang krung chonthung samai plianplaeng rabop kanpokkhrong" [The evolution of Bangkok's plan, from the initial settlement to 1932], *Warasan mahawitthayalai sinlapakorn* 4–5 (1980–1982): 221–244.

11. Robert Heine-Geldern, *Conceptions of State and Kingship in Southeast Asia* (Ithaca, N.Y.: Cornell University Southeast Asia Program, 1956). With reference to Siam, Riggs (*Thailand,* pp. 70–77) sketched a historical model of the traditional Siamese bureaucracy based on the cosmological ideal; and Tambiah (*World Conqueror,* chaps. 7 and 8) relied on both Heine-Geldern and Riggs to outline his model of the Ayutthayan kingdom as a "galactic polity."

12. Naengnoi, *Phraratchawang,* pp. 11–12.

13. The madness of King Taksin appears to a large extent a historical myth created to legitimate the foundation of the Chakri dynasty. For a revisionist interpretation of Taksin's reign, see Nidhi Aeusriwongse, *Kanmuang thai samai phrachao krung thonburi* [Thai politics in the Thonburi reign] (Bangkok: Sinlapa Watthanatham, 1986).

14. Thipakorawong, *The First Reign,* 1:59.

15. Clifford Geertz, *Negara* (Princeton, N.J.: Princeton University Press, 1980). About the seats of power of the Siamese kings, Richard O'Connor ("Place, Power, and Discourse in the Thai Image of Bangkok," *Journal of the Siam Society* 78, 2 [1990]: 70) claims, "Only a leap of faith can make them [Ayutthaya and Bangkok] into cosmological cities anywhere near as perfect as their [Khmer] neighbours built." However, O'Connor's explanation for such a lack of cosmological precision is a tautological one: "Thai were never rigorously cosmological anyway." On the discrepancy between the theory of town planning of royal capitals of Theravada Buddhist courts and Ayutthaya's actual plan, see Larry Sternstein,

"Krung Kao: The Old Capital of Ayutthaya," *Journal of the Siam Society* 53, 1 (1965): 83–121.

16. Akin, *Organization of Thai Society*, pp. 44–45.

17. Prince Damrong Rajanubhap, "Athibai ruang tamnan wang kao," [History of old palaces], in *Prachum phongsawadan* [Collected chronicles], vol. 15, sect. 26 (Bangkok: Khurusapha, 1964), pp. 144–149. Saranrom Palace was completed only in the Fifth Reign. It was, for a brief period, the residence of Crown Prince Vajiravudh following his return from Europe in January 1902 and was later transformed during his reign into the seat of the Ministry of Foreign Affairs.

18. Thipakarawong, *The Fourth Reign*, 2:492–493, 518–519, 521–524, 527–530; Damrong, "Tamnan wang kao," pp. 154–156.

19. Anake Nawigamune, *Raek mi nai sayam* [First in Siam], vol. 1 (Bangkok: Saengdaet, 1989), pp. 100–102; 127–129.

20. Larry Sternstein, "Bangkok at the Turn of the Century: Mongkut and Chulalongkorn Entertain the West," *Journal of the Siam Society* 54, 1 (1966): 68–69.

21. Thiphakorawong, *The Fourth Reign*, 2:319.

22. Cited by Charnvit, "Siam/Civilization." Bradley's article (in Thai) was published in December 1866.

23. For a description of the Bangkok cityscape in the early 1870s, see Vincent, *Land of the White Elephant*, pp. 130–132.

24. Reid, *Age of Commerce*, 1:62–66.

25. The recycling of Ayutthaya's buildings is actually mentioned by Prince Chula Chakrabongse, *Lords of Life*, p. 90.

26. Apinan, "Modern Art," pp. 13–22; Naengnoi, *Palaces of Bangkok*, pp. 60–66.

27. *The Graphic*, issue of 7 May 1881 (reproduced in Anake, *Chulalongkorn*, p. 111).

28. It is said that Chaophraya Si Suriyawong imposed the *prasat* on the Chakri Throne Hall on the basis of two arguments. First, in Ayutthaya there used to be three spire-roofed buildings but in Bangkok there were only two; second, every Chakri king had built a *prasat*, and Chulalongkorn should follow suit. Naengnoi Saksi, *Satthapatayakam phraborom maharatchawang* [The architecture of the Grand Palace] (Bangkok: His Majesty's Private Secretariat, 1988), pp. 100–101.

29. Finn, *Meiji Revisited*, p. 98.

30. On the occasion of a visit to the palace of Nakhon Khiri some twenty years after its construction, Carl Bock (*Temples and Elephants*, p. 82) wrote, "It is a curious fact that the Siamese, though ever building, seem seldom, if ever, to take steps to keep their edifices, sacred or secular, in repair. And more often than not what they do build they leave uncompleted. It is quite an exception to see any building which has been completed 'out of hand,' and still more exceptional to find repairs going on."

31. Buls, *Siamese Sketches*, p. 12.

32. Suchrit Thawansuk, *Nangsu prakuat ruang phraprawat lae nangsilpa khong somdet phrachao boromwongthe chaofa kromphraya naritsara nuwattiwong* [The life and

work of Prince Naritsara Nuwattiwong] (Bangkok: Thai Watthana Phanich, 1966), p. 68.

33. Ibid., p. 110.

34. Prince Damrong wrote a detailed biography of Pan Sukhum as the introduction to the collection of letters addressed to him by Chulalongkorn, *Phraratchahatthalekha . . . chaophraya yomarat*; see also Yomarat's biography in Prayut Sitthipan, *Chomna prawattisat khut khunnang sayam* [Biographies of Siamese nobles] (Bangkok: Samnakphim Sayam, 1987), pp. 303–313.

35. *Prachum kotmai* [Collected acts], vol. 21, pt. 1 (Rattanakosin era 125 [1906/7]) (Bangkok: 1935), pp. 30, 115.

36. *Siam Directory* (Bangkok, 1892, 1893).

37. NA, Ministry of Foreign Affairs 35.7/39.

38. The Engineering Section included besides Gollo, G. Canova, E. Roberto, A. Spigno, M. Salao, G. Levi, and A. Facchinetti; and as assistants, L. Giacone, P. Coletti, G. Guasco, and L. Boghini. The Architectural Section besides Tamagno, A. Rigotti, G. Salvatore, A. Rigazzi, O. Tavella, E. Manfredi, B. Moreschi, and P. Remedi. The sculptors Tonarelli and Novi, the decorators G. Innocenti, A. Parodi, R. Nolli and G. Clessi, and the marble cutter G. Di Prato were also employed in the early 1910s, in connection with the decoration of the Ananta Samakhom. Pietro Jansen, "Costruttori e artisti italiani nel Siam," *Le vie d'Italia e del mondo* 1, 10 (1933): 1279–1294.

39. Leopoldo Ferri de Lazara and Paolo Piazzardi, *Italians at the Court of Siam* (Bangkok: Amarin Press, 1996). This coffee-table book, written by the Italian ambassador and cultural attaché in Bangkok and published for King Bhumibol's Golden Jubilee, contains some valuable information on these individuals but very little on their activity as employees of the Siamese government.

40. Charles A. Ward, *Moscow and Leningrad* (München and London: K. G. Saur, 1989); and Ellen P. Conant, "Principles and Pragmatism: The *Yatoi* in the Field of Art," in *Foreign Employees in Nineteenth-century Japan,* ed. E. R. Beauchamp and Akira Iriye (Boulder, Colo.: Westview, 1990), pp. 137–170.

41. Somchart Chungsiriarak, "Satthapatayakam khong kharl duhring" [The architecture of Karl Döhring], *Muang Boran* 19, 3 (1993): 66–101.

42. NA, RV, Ministry of Public Works 1/32 (esp. pp. 3–8, 9–10) and 1/36.

43. In a letter dated 21 March 1906, Allegri complained that during the first ten years of service (1890–1900) he had received a monthly salary of 550 baht against the 1,200 baht earned by the engineer in chief of the Railways Department, which was part of the same ministry (NA, RVI, Miscellany 5/124). In 1934 Allegri successfully petitioned the regent, Prince Narit, against a planned 30 percent reduction of his pension (NA, RVI, Ministry of Municipal Government 7.2/18). Allegri retired at fifty-four, even though the retirement age for government employees was fifty.

44. Malcolm Smith, *Physician,* p. 57.

45. Jottrand, *In Siam,* p. 312.

46. Naengnoi, *Palaces of Bangkok,* 228–231.

47. *Prachum kotmai,* vol. 17, pt. 1 (Rattanakosin era 118 [1899–1990]), pp. 71–77; and vol. 18, pt. 1 (Rattanakosin era 120 [1901–1902]), pp. 138–144.

48. A. Cecil Carter, ed., *The Kingdom of Siam* (repr. Bangkok: Siam Society, 1988), p. 108.

49. The three bridges were named, respectively, Phanphi Phoplila, Phanphi Lilat, and Makhawan Rangsan.

50. Naengnoi, *Palaces of Bangkok,* p. 195.

51. Anake, *Raek mi nai sayam,* 1:212, referring to a passage from *Phraratchahatthalekha phrabat somdet phrachulachomklao chaoyuhua lae ruang khong set athibodi fainai* (Bangkok, 1910), p. 34, in which the expression occurs "to go by lift" (*pay khun lif*).

52. Apinan, "Modern Art," pp. 113–116.

53. Debora Silverman, *Art Nouveau in Fin-de-Siècle France* (Berkeley: University of California Press, 1989), p. 77.

54. *Bangkok Times,* 18 February 1907. As part of the entertainments for the inauguration of Amphon Sathan, King Chulalongkorn's play *Ngo pa* (People of the forest) was staged.

55. Phra Thammakit Sophana, ed., *Phraphuttha chaoluang kap wat benchamabophit* [Rama V and Wat Benchama Bophit] (Bangkok: Wat Benchama Bophit, 1988), pp. 15, 23.

56. Ibid., pp. 131–146.

57. Apinan, "Modern Art," p. 138.

58. NA, RV, Ministry of Public Works 1/26 (memo dated September 1901). White marble was the cheapest option (estimated cost 48,200 baht for common marble and 61,346 baht for polished marble). As an alternative, Allegri proposed either white marble for the walls and colored marble for the basement, or colored marble slabs throughout.

59. Chulalongkorn, letter of 23 May 1907, *Phraratchahatthalekha . . . chaophraya yomarat,* p. 38. At that time the problem arose of employing a Japanese artisan, as Rama V wanted someone from that country for the gilding of the seated Buddha image placed inside the *ubosot,* a copy of the venerated Buddha Chinarat image in Phitsanulok. Upon an inquiry by the Siamese chargé d'affaires in Tokyo, the principal of the Tokyo School of Fine Arts recommended the service of Kenzaburo Tsuruharu. Included in his contract was the provision that the Japanese decorator would also teach his technique to local artisans, a fact that indicates the lower standards of Thai artisans at that time. The contract, signed on 13 January 1910, provided for two months' employment at 8 yen per day, extendable at the lower rate of 6 yen. NA, RV, Miscellany 9/65.

60. Damrong, "Tamnan wang kao," p. 192.

61. Naengnoi, *Palaces of Bangkok,* pp. 245–265.

62. Naengnoi, *Phraratchawang,* pp. 439–459, 470–473.

63. Chula Chakrabongse, *Twain Have Met,* pp. 69–73.

64. Damrong, "Tamnan wang kao," pp. 181–182.

65. Chula Chakrabongse, *Twain Have Met,* p. 64.

66. Naengnoi, *Palaces of Bangkok,* pp. 301–307.

67. Ibid., pp. 19–20, 245, 264.

68. J. Antonio, *The 1904 Traveller's Guide to Bangkok and Siam* (Bangkok: White Lotus, 1997), p. 20.

69. Arnold Wright, ed., *Twentieth-Century Impressions of Siam* (London: Lloyd's Greater Britain Publishing Co., 1908), p. 256.

70. NA, provisional collection of Fifth Reign and Sixth Reign documents, vol. 2, pt. 8, p. 1552.

71. Jottrand, *In Siam*, p. 418.

72. Ibid., p. 284.

73. Richard Bentmann and Michael Müller, *The Villa as Hegemonic Architecture*, trans. Tim Spence and David Craven (New Jersey and London: Humanities Press, 1992). See also James S. Ackerman, *The Villa* (Princeton, N.J.: Princeton University Press, 1990), according to whom (p. 10) the villa represents "a paradigm not only of architecture but of ideology . . . a myth or fantasy through which over the course of millennia persons whose position of privilege is rooted in urban commerce and industry have been able to expropriate rural land, often requiring for the realization of the myth the care of a laboring class or of slaves."

74. Lewis Mumford, *The Story of Utopias* (repr. Gloucester, Mass.: P. Smith, 1959), p. 202.

75. Chulalongkorn, *Phraratchahatthalekha . . . prapat yurop pho.so. 2440,* 2:27.

76. Sakda, *Kasattri,* pp. 142–143.

77. Dean MacCannel, "Staged Authenticity: Arrangements of Social Space in Tourist Settings," *American Journal of Sociology* 79, 3 (1973): 589–603.

78. Vella, *Chaiyo!,* p. 75.

79. Pin Malakun, M.L., *Dusit thani muang prachathipatai phrabat somdet phra mongkutklaochaoyuhua* [Dusit Thani, the democratic city of Rama VI] (Bangkok: National Library, 1970).

80. Vella (*Chaiyo!,* pp. 75–76) described Dusit Thani as "one of the world's most unusual expressions of political thought," though admitting that "certainly much of the miniature city was for fun."

81. Susan Stewart, *On Longing* (Baltimore: Johns Hopkins University Press, 1984), p. 163.

82. Jottrand, *In Siam,* pp. 318–320.

83. Five gold, thirty silver, and sixty-eight bronze medals were awarded at the competition, the five top prizes going to Rama V, a prince, and three foreigners. Sakda, *Kasattri,* pp. 96–102.

84. *Bangkok Times,* 14 December 1907.

Chapter 4: Field of Glory

1. David Cannadine, "The Transformation of Civic Ritual in Modern Britain: The Colchester Oyster Feast," *Past and Present* 94 (1982): 107–130.

2. Geertz, "Centers, Kings, and Charisma," p. 20.

3. Eric Hobsbawm, *Nations and Nationalism since 1780* (Cambridge: Cambridge University Press, 1990), p. 84.

4. Fujitani, *Splendid Monarchy,* p. 81.

5. Breckenridge, "Aesthetics and Politics," p. 214.

6. Nidhi Auesriwongse, "Songkhram anusaori kap rat thai" [The war of monuments and the Thai state], repr. in his *Chat thai muang thai baeprian lae anusaori* [Thai nation, "Thailand," textbooks, and monuments] (Bangkok: Matichon, 1995), esp. pp. 97–103.

7. NA, RVI, Ministry of Municipal Government 17.5/3.

8. Pierre Nora, "General Introduction: Between Memory and History," in *Realms of Memory,* gen. ed. P. Nora, English-language ed. and intr. Lawrence D. Kritzman, trans. Arthur Goldhammer (New York: Columbia University Press, 1996–1998), 1:1–23. *Realms of Memory* is an abridged translation in three volumes of the seven-volume cultural history of France edited by Nora, *Les lieux de mémoire* (Paris: Seuil, 1984–1992). Nora's introduction was first published in English translation in *Representations* 26 (1989): 7–25.

9. *Ratchakitchanu bekkasa* [Royal government gazette], vol. 24 (8 March 1908): 1321, cited in Songsan Nilkamhaeng and Phrani Sunthrayot, "Khrongkan burana prapprung phrathinang ananta samakhom raya raek pho.so. 2519–2522" [The original project and the first stage of restoration of the Ananta Samakhom Throne Hall, 1976–1979], *Sinlapakorn* 21, 5 (1979): 2.

10. This is the grand total of sums that were apportioned in the annual budget reports as follows: 1909–1910 to 1912–1913: 500,000 baht per year; 1913–1914: 1,162,569 baht; 1914–1915: 842,030 baht; 1915–1916: 1,137,547 baht; 1916–1917: 349,762 baht; 1917–1918: 1,032 baht. NA, Office of the Financial Adviser, Budget Report, Rattanakosin era 127 (1909–1910) to Buddhist era 2462 (1919–1920). Starting with B.E. 2456 (1913/14), when they are first given in the reports, I have calculated actual expenditure figures rather than the budgeted sums apportioned in the financial budget for the coming year.

11. See FAD, comp., *Chelim phrathinang ananta samakhom* [A celebration of the Ananta Samakhom Throne Hall], Cremation volume (Bangkok, 1979), p. 97; Thongthong Chansangsu, *Phrathinang ananta samakhom* [The Ananta Samakhom Throne Hall] (Bangkok: Akson Samphan, 1987), p. 83; Apinan, "Modern Art," p. 128.

12. Piriya Krairikish, *Prawattisat sinlapa nai prathet thai chabap khumu naksuksa* [History of art in Thailand: A student's textbook] (Bangkok: Amarin Press, 1985), p. 334.

13. Chaophraya Thammasak Montri, "Phraong song saedong phraratchathomnat mak thung kae rapsang wa topai khangna khao khong phakan tichan wa samai phrachulachomklao ni chang prottuk farang sia chring," in Songsan and Phrani, "Khrongkan burana," p. 3. Thammasak was educated overseas in the years 1896–1898, and from 1916 to 1926 he was minister of education. A versatile author and journalist, he was among the first to write about economics in Siam, under the pseudonym of Khru Thep. Phraya Ratcha Songkhram, who is mentioned in the poem, was the honorific title granted to Kon Hongsakun, the chief court draughtsman.

14. Chulalongkorn, letter of 25 March 1907, *Phraratchatthalekha . . . chaophraya yomarat,* pp. 28–29.

15. Ministry of Public Works, memo of 24 June 1909, NA, RV, Miscellany 9/64. Rigotti was employed for this project under a temporary contract (at a monthly salary of 1,200 baht) that ran initially from November 1907 to September 1909 and was later extended but at lower pay.

16. Erik Seidenfaden, *Guide to Bangkok,* 3d ed. (Bangkok: The Royal State Railways of Siam, 1932), p. 252.

17. Emilio E. Rodio, "La perla di Bangkok," *Art e dossier* 19 (December 1987): 18–19.

18. In relation to Chulalongkorn's jubilee, Prince Chula Chakrabongse wrote in *Lords of Life* (p. 266), "It is said they wanted a vast and grandiose marble memorial like the one in Rome for King Victor Emmanuel II."

19. Chulalongkorn, letter of 24 April 1909, *Pharatchahatthalekha . . . chaophraya yomarat,* p. 134.

20. Ibid., letters of 24 and 25 October 1909, pp. 166–167, 168. Ellipsis in original.

21. Apinan, "Modern Art," p. 122.

22. Carlo Allegri, letter to Chaophraya Yomarat of 19 October 1909, with enclosed "Proposals made by Mr. Ferro in regard to the painting of the Phrathinang Ananta Samakhom" (in English). NA, RV, Miscellany 9/64.

23. Chulalongkorn, letter of 25 October 1909, *Phraratchahatthalekha . . . chaophraya yomarat,* p. 168. Apinan (*Modern Art,* p. 18) erroneously contends that Ferro actually worked at the decoration of the Ananta Samakhom. Ferro did go back to Bangkok but in 1923 to work at the decoration of Norasing Villa, a grand mansion in the Venetian gothic style designed by Annibale Rigotti for King Vajiravudh's favorite, Chaophraya Ramrakop (later converted to use as the prime minister's residence).

24. F. Dalmaso, P. Gaglia, and F. Poli, *L'Accademia Albertina di Torino* (Turin: Istituto Bancario S. Paolo, 1982), p. 64.

25. Gianni Vianello, *Galileo Chini e il Liberty in Italia* (Florence: Sansoni, 1964).

26. *Bangkok Times,* 22 June 1907.

27. The suggestion is made by Apinan, "Modern Art," p. 123.

28. NA, RVI, Miscellany 5/124.

29. E. G. Gollo (acting engineer in chief, Public Works Department), letter to Chaophraya Yomarat of 28 July 1910, where mention is made of a telegram sent by Allegri from Italy. NA, RV, Miscellany 5/15.

30. Chulalongkorn, letter of 28 July 1910, *Phraratchahatthalekha . . . chaophraya yomarat,* p. 235. It is worth noting that the date of the king's letter is the same as that of the memorandum by Gollo cited in note 29. This means that on the very same day Chaophraya Yomarat was informed by Gollo of Chini's availability to take up the job, he transmitted the information to Rama V and received his answer on the issue. Mindful of Ferro's slow working pace, Rama V stated that Chini should receive a monthly salary of 1,500 baht only for the duration of the contract (thirty months) with the remaining sum of 8,000 baht to be paid at the work's completion.

31. Vianello, *Galileo Chini,* p. 36.

32. Public Works Department, memorandum of 26 September 1911. NA, RVI, Miscellany 5/15.

33. Carlo Allegri, letter to Chaophraya Yomarat of 22 November 1911. NA, RVI, Ministry of Municipal Government 39.1/6.

34. Chronology established by Anna Imponente, "Liberty e orientalismo nelle collezioni di corte in Siam," *Aspetti del collezionismo in Italia* (Trapani: Quaderni Museo Regionale Pepoli, 1993): 185–203.

35. For excellent reproductions of Chini's frescoes see Apinan, *Western-style Paintings in the Thai Royal Court.*

36. Apinan, "Modern Art," p. 154.

37. King Vajiravudh, letter to Chaophraya Yomarat of 30 April 1915; Mario Tamagno, letter to Chaophraya Yomarat of 4 May 1915; minister of finance, letter to Chaophraya Yomarat of 5 May 1915. NA, RVI, Ministry of Municipal Government 7.7/14.

38. *Ratchakitchanu bekkasa*, vol. 33 (14 January 1917): 2808–2815; *Bangkok Times*, 8 and 13 January 1917.

39. NA, RVI, Ministry of Royal Household 17/32.

40. See Copeland, "Contested Nationalism," chaps. 3–4.

41. Vella, *Chaiyo!*, p. 234, quoting a Thai source.

42. See Davis, *Postcards of Old Siam*, pp. 16, 19, 20, for postcards featuring the Ananta Samakhom from 1917 to 1920.

43. Seidenfaden, *Guide to Bangkok*, p. 252.

44. See Thongthong, *Phrathinang ananta samakhom*, pp. 73, 83–89.

45. King Chulalongkorn, *Phraratchadamrat nai phrabat somdet phrachula-chomklaochaoyuhua song thalaeng phraborom ratchathibai kaekhai kanpokkhrong phaendin* [The king's speech explaining the reform of the government], Cremation volume (Bangkok, 1927), pp. 62–63.

46. Prince Damrong, "Ruang sang phraborom rup songma" [The king's equestrian statue], in *Prachum phraniphon betthalet* [Miscellaneous writings] (Bangkok: Kurusapha, 1961), in 59–62.

47. Chulalongkorn, letter of 15 April 1907, *Phraratchathatthalekha . . . chaophraya yomarat*, pp. 30–32. Before being appointed acting minister of public works for 1905–1906, Phraya Suriya had been the ambassador to Berlin, and it is quite clear that his extravagant proposal was inspired by the Brandenburg Gate (built 1788–1791).

48. *Bangkok Times*, 18 November 1907 and 27 October 1908.

49. See entries "Masson" and "Saulo" in Emmanuel Bénézit, *Dictionnaire des peintres, sculpteurs, dessinateurs et graveurs*, 5 vols (N.p.: Libraire Gründ, 1954–1959).

50. Chulalongkorn, *Klai ban*, chaps. 85 (19 June 1907), 146 (19 August), 149 (22 August).

51. Ibid., chap. 149 (22 August 1907), pp. 328–329.

52. NA, RV, Miscellany 8.3/17. The shipment of the statue was done by a Hamburg firm, Brasch and Rothenstein. NA, RV, Ministry of Public Works 8.2/8.

53. Phraya Si Sahathep, *Sadet prapat yurop ro.so. 116* [The royal tour of Europe in 1897], 5 vols. (Bangkok: Kurusapha, 1972), 2:94, 98.

54. John Colet and Joshua Eliot, *Cambodia Handbook* (Bath: Footprint,

1997), p. 89. I thank Craig Reynolds for bringing to my attention King Norodom's statue. Its present location, under a spire-roofed concrete pavilion in a corner of the palace compound, may have not been the original one. The date of the statue's erection is also questionable. The base carries the inscription "À Norodom premier roi du Cambodge ses mandarins et son peuple reconnaissants 1860." In fact, the statue must have been erected after 1863, when the French protectorate over Cambodia was established, and perhaps even after 1870, when the fall of the Second Empire arguably opened the way for the recycling of Napoleon III's statue. On the construction of Phnom Penh's royal palace, see Pierre-Lucien Lamant, "La creation d'une capitale par le pouvoir colonial: Phnom Penh," in *Peninsule indochinoise, Études urbaines,* ed. P. B. Lafont (Paris: L'Harmattan, 1991), pp. 59–102, which, however, makes no mention of King Norodom's statue.

55. Peter Kenez, *The Birth of the Propaganda State* (Cambridge: Cambridge University Press, 1985), p. 153.

56. NA, RV, Ministry of Municipal Government 7.10/1–24.

57. Maurice Agulhon, "La statuomanie et l'historie," *Ethnologie française* 2–3 (1978): 145–172; Fujitani, *Splendid Monarchy,* pp. 124–125.

58. Corrado Feroci (1883–1962) arrived in Bangkok in 1923, the last in the wave of Italian architects and decorators. A native of Florence, Feroci was instrumental in the establishment of the Academy of Fine Arts, Silpakorn. Under his direction, the academy began realizing the monuments and statuary commissioned by the Phibun Songkhram government for Bangkok and the provinces. In the early 1950s Feroci, who two decades earlier had sculpted the statue of Rama I, realized the only other equestrian statue in Bangkok, that of King Taksin. This statue was an attempt by Phibun to appropriate the figure of the Thonburi king as a potential anti-Chakri symbol (Taksin was deposed and executed by the founder of the Bangkok dynasty). Notably, Taksin is represented with a fierce expression while brandishing his sword pointing skyward. Feroci, who in the 1940s assumed the Thai name of Silpa Bhirasri along with Thai citizenship, is honored as "the father of Thai modern art." This circumstance has considerably hindered a critical approach to Feroci's role as *the* regime's artist in Thailand for more than forty years. Mildly appreciative of this role is Apinan, *Modern Art,* chap. 2; for a more critical account, see Helen Michaelsen, "State Building and Thai Painting and Sculpture in the 1930s and 1940s," in *Modernity in Asian Art,* ed. John Clark (Sydney: Wild Peony Press, 1993), pp. 60–74.

59. Maurice Agulhon, "Politics, Images, and Symbols in Post-Revolutionary France," in *Rites of Power,* ed. Sean Wilentz (Philadelphia: University of Pennsylvania Press, 1985), p. 185.

60. Keith M. Baker, *Inventing the French Revolution* (New York: Cambridge University Press, 1990), pp. 225–226.

Chapter 5: Refashioning the Theater of Power

1. Chulalongkorn, *Phraratchaphiti sipsong duan* [Royal ceremonies of the twelve months] (Bangkok: Khurusapha, 1985); Wales, *Siamese State Ceremonies.*

2. For the influence of nineteenth-century historicism on the Siamese elite, see Atthachak, *Kanpliangplaeng lokathat,* pp. 28–45.

3. Eric Hobsbawm, *The Age of Capital, 1848–1875* (London: Weidenfeld and Nicolson, 1975), p. 32.

4. Eiji Murashima, "The Origin of Modern Official State Ideology in Thailand," *Journal of Southeast Asian Studies* 19, 1 (1988): 80–96.

5. *Bangkok Times Weekly Mail,* 23 and 24 April 1908, cited in Sakda, *Kasattri,* p. 117. Photographers included Prince Damrong at Paknam, the Bangkok-based professional Mr. de la Roca at Chantaburi and Paknam, and several others in locations such as the royal landing, the Grand Palace and Wat Phra Keo, and each of the triumphal arches. Included in the album were also photographs taken in Ayutthaya in December 1907.

6. Prince Damrong Rajanubhap, *Chotmaihet prakop ruang klai ban* [Chronicles concerning the narrative of "Klaiban"], Cremation volume (Bangkok, 1962), chap. 4. For a report on the progress with an English translation of the welcoming speeches see the *Bangkok Times,* 18 November 1907 (references in the main text are to this issue unless noted otherwise). The translation of the excerpts from the speeches given at the progress, as found in Damrong's chronicle, is mine and was done with the objective of avoiding the flavor of early-twentieth-century English prose.

7. Damrong, *Prakop ruang klai ban,* pp. 53–68.

8. The provision of the service was announced by the *Bangkok Times,* 11 November 1907.

9. Damrong, *Prakop ruang klai ban,* pp. 78–80.

10. Ibid., pp. 84–91.

11. Ibid., pp. 92–97.

12. Ibid., pp. 98–99. Here and elsewhere the usage of "*pluralis maiestatis*" ("royal we") follows that of "*rao*" in the original text of Rama V's speeches.

13. A meeting of officials from European banks and firms had been held to consider ways of celebrating Rama V's return on 16 August at the Hong Kong and Shanghai Bank; a committee was appointed to consider proposals (*Bangkok Times,* 17 August 1907). A similar move was made by the Chinese entrepreneurs on 1 September (*Bangkok Times,* 3 September 1907).

14. The basket, chased with figures from the *Ramakien* and Chulalongkorn's monogram in gold, rested on a wooden base inscribed "From the foreign banks and mercantile community in Bangkok in commemoration of His Majesty's return to His Kingdom, November 1907." Before the celebrations, the basket was put on display at the premises of the goldsmith who had made it (*Bangkok Times,* 12 November 1907).

15. Damrong, *Prakop ruang klai ban,* pp. 100–102.

16. Ibid., pp. 102–107. This never uttered speech has been taken as the most explicit statement on the Fifth Reign policy on the Chinese. See Skinner, *Chinese Society in Thailand,* pp. 161–162. Coincidentally, the year 1907–1908 (B.E. 2450) registered the highest number of Chinese entries in Siam prior to the establishment of the Chinese Republic in 1911 (ibid., p. 61).

17. Damrong, *Prakop ruang klai ban,* pp. 109–112.

18. The *Bangkok Times* reported the intention of having this arch rebuilt in marble at a later stage as a monument to the reign. On the idea for a monumental gate to Dusit Park, see also King Chulalongkorn, letter to Chaophraya Yomarat of 15 April 1907, in *Phraratchatthalekha . . . chaophraya yomarat,* pp. 30–32.

19. The elaborate fireworks show, staged by a London firm on a site adjacent to Dusit Park, comprised almost forty items, including the ascent of a magnesium balloon, the devising of the mottos "Welcome home to His Majesty the King" and "Prosperity to Siam," fire portraits of the king, the queen, the crown prince, the royal arms, and the Chakri emblem, and the grand naval combat finale (*Bangkok Times,* 13 November 1907). It is significant that, in a city with such a large Chinese community as Bangkok, the fireworks display was entrusted to the London firm of Mr. J. Pain and Sons. The *Bangkok Times* had earlier pointed out (27 August 1907), "By the desire of the Siamese themselves, the whole display will be as European as possible, although portraits of their Majesties and the Crown Prince will be shown in the fireworks."

20. *Bangkok Times,* 19 November 1907.

21. Ibid. The two companies were the Siam Electricity Company, a Danish company, and the Siamese Tramway Company, established in 1905 by Prince Norathip as a joint-stock company but whose majority share was bought in 1907 by the Siam Electricity Company. Wright, ed., *Twentieth-Century Impressions of Siam,* p. 192.

22. Geertz, "Centers, Kings, and Charisma," p. 20. The *Negarakertagama* was written in 1365 by a Buddhist cleric resident in the court of King Hayam Wuruk (1350–1389).

23. Wales, *Siamese State Ceremonies,* pp. 106–115, 200–208; Reid, *Age of Commerce,* 1:179–180. Bock, *Temples and Elephants,* pp. 108–110. Bock described (p. 110) the impression the procession of barges made on him as follows: "The effect of the scene and its surroundings, the deep, wide river reflecting the brilliancy of the sunny sky, and doubling every gay object upon its surface, while ashore, on either side, flags fluttered and gilt spires glittered, will never be effaced from my mind."

24. Roy Strong, *Splendour at Court* (London: Weidenfeld and Nicolson, 1973), pp. 23, 36. In the Renaissance, the staging of these spectacles had the collaboration of eminent artists such as Tintoretto and Palladio (for Henry III's entry into Venice in 1574), Leonardo (for the entries of Louis XII into Milan and Francis I into Pavia), and Rubens (for the entry of Archduke Ferdinand into Antwerp in 1635).

25. Wortman, *Scenarios of Power,* p. 46.

26. The similarities between the spectacle of the exhibitions and the celebrations for the opening of the Suez Canal in 1869 have been pointed out by Timothy Mitchell, *Colonising Egypt* (Berkeley: University of California Press, 1991), p. 17. The effect of nocturnal lighting by electricity instead of gas was initially revealed at international exhibitions (Rosalind Williams, *Dream Worlds* [Berkeley: University of California Press, 1982], p. 85). A permanent triumphal arch in the sixteenth-century Gujarati style, the so-called Gateway of India, was built in Bombay to commemorate the visit of George V and Queen Mary in 1911.

27. *Bangkok Times,* 2 December 1907.

28. NA, RV, Department of Royal Secretariat 2/24.

29. Peter A. Thompson, *Lotus Land* (London: Lippincott, n.d. [c. 1906]), p. 218.

30. *Bangkok Times,* 5 March 1907.

31. Ibid., 14 October 1907.

32. Five hundred silver pendants and thirty gold pendants were also made for distribution to provincial officials and high-rank dignitaries. Royal Siamese Legation in Paris, letters of 23 November and 5 December 1907. NA, RV, Ministry of the Privy Seal 16.1/115.

33. These rewards were a medal for officials of royal rank, 6 baht per head for the 120 headmen (*kamnan*), and 4 baht for the 1,400 village chiefs (*phuyai*). Ministry of Interior, letter of 7 January 1908 to Phraya Boran Boranurak. NA, RV, Department of Royal Secretariat 2/24.

34. *Bangkok Times,* 2 December 1907. The newspaper report imputed the scant participation of Europeans to the rudimentary accommodation and food available in Ayutthaya, but remarked, "Those who did go were well repaid."

35. National Archives (NA), comp., *Chotmaihet phraratchaphiti ratchamangkhla phisek ro.so. 126, 127* [Documents concerning the celebrations for the royal jubilee, 1907 and 1908] (Bangkok: Fine Arts Department, 1984), pp. 23–25.

36. Ibid., pp. 34–36.

37. Ibid., pp. 37–38.

38. Ibid., pp. 25–31.

39. King Chulalongkorn, "Samakhom subsuan khong buran nai prathet sayam" [The society for archaeological investigation in Siam]. NA, RV, Miscellany 15/5; also published in *Sinlapakorn* 12, 2 (1968): 42–46.

40. Halbwachs (1877–1945), a disciple of Durkheim and Bergson, developed his concept in the books *La mémoire collective* (*The Collective Memory,* trans. Francis D. Ditter, Jr., and Vida Yadzi Ditter [New York: Harper Colophon, 1980]), *Les cadres sociaux de la mémoire,* and *La topographie legendarie des Évangiles en Terre Saint* (a selection of which has been published in English as *On Collective Memory,* trans. and edit. Lewis A. Coser [Chicago: University of Chicago Press, 1992]).

41. Bonnie Davis, *The Siam Society under Five Reigns* (Bangkok: Siam Society, 1989).

42. Thongchai, *Siam Mapped,* pp. 162–163; idem, "Changing Landscape," p. 119, n. 76. Thongchai points out that Chulalongkorn's view of premodern Siam bears a striking similarity to that of the 1980s historiographical endeavor of Local History (*prawattisat thongthin*).

43. Although the expression "*ratchamangkhla phisek*" is generally translated as "jubilee," the expression used by Bangkok's English-language press to refer to the event was "record reign." King Chulalongkorn's first coronation took place on 11 November 1868; a second coronation was performed on 16 November 1873, when the king came of age.

44. Hobsbawm, "Mass Producing Traditions," p. 281. Probably the first to celebrate his fortieth anniversary of reign (later designated "silver jubilee") was the Rumanian monarch in 1906 (ibid.).

45. Richard Mullen and James Munson, *Victoria* (London: BBC Books, 1987), pp. 133–135; *Bangkok Times,* 17 August 1897.

46. Crown Prince Vajiravudh, memorandum of 8 October 1908, NA, RV, Royal Secretariat Department 2/25. The budget of 200,000 baht was to be allocated as follows: 10,000 baht to the Ministry of Public Works; 20,000 baht to the army and 40,000 baht to the navy; 10,400 baht for the entertainment; 13,000 baht for the fireworks; 400 baht to each of the sixty-eight groups taking part in the pageant; and 79,400 baht to the Ministry of the Royal Household.

47. For this last figure see NA, Budget Reports of the Financial Adviser, B.E. 2456 [1913/4], p. 14 (3,781,675 baht and 93 satang), and B.E. 2457 [1914/5], p. 18 (1,103,066 baht).

48. These were a special fund for the reception of guests and the advances in the salary of state officials. Office of Royal Treasury, memo of 15 October. NA, RV, Royal Secretariat Department 2/25.

49. *Bangkok Times,* 16 November 1908.

50. *Ratchakitchanu bekkasa*, vol. 25 (29 November 1908), repr. in NA, comp., *Chotmaihet phraratchaphiti,* pp. 99–101; *Bangkok Times,* 18 November 1908.

51. NA, RV, Ministry of Municipal Government 48.2/12. The English translation of the crown prince's speech, published in the *Bangkok Times* (12 November 1908), was made by Phraya Borirat, corrected by J. Westengard (general adviser to the Ministry of Foreign Affairs), and revised by Vajiravudh himself.

52. NA, RV, Ministry of the Royal Household 21/13. The English translation of the speech, originally published in the *Bangkok Times* (12 November 1908), is reproduced in NA, comp., *Chotmaihet phrarachaphiti,* pp. 125–131.

53. The inscription on the statue's pedestal, in the translation given by the *Bangkok Times* (12 November 1908), reads as follows:

> In the year 2451 of the Buddhist Era and the 127th of the Rattanakosin Era, His Most Gracious Majesty King Chulalongkorn attained a reign of forty years over his Kingdom. This period of rule has never been reached by any other monarch in the history of the Siamese nation. His Majesty is endowed with all the greatest attributes of a wise ruler. He has ruled his country with an unswerving sense of equity. He has devoted his whole heart to the care of his dominions, to preserve them in a state of national independence and to promote the unity and contentment of his people. He is highly gifted with a keen perception of all that is good and evil in the manners and customs of His country, and has always eliminated the bad and introduced nought but what is good and beneficial. He has always set himself as a meritorious example and guided his people in the path of progress and lasting benefits. He has succeeded by his high personal qualities in conferring happiness and contentment upon his people. He has never been deterred by any obstacle, however great, nor has he hesitated to sacrifice his own personal comfort, whenever the welfare and advancement of the people and the State were concerned. He has been the true father of his people. His great qualities and exalted traits of char-

acter have brought the Kingdom of Siam to the high state of prosperity and independence which she enjoys at the present time, and earned the undying love and gratitude of his people. Now that His Majesty has attained this unprecedented historical distinction by the great length of time he has sat upon the Throne, we, his grateful people, from the highest to the lowest, have felt deeply moved by the remembrance of all the immeasurable blessings conferred upon us all during his long reign, and have heartily united in erecting this royal statue as a token which shall be preserved for all generations of our supreme appreciation, gratitude and love for Our Great and Good King Chulalongkorn. Long live the king!

54. NA, comp., *Chotmaihet phraratchaphiti,* pp. 140–162; for photographs of the king's car, pp. 165, 176. This peculiar spectacle appears redolent of a *kathin* fluvial procession that, according to Prince Chula Chakrabongse (*Lords of Life,* p. 113), was held in 1807, on whose occasion Rama I "asked the princes and the nobles to join him in decorating boats as living creatures of the water, such as crocodiles, shells, lobsters, crabs, and all kinds of fish."

55. NA, comp., *Chotmaihet phraratchaphiti,* pp. 138–139, 174–175.

56. *Bangkok Times,* 14 November 1908.

57. Ibid.; and NA, comp., *Chotmaihet phraratchaphiti,* pp. 178–180.

58. *Bangkok Times,* 14 November 1908.

59. Murashima, "State Ideology," pp. 88–89; also Copeland, "Contested Nationalism," chap. 2. On modern Siamese state ideology as a form of "official nationalism," see the comments by Benedict Anderson, *Imagined Communities,* rev. ed. (London: Verso, 1991), pp. 99–101.

60. Atthachak, *Kanplianplaeng lokathat,* pp. 179–181. Rama V's speech, "Phraborom ratchathibai khwamsamakkhi keakhwam nai khatha thi mi nai ham phaendin" [The royal discourse on unity], is reprinted in the anthology *Prawattisat lae kanmuang* [History and politics] (Bangkok: Thammasat University Press, 1973). I thank Bruce Lockhart for suggesting "solidarity" as an alternative to "unity" as a meaning of "*samakkhi.*"

61. In 1906 it was established that candidates should be the offspring of reputable parents and be sponsored by a commissioned government official; in 1909, admission to the academy's three preparatory grades was restricted to scions of the royal family and to officers' sons, and a separate class—exempted from examination—was created for royal princes and the sons of officers of commissioned or warrant ranks. Battye, "The Military, Government and Society in Siam," pp. 494–495.

62. *Bangkok Times,* 24 October 1910; see also Malcolm Smith's firsthand account, *Physician,* pp. 96–97. Smith claims (p. 94) that the arrangement of the funeral procession and the search for precedents in old documents involved a considerable delay in the conveyance of the king's corpse to the Grand Palace. The illustrated supplement of the Parisian magazine *Petit Journal* had, on the cover of the 6 November issue, an engraving of the funeral procession, in which the exoticism of the scene was somewhat exaggerated by depicting two elephants marching along.

63. NA, RVI, Ministry of Municipal Government 17.3/7. Besides the messages of condolence from diplomatic and commercial bodies, there were those of two Russian gentlemen and their wives on a private visit to Bangkok and of the Italian firm that had supplied part of the marble for the Ananta Samakhom Throne Hall.

64. *Bangkok Times,* 26 October 1910.

65. *Bangkok Times,* 16 November 1910. This bridge was built for Chulalongkorn's fifty-seventh birthday on 20 September 1910, his last. In fact, another birthday bridge, Saphan Chelim Sawan 58, at the northern end of Khlong Lot, was opened posthumously; it is considered the most imposing of the series.

66. "Black-edged royal memorandum informing the entire population," issued on 9 December 1910. NA, RVI, Ministry of Municipal Government 17.3/1.

67. "Royal proclamation announcing the royal permission for the populace to have the opportunity for making merit at the funeral of King Chulalongkorn," issued on 28 February 1911; and "Words of explanation and advice to those who will follow the king's funeral," issued on 1 March 1911. NA, RVI, Ministry of Municipal Government 17.3/3.

68. Wales, *Siamese State Ceremonies,* pp. 138, 145. Witnessing the cremation of Rama VI in March 1926, Wales reported that the expenditure for his pyre was one-eighth of that for King Chulalongkorn's.

69. Photos of both pyres are reproduced in Anake, *Chulalongkorn,* p. 75 and p. 280, respectively.

70. Somphop Phirom, *Phra meru rat phra meru lae meru samai krung rattanakosin* [Funeral pyres of state and royal cremations in the Bangkok period], Cremation volume (Bangkok, 1985), pp. 172–213.

71. On the abolition of entertainments at royal funerals, Wales (*Siamese State Ceremonies,* p. 147) opined, "This interference with tradition seems to me to be a mistake; such entertainments are highly appreciated by the people, and even commoners, unless very poor, do their best to provide at their cremations at least one theatrical performance, or nowadays [late 1920s] a cinema. Such a reduction in the grandeur of the royal obsequies cannot fail to decrease the popularity of a Royal Cremation, and, what is more, decrease its impressiveness and sociological value."

72. *Bangkok Times,* 17 March 1911.

73. "Phratham thesana lae thambanyai satthaphrot." Front cover reproduced in Anake, *Chulalongkorn,* p. 281.

74. Ibid.; and Somphop, *Phra meru rat,* pp. 214–236.

75. *Bangkok Times,* 17 March 1911 (*ratsadorn* without italics in original). A guess of the number of ordinary people who gathered for the funeral is given by the takings of Bangkok's two tram companies on 16 March, which totalled 7,378 baht against the daily average of 7,200 baht in the five days of the jubilee in November 1908.

76. Jottrand (*In Siam,* p. 258) reports that Handel's piece was played at the funeral of a prince in February 1900.

77. Fujitani, *Splendid Monarchy,* pp. 145–154.

78. Ibid., p. 148.

79. Carol Breckenridge and Peter van der Veer, "Introduction," in *Orientalism and the Post-Colonial Predicament,* ed. Breckenridge and van der Veer, pp. 14–15.

Chapter 6: On the World Stage

1. On international exhibitions in general, see Paul Greenhalgh, *Ephemeral Vistas* (Manchester: Manchester University Press, 1988); on the Crystal Palace Exhibition, Richards, *Commodity Culture,* chap. 1. On exhibitions in America, Robert Rydell, *All the World's a Fair* (Chicago: University of Chicago Press, 1984). On the display of Indian artifacts, Breckenridge, "Aesthetics and Politics"; and Metcalf, *Imperial Vision,* chap. 5. On colonial displays at French exhibitions, Sylviane Leprun, *Le théâtre des colonies* (Paris: L'Harmattan, 1986); and Panivong Norindr, *Phantasmatic Indochine* (Durham, N.C.: Duke University Press, 1996), chap. 1. On the exhibition of Islamic countries, Mitchell, *Colonising Egypt,* chap. 1; and Zeynep Çelik, *Displaying the Orient* (Berkeley: University of California Press, 1992). On the display of so-called primitive cultures, Benedict Burton, ed., *The Anthropology of World's Fairs* (Berkeley: University of California Press, 1983).

2. Neil Harris, "All the World's a Melting Pot? Japan at American Fairs, 1894–1904," in *Mutual Images,* ed. Akira Iriye (Cambridge: Harvard University Press, 1975), pp. 24–54; Judith Snodgrass, "The Representation of Japanese Buddhism at the World Parliament of Religions, Chicago 1893" (Ph.D. diss., University of Sydney, 1994); *Official Report of the Japan-British Exhibition 1910 at the Great White City* (London: Unwin, 1911).

3. Bock, *Temples and Elephants,* chap. 31.

4. Sakda, *Kasattri,* p. 171.

5. *Souvenir of the Siamese Kingdom Exhibition at Lumbini Park* (Bangkok: Siam Free Press, n.d.).

6. The invitation to the Glasgow Exhibition (1901), the only one in the records, was declined on the grounds it was received too late. NA, RV, Miscellany 11/60.

7. Amedee A. Gréhan, *Le royaume de Siam* (Paris: Simon Raçon, 2d ed. 1868 [with notes on the Paris Expo of 1867]; 3d ed. 1869 [with notes on the Havre Maritime Expo of 1868]; 4th ed. 1878 [with notes on that year's Paris Expo]).

8. Boyer, *City of Collective Memory,* pp. 262–269.

9. Giovanni Sacheri, *Le costruzioni moderne di tutte le nazioni alla esposizione universale di Parigi del 1878* (Turin: Camilla and Bortolero Editori, 1883), p. 92.

10. *Siamese Exhibits to the Exhibition of Paris, 1878* (Bangkok: Press of D. B. Bradley, n.d.).

11. Ibid., pp. 5–6.

12. Étienne-Gallois, *Le royaume de Siam au Champ de Mars en 1878 et à la cour de Versailles en 1686* (Paris: Challamel Ainé, 1878–1879), pp. 138–140.

13. E. Monod, *L'Exposition Universelle de 1889* (Paris: E. Dentu, 1890), 3:64–71.

14. "La sezione Siamese," *Parigi e l'Esposizione del 1889* (Milan: Treves, 1889), 19:147.

15. Leprun, *Théâtre des colonies,* p. 261.

16. Quoted in the *Bangkok Times,* 1 May 1907.

17. NA, RV, Miscellany 11/29.

18. Ibid., 11/17.

19. This threefold typology comprises replicas of actual buildings; composite assemblages, which presented a synthetic image of a given architectural tradition; hybrid buildings made of "*signes interprétes,*" allowing easy identification despite bearing no resemblance to any actual building or architectural style. Leprun, *Théâtre des colonies,* p. 96.

20. *Le Siam. Exposition Universelle de 1900* (Paris: N.p., 1900).

21. *Esposizione universale del 1900 a Parigi* (Milan: Treves, 1901), 1:6, 132.

22. Quoted in Williams, *Dream Worlds,* p. 61.

23. Wright, *Impressions of Siam,* pp.121–127. At his retirement, McCarthy was replaced by the Australian R. W. Giblin.

24. Thongchai, *Siam Mapped,* p. 128.

25. *Bangkok Times,* 14 January 1898.

26. From October 1902 to the end of March 1903, an exposition devoted exclusively to France's colonies was held in Hanoi, following a vogue initiated by the British with the 1886 Colonial and Indian Exhibition and first taken up by the French with the Colonial Exposition of Lyon in 1894. Besides displaying products from Indochina and other French colonies, the Hanoi Exposition also saw the participation of the British colony of Hong Kong; the federated states of North Borneo; the cities of Canton, Shanghai, Tianjin, and Peking; Japan, Korea, the Philippines, and Siam. Siam was given a four-hundred-square-meter exhibit space where products presented by some hundred exhibitors were on display. NA, RV, Miscellany 11/31; and *L'Exposition de Hanoi,* no. 2 (15 October 1902), p. 21.

27. Greenhalgh, *Ephemeral Vistas,* p. 127.

28. Rydell, *World's a Fair,* p. 29 (quoting *The Press,* 9 July 1873; and the *Philadelphia Enquirer,* 2 August 1873).

29. Abbot Low Moffat, *Mongkut the King of Siam* (Ithaca, N.Y.: Cornell University Press, 1961), pp. 87–88, 189–191.

30. Lisa McQuail Taylor, " 'Articles of Peculiar Excellence': The Siam Exhibit at the U.S. Centennial Exposition (Philadelphia, 1876)," *Journal of the Siam Society* 79, 2 (1991): 13–23.

31. *Siamese Exhibits to the International Centennial Exhibition of 1876* (Philadelphia: J. B. Lippincott, 1876).

32. "Le coppe del Re del Siam," *L'Esposizione universale di Filadelfia del 1876* (Milan: Sonzogno, 1876), p. 338.

33. NA, RV, Miscellany 11/45; see also the booklet *Royal Siamese Commission to the World's Columbian Exposition Chicago 1893* (N.p., n.d.).

34. NA, RV, Miscellany 11/46; Jacob Child, *Pearl of Asia* (Chicago: Donohue Hanneberry, 1892).

35. The Chicago World's Columbian Exposition occasioned a large num-

ber of publications; one of the most exhaustive is Hubert H. Bancroft, *The Book of the Fair,* 2 vols. (New York: Bancroft Books, 1894), which describes the Siamese exhibits in the fair's various sections. For an overall discussion of the Chicago Exposition, see Rydell, *World's a Fair,* chap. 2.

36. Frederic Mayer, *The Siamese Exhibits at the World's Columbian Exposition* (Chicago: N.p., 1893), p. 4.

37. Ibid., pp. 7–15.

38. NA, RV, Miscellany 11/46. On the Women's Building, see Mona Domosh, "A 'Feminine' Building? Relations between Gender Ideology and Aesthetic Ideology in Turn-of-the-Century America," *Ecumene* 3 (1996): 305–324.

39. Bertha Palmer, letter of 7 April 1892. NA, RV, Miscellany 11/45.

40. Phraya Suriya to Prince Devawongse, letter of 2 September 1892. NA, RV, Miscellany 11/46. Suriya pointed out that in Germany the compilation of a similar survey had been entrusted to a group of princesses and not one person alone.

41. Mayer, *Siamese Exhibits,* pp. 12–13.

42. Domosh, "A 'Feminine' Building?" p. 313.

43. Wyatt, *Politics of Reform,* pp. 163–166.

44. Suwadi Tanaprasitpatana, "Thai Society Expectations of Women, 1851–1935" (Ph.D. diss., University of Sydney, 1989); Barmé, "Social History of Bangkok," p. 17.

45. See Craig J. Reynolds, "A Nineteenth-Century Thai Buddhist Defense of Polygamy and Some Remarks on the Social History of Women in Thailand," *Proceedings, Seventh International Association of the Historians of Asia Conference* (Bangkok: Chulalongkorn University, 1979).

46. On bondage in Siam see Chatchai Pananon, "Siamese 'Slavery': The Institution and Its Abolition" (Ph.D. diss., University of Michigan, 1982); and Baas Terwiel, "Bondage and Slavery in Early Nineteenth-Century Siam," in *Slavery, Bondage and Dependency in Southeast Asia,* ed. Anthony Reid (St. Lucia: University of Queensland Press, 1983): 118–137.

47. *Chicago Sunday Times,* 1 October 1893. Clipping in NA, RV, Miscellany 11/47.

48. NA, RV, Miscellany 11/49–51.

49. NA, RV, Miscellany 11/52.

50. Rydell, *World's a Fair,* chap. 6.

51. J. H. Gore, letters of 17 June to C. A. Carter and 6 July 1904 to the Siamese Royal Commission for the Louisiana Purchase Exposition. NA, RV, Miscellany 11/53.

52. NA, Budget Reports of the Financial Adviser, r.e. 123 to r.e. 127 (1904–1905 to 1908–1909).

53. Carter, ed., *Kingdom of Siam*; J. H. Gore, letter to A. C. Carter, 17 June 1904. NA, RV, Miscellany 11/53.

54. Siamese exhibits were awarded prizes in the following categories: Liberal Arts, seven gold medals, three silver medals, and one bronze medal; Fish and Game, two gold medals and one bronze medal; Forestry, one grand prize and

six bronze medals; Transportation, one gold medal, one silver medal, and one bronze medal; Manufacture, two grand prizes, fifteen gold medals, nineteen silver medals, and seventeen bronze medals; Mines, two gold medals, two silver medals, and four bronze medals; Education, one silver medal; Anthropology, one grand prize; Agriculture, four gold medals, eight silver medals, and seventeen bronze medals.

55. Smithsonian Institution, letter of 8 September 1905; American legation in Bangkok, letter of 6 November 1905. NA, RV, Miscellany 11/53.

56. NA, RV, Miscellany 11/52 (typewritten copy of the article).

57. J. H. Gore, letters of 6 and 24 December 1904 to the Siamese Royal Commission. NA, RV, Miscellany 11/53.

58. See photographs of the postcard in Davis, *Siam Society,* p. 53.

59. NA, RV, Miscellany 11/63. The Siamese government also declined to participate at the Milan exposition of 1906 celebrating the opening of the Simplon Tunnel and mostly devoted to transportation. NA, RV, Miscellany 11/64.

60. NA, RV, Miscellany 11/1.

61. Among Gerini's scholarly works, see *A Retrospective View and Account of the Origin of the That Mahachat Ceremony* (Bangkok: *Bangkok Times,* 1892); *Chulakantamagala, or the Tonsure Ceremony as Performed in Siam* (Bangkok, 1895 [repr. Bangkok: Siam Society, 1976]); "Trial by Ordeal in Siam and the Siamese Law of Ordeals," *Asiatic Quarterly Review* (April and July 1895); "A Historical Retrospect of Junkceylon Island," *Journal of the Siam Society* 2, 2 (1905) and 3, 1 (1906) (repr. as one volume, Bangkok: Siam Society, 1986).

62. Gerolamo E. Gerini, ed., *Catalogo descrittivo della Mostra Siamese alla Esposizione Internazionale delle Industrie e del Lavoro in Torino, 1911* (n.p., n.d.). In the preface to the English edition, *Siam and Its Productions, Arts, and Manufactures* (Hertford: Stephen Austin, 1912), Gerini specified that "this catalogue is a translation of the preceding Italian one only in so far as the articles from the Editor's pen are concerned. The others are given in the original English in which they have been written by their respective authors . . . except those . . . translated by the Editor from the Siamese language. In many respects the present edition is a revised and enlarged one, and may on this score be considered an improvement upon its Italian prototype" (p. vii). Quotations are from the catalogue's English edition.

63. NA, RV, Miscellany 11/1. A memorandum signed 23 December 1908 states that this overall sum was to be apportioned in the financial years' budgets as follows: R.E. 127 (1908–1909): 10,000 baht; R.E. 128 (1909–1910): 21,000 baht; R.E. 129 (1910–1911): 52,000 baht; R.E. 130 (1911–1912): 42,000 baht.

64. *Bangkok Times,* 24 December 1910.

65. *La Stampa,* 29 April 1911.

66. The following were the sizes of the national pavilions in Turin: United States: 5,000 square meters; Latin America (Chile, Dominica, Equador, Peru, Uruguay, Venezuela): 6,000 square meters; Brazil: 8,000 square meters; Belgium and Germany: each 9,000 square meters; France: 13,990 square meters; Great Britain: 20,000 square meters. *Guide pratique pour visiter l'Exposition Internazionale de l'industrie et du travail établie à Turin* (Turin: Jassa and Ferruto, 1911).

67. Gerini, *Siam,* p. xlix.

68. *Catalogue of Educational Exhibits Prepared in the Schools of the Education Department to be Shown at the International Exhibition of Industry and Labour, Turin* (Bangkok: printed at the American Presbyterian Mission Press, n.d.).

69. Gerini, *Siam,* pp. liv–lxiv.

70. Ibid., pp. 282–294. The remaining eighty-four prizes included ten *diplômes d'honneur,* twenty-one gold medals, twenty-five silver medals, eighteen bronze medals, and ten special mentions. Four prizes were also awarded to participants from Siam as part of a photographic competition.

71. Ibid. Diplomas of high merit went to the ministers of public works, interior, finance, justice, education, and agriculture; and another fifteen awards to Thai as well as foreign officials in the public service.

72. Ibid., pp. 276–277.

Epilogue

1. Barmé, "Social History of Bangkok," chaps. 1–3; and Copeland, "Contested Nationalism," esp. chap. 2.

2. During Phibun's premiership (1938–1944) court ceremonies were suspended, the Ministry of the Royal Household declassed, the palace's employees drastically reduced, the display of Rama VII's images prohibited and his properties confiscated, and Prince Rangsit (a son of Chulalongkorn) even sentenced to death (later commuted to life imprisonment) for conspiracy. Pitipat Supamit, "The Evolution of the Thai Monarchy in the Constitutional Period, 1932–present" (M.A. thesis, American University, 1990).

3. Kevin Hewison, "The Monarchy and Democratization," in *Politics in Thailand,* ed. Hewison (New York: Routledge, 1997), p. 59.

4. Thak Chaloemtiarana, *Thailand* (Bangkok: Social Sciences Association, 1979), pp. 309–325, 397–402.

5. The royal household's financial assets were recently estimated at US$2–US$8 billion, invested mostly in landed estates and stocks. Terry McCarthy, "Thailand: The King and Ire," *Time,* 6 December 1999, p. 19.

6. The artfully spread news that students at Thammasat University had allegedly performed the mock hanging of an effigy of the crown prince gave the military and right-wing paramilitary groups the excuse to storm the campus on the early morning of 6 October 1976, bringing to a bloody end three years of open politics. Charles F. Keyes, *Thailand* (Boulder, Colo.: Westview, 1987), p. 99.

7. King Narai too enjoys the *maharat* title but as a posthumous bestowal arguably prompted by his being a contemporary of Louis XIV.

8. For two of the many examples of the media celebration of the Fifth Reign court's conspicuous lifestyle, see the already cited Thongthong, *Khong suay khong di;* and Phisanu Chanwithan, "Wai khun to sewey ratchakan thi 5" [Wine on Rama V's table], *Sinlapa watthanatham* 17, 1 (1995): 104–115 (which was also the issue's cover story).

9. See Donald Horne, *The Great Museum* (London: Pluto Press, 1984), pp. 95–99.

10. Nidhi Aeusrivongse, *Latthi phiti sadet pho ro. 5* [The worship of Rama V], 2d ed. (Bangkok: Sinlapa watthanatham, 1993); see also Peter Jackson, "Royal Spirits, Chinese Gods, and Magic Monks: Thailand's Boom-Time Religions of Prosperity," *South-East Asia Research* 7, 3 (1999), esp. pp. 266–268.

11. Ibid., 301–304.

12. From 1996, Princess Sirindhorn's books, published by Thai Phanich in both hard- and soft-cover editions, can even be bought on the "Travel with the Princess" Web site: <http://princessbook.or.th/>.

13. Golden Jubilee Network, <http://kanchanapisek.ot.th/index.en. html>; Thai Monarchy Web Page, <http://thaimain.org/eng/monarchy/family. html>.

14. Nora, "General Introduction," p. 8.

Bibliography

Sources from the National Archives of Thailand (NA)

The numeration and titles of files (here given only in English translation) are the National Archives of Thailand's. The number on the left of the stroke indicates the section a given file belongs to; a second number after a full stop indicates a subsection; the number on the right of the stroke indicates the numeration of the file within a record's section.

Records of the Fifth Reign (RV)

Ministry of Municipal Government *(krasuang nakhonban)*
7.10/1–24. Funds for the construction of the equestrian statue (1908–1917).
48.2/12. The prince's speeches (17 November 1907–13 November 1908).

Ministry of Public Works *(krasuang yothatikan)*
1/26. Ensuring protection of the crumbling bank in front of the Revenue Department and Allegri's examination of protection methods in Europe (11 April–3 December 1901).
1/32. Phraya Suriya's ideas about the management of the Ministry of Public Works (7 November 1905–9 February 1906).
1/36. Phraya Sukhum's ideas about the management of the Ministry of Public Works (2 September 1906).
3.5/3. Postage hallmarks (31 August 1899–9 April 1910).
8.2/8. The king's equestrian statue (5 December 1907–14 September 1910).

Ministry of Privy Seal *(krasuang munthathan)*
16.2/92. Conferring of a royal decoration on the painter Professor Gelli (9 August–23 November 1899).
16/13. The jubilee medal (23 November 1907–12 February 1909).
16.1/115. Medals for the Ayutthaya celebrations (10 October 1907–10 November 1908).

Ministry of the Royal Household *(krasuang wang)*
21/11. The king's speeches at his return from Europe (17–18 November 1907).
21/13. The king's speech at the inauguration of the equestrian statue (11 November 1908).
21/14. The king's reply to foreign ambassadors and consuls at the jubilee (13 November 1908).

Department of Royal Secretariat *(krom ratchalekhathikan)*
2/24.   Celebrations for the fortieth anniversary of reign (5 September 1906–8 January 1908).
2/25.   Celebrations for the royal jubilee (10 March 1906–19 December 1908).

Miscellany *(bettalet)*
8.3/17.   Freres Brothers (21–29 April 1908).
9/64.   Foreigners hired for the construction of Amphorn Palace, Ananta Throne Hall, Dusit Royal Palace: Ferro, Natali, Rigotti (21 October 1903–14 February 1910).
9/65.   Employment of a Japanese gilder for Wat Benchama Bophit's ordination hall.
11/1.   Exhibitions of Tokyo, Rome, and Turin, and Vienna Shooting and Field Sports Exhibition (April 1907–December 1908).
11/17.   The Paris Exposition, 1900.
11/26–28.   The Paris Exposition, 1889 (1890–1893).
11/29–30.   The Paris Exposition, 1900 (1898–1899).
11/31.   The French open the Hanoi Exhibition; Exhibitions of Glaslow, Paris, Berlin (16 January 1899–2 March 1901).
11/32–36.   Paris Exposition (1899–1902).
11/45–48.   The 1893 Chicago Exposition (1890–1896).
11/49.   Tennessee centennial exhibition (30 June–2 July 1896).
11/51.   Commercial exhibition of Philadelphia (1–9 June 1899).
11/52.   St. Louis Exhibition (22 August 1901–3 January 1902).
11/53.   Exhibitions of St. Louis and Philadelphia (10 July 1902–8 March 1909).
11/60.   Glasgow Exhibition (8–16 March 1899).
11/63.   Turin Exposition, Italy (20–23 May 1901).
11/64.   Milan Exhibition (31 March 1904–16 December 1905).
15/5.   Society for archaeological investigation in Siam (29 December 1907).

Records of the Sixth Reign (RVI)

Ministry of Municipal Government
7.1/10.   Mr. Allegri's request for payment (21–24 March 1914).
7.2/18.   Granting of pensions to European officers of the Sanitary Department (24 May 1919).
7.7/14.   Report of the Ministry of Finance on the cost of Ananta Throne Hall (16 April 1914–27 March 1916).
17.3/1–38.   Funeral of Rama V (1910–1915).
17.5/3.   Commemoration at the king's equestrian statue (14 October–19 November 1912).
39.1/6.   Mr. Chini asks for authorization to study temples, museum, and the royal library (22–23 November 1911).

Ministry of the Royal Household
17/32. Celebrations for Ananta Samakhom (26 December 1916–8 February 1917).

Miscellany
5/15. Employment of Professor Chini (28 July 1910–26 September 1913).
5/124. Engineer Allegri (15 July 1903–13 June 1916).

Provisional Collection of Loose Documents of the Fifth and Sixth Reigns

Vol. 2/8. Budget for the building of Ratcha Damnoen Avenue (29 September 1899).

Records of the Ministry of Foreign Affairs

35.7/39. Mr. Allegri, public servant in the Ministry of Communication (1924–1935).

Office of the Financial Adviser: Budget Reports

Rattanakosin era (R.E.) 120 (1901/2) to Buddhist era (B.E.) 2462 (1919/20).

Newspapers

Bangkok Times.

Contemporary Sources

The date of publication of books printed in Thailand is given also according to the Buddhist era (B.E.). Following common usage, Thai authors are listed alphabetically according to their first name.

Antonio, J. *The 1904 Traveller's Guide to Bangkok and Siam*. Bangkok: White Lotus, 1997.
Armstrong, William N. *Around the World with a King*. Repr. ed. Honolulu: Mutual Publishing, 1995.
Bancroft, Hubert H., *The Book of the Fair*. 2 vols. New York: Bancroft Books, 1894.
Bock, Carl. *Temples and Elephants*. Singapore: Oxford University Press, 1986 (orig. ed. London, 1884).
Bowring, John. *The Kingdom and People of Siam*. 2 vols. Kuala Lumpur: Oxford University Press, 1969 (orig. ed. London, 1857).
Buls, Charles. *Siamese Sketches*, trans. and intr. by Walter E. J. Tips. Bangkok: White Lotus, 1994 (orig. ed. Paris, 1901).

Caddy, Florence. *To Siam and Malaya in the Duke of Sutherland's Yacht "Sans Peur."* Singapore: Oxford University Press, 1992 (orig. ed. London, 1889).

Carter, A. Cecil, ed. *The Kingdom of Siam.* Bangkok: Siam Society, 1988 (orig. ed. New York, 1904).

Catalogue of Educational Exhibits Prepared in the Schools of the Education Department to be Shown at the International Exhibition of Industry and Labour, Turin. Bangkok: printed at the American Presbyterian Mission Press, n.d. (c. 1911).

Chulalongkorn, King. "Phraborom ratchathibai khwamsamakkhi nai khatha thi mi nai ham phaendin" [The royal discourse on unity]. In *Prawattisat lae kanmuang* [History and politics]. Bangkok: Thammsat University, B.E. 2516 (1973).

———. *Phraratchadamrat nai phrabatsomdet phrachulachomklaochaoyuhua song thalaeng phraborom ratchathibai kaekhai kanpokkhrong phaendin* [The king's speech explaining the reform of the government]. Cremation volume. Bangkok, B.E. 2470 (1927).

———. *Phraratchaniphon klai ban* [The king's writings from overseas, or Far from home]. 2 vols. Bangkok: Khurusapha, B.E. 2498 (1955).

———. *Phraratchaphiti sipsong duan* [Royal ceremonies of the twelve months]. Bangkok: Khurusapha, B.E. 2528 (1985).

———. *Phraratchahatthalekha phrabat somdet phrachulachomklaochaoyuhua phraratchathan chaophraya yomarat (pan sukhum)* [The king's correspondence to Chaophraya Yomarat (Pan Sukhum)]. Bangkok: Cremation volume for Police General Trinit Sukhum, B.E. 2529 (1986).

———. *Phraratchahatthalekha phrabat somdet phrachulachomklaochaoyuhua phraratchathan somdet phrachao boromwongthe kromphraya damrong ratchanuphap nai wela sadet phraratchadamnoen prathet yurop khrang thi song pho.so. 2450* [The king's correspondence to Prince Damrong Rajanubhap from his second journey to Europe in 1907]. Cremation volume for Kromluang Singwi Kromnang Krai. Bangkok, B.E. 2491 (1948).

———. *Phraratchahatthalekha suan phraong sang mi phraratchathan dae somdet phrasi phacharinthra boromratchaninat mua saedet phraratcha damnoen praphat yurop pho.so. 2440* [The king's correspondence to Queen Si Phacharinthra when regent from the 1897 journey to Europe]. 2 vols. Bangkok: Khurusapha, B.E. 2505 (1962).

———. *Rayathang thiao chawa kwa song duan* [Narrative of a journey to Java of over two months]. Cremation volume. Bangkok, B.E. 2468 (1925).

———. "Samakhom subsuan khong buran nai prathet sayam" [The Society for Archaeological Investigation in Siam]. *Sinlapakorn* 12, 2 (B.E. 2511 [1968]): 42–46.

"Le Coppe del Re del Siam." In *L'Esposizione universale di Filadelfia del 1876.* Milan: Sonzogno, 1876.

Crawfurd, John. *Journal of an Embassy from the Governor-General of India to the Courts of Siam and Cochin-China.* Kuala Lumpur: Oxford University Press, 1967 (orig. ed. London, 1828).

Damrong Rajanubhap, Prince. "Athibai ruang tamnan wang kao" [History of old palaces]. In *Prachum phongsawadan* [Collected chronicles], vol. 15, sect. 26, pp. 61–204. Bangkok: Khurusapha, B.E. 2507 (1964).

———. *Chotmaihet prakop ruang klai ban* [Chronicles concerning the narrative of "Klaiban"]. Cremation volume for Somdet Ariyawong Sawakhatayan. Bangkok, B.E. 2505 (1962).

———. *Chotmaihet ratchawang ban pa'in lae wat niwet* [Documents on the royal palace of Bang Pa-in and Wat Niwet]. Bangkok: Fine Arts Department, B.E. 2537 (1994).

———. *Khwamsongcham* [Recollections]. Bangkok: Phrae Phittaya, B.E. 2514 (1971).

———. *Phraratcha phongsawadan krung rattanakosin ratchakan thi 5* [Chronicles of the Fifth Reign]. Cremation volume for Thiti Bunnak. Bangkok, B.E. 2522 (1979).

———. "Ruang sang phraboromrup songma" [The king's equestrian statue]. In *Prachum phraniphon bettalet* [Miscellaneous writings], 59–62. Bangkok: Kurusapha, B.E. 2504 (1961).

Esposizione Internazionale del 1900 a Parigi. Milan: Treves, 1901.

Étienne-Gallois. *Le royaume de Siam au Champ de Mars en 1878 et à la cour de Versailles en 1686.* Paris: Challamel Ainé, 1878–1879.

L'Exposition de Hanoi. No. 2 (15 October 1902). Hanoi: F-H. Schneider, 1902–1903.

Fine Arts Department (FAD), comp. *Chelim phratinang ananta samakhom* [A celebration of the Ananta Samakhom Throne Hall]. Cremation volume for Nangchitra Bamrung. Bangkok, B.E. 2522 (1979).

———. *Chotmaihet sadet praphat tang prathet nai ratchankan thi 5 muang singkhapo lae muang betawia khrang ae lae sadet praphat india* [Chronicles of the royal journey to Singapore, Batavia, and India in the Fifth Reign]. Cremation volume. Bangkok, B.E. 2509 (1966).

———. *Prawat kanthunklao thawai parinya nitisan dusathibanthit kittimosak* [Report on the conferral of an honorary doctorate in law to the king]. Cremation volume for Khun Maewat Burokham. Bangkok, B.E. 2519 (1976).

———. *Samnao raignan phrachao boromwongthe khromphraya naretworarit sadet prathet amerika pho.so. 2427* [Itinerary of Prince Naret Worarit's tour of America in 1884]. Cremation volume for Prince Naret Worarit. Bangkok, B.E. 2469 (1926).

———. *Somdet phrachao boromwongthe kromphraya damrong ratchanuphap sadet tawip yurop pho.so. 2434* [Prince Damrong Rajanubhap's journey to Europe in 1891]. Cremation volume for M. C. Dissanuwat Diskul. Bangkok, B.E. 2511 (1968).

Finlayson, George. *The Mission to Siam and Hué the Capital of Cochin-China in the Years 1821–1822.* Singapore: Oxford University Press, 1988 (orig. ed. London, 1826).

Gerini, Gerolamo E., ed. *Catalogo descrittivo della Mostra Siamese alla Esposizione Internazionale delle Industrie e del Lavoro in Torino, 1911.* N.p., n.d. [1911].

———. *Siam and Its Productions, Arts, and Manufactures.* Hertford: Stephen Austin, 1912.

Gréhan, Amedee A. *Le royaume de Siam.* 2d ed. Paris: Simon Raçon, 1868. 3d ed. Paris: Simon Raçon, 1869. 4th ed. Paris: Simon Raçon, 1878.

Guide pratique pour visiter l'Exposition Internazionale de l'industrie et du travail établié à Turin. Turin: Jassa and Ferruto, 1911.

Jottrand, Émile. *In Siam*, trans. and intr. Walter E. J. Tips. Bangkok: White Lotus, 1996 (orig. ed. Paris, 1905).

Leonowens, Anna. *The English Governess at the Siamese Court.* Singapore: Oxford University Press, 1988 (orig. ed. London, 1870).

Mayer, Frederic. *The Siamese Exhibits at the World's Columbian Exposition.* Chicago: N.p., 1893.

Monod, E. *L'Exposition Universelle de 1889.* 4 vols. Paris: E. Dentu, 1890.

Mouhot, Henri. *Travels in the Central Parts of Indo-China (Siam), Cambodia and Laos.* 2 vols. Singapore: Oxford University Press, 1992 (orig. ed. London, 1864).

National Archives (NA), comp. *Chotmaihet phraratchaphiti ratchamangkhla phisek ro.so. 126, 127* [Documents concerning the celebrations for the royal jubilee, 1907 and 1908]. Bangkok: Fine Arts Department, B.E. 2527 (1984).

Official Report of the Japan-British Exhibition 1910 at the Great White City. London: Unwin, 1911.

Ookhtomsky, Prince Esper Esperovitch. *Travels in the East of Nicholas II Emperor of Russia when Cesarevetich, 1890–1891*, ed. and trans. Sir George Birdwood. 2 vols. London: Archibald Constable, 1896.

Pallegoix, Jean Baptiste, Mgr. *Description du royaume Thai ou Siam.* Westmead: Gregg International, 1969 (orig. ed. Paris, 1854).

Prachum kotmai [Collected acts]. Vol. 17, pt. 1 (R.E. 118 [1899/1900]); vol. 18, pt. 1 (R.E. 120 [1901/2]); vol. 21, pt. 1 (R.E. 125 [1906/7]). Bangkok, B.E. 2478 (1935).

Royal Siamese Commission to the World's Columbian Exposition Chicago 1893. N.p., n.d.

Sacheri, Giovanni. *Le costruzioni moderne di tutte le nazioni alla esposizione universale di Parigi del 1878.* Turin: Camilla and Bertolero Editori, 1883.

Seidenfaden, Erik. *Guide to Bangkok.* 3d ed. Bangkok: Royal State Railways of Siam, 1932.

Seni Pramoj, M. R., and Kukrit Pramoj, N. R., eds. *A King of Siam Speaks.* Bangkok: Siam Society, 1987.

"La Sezione Siamese." In *Parigi e l'Esposizione del 1889.* Vol. 19. Milan: Treves, 1889.

Siam Directory. Bangkok, 1892, 1893, 1896, 1897.

Le Siam. Exposition universelle de 1900. Paris: N.p., 1900.

Siamese Exhibits to the Exhibition of Paris, 1878. Bangkok: Press of D. B. Bradley, n.d.

Siamese Exhibits to the International Centennial Exhibition of 1876. Philadephia: J. B. Lippincott, 1876.

Si Sahathep, Phraya. *Sadet prapat yurop ro.so. 116* [The royal tour of Europe in 1897]. 5 vols. Bangkok: Khurusapha, B.E. 2515 (1972).

Souvenir of the Siamese Kingdom Exhibition at Lumbini Park. Bangkok: Siam Free Press, n.d.

Thipakorawong, Chaophraya. *The Dynastic Chronicles of the Bangkok Era: The First*

Reign, trans. and ed. Thadeus and Chadin Flood. 2 vols. Tokyo: Centre for East Asian Culture, 1978–1990.

———. *The Dynastic Chronicles of the Bangkok Era: The Fourth Reign*, trans. and ed. Chadin Flood. 5 vols. Tokyo: Centre for East Asian Culture, 1965–1974.

Thompson, Peter A. *Lotus Land: Being an Account of the Country and People of Southern Siam.* London: Lippincott, n.d. [c 1906].

Thomson, John W. *The Straits of Malacca, Indo-China, and China, or Ten Years Travels, Adventures, and Residence Abroad.* London: Sampson Low, 1875.

Vincent, Frank. *The Land of the White Elephant.* Singapore: Oxford University Press, 1988 (orig. ed. London, 1873).

Wachirayan Warorot, Prince. *Autobiography: The Life of Prince-Patriarch Vajiranana of Siam, 1860–1921*, trans., ed., and intr. Craig J. Reynolds. Athens: Ohio University Press, 1979.

Wright, Arnold, ed. *Twentieth-Century Impressions of Siam: Its History, People, Commerce, Industries and Resources.* London: Lloyd's Greater Britain Publishing Co., 1908.

Secondary Sources

Ackerman, James S. *The Villa: Form and Ideology of Country Houses.* Princeton, N.J.: Princeton University Press, 1990.

Adams, David B. "Monarchy and Political Change: Thailand under Chulalong-korn (1868–1885)." Ph.D. diss. University of Chicago.

Agulhon, Maurice. "Politics, Images, and Symbols in Post-Revolutionary France." In *Rites of Power: Symbolism, Ritual, and Politics Since the Middle Ages*, ed. Sean Wilentz, 177–205. Philadelphia: University of Pennsylvania Press, 1985.

———. "La statuomanie et l'historie." *Ethnologie française* 2–3 (1978): 145–172.

Akin Rabhidana. *The Organization of Thai Society in the Early Bangkok Period, 1782–1873.* Data paper, no. 74. Ithaca, N.Y.: Southeast Asia Program, Cornell University, 1969.

Amphon Chirattikon. *Tamsadet Klaiban* [On the footsteps of *Klaiban*]. Bangkok: Matichon, B.E. 2541 (1998).

Anake Nawigamune. *Laoruang thairup* [On photography]. Bangkok: Saengdaet, B.E. 2538 (1995).

———. "Poska khlatsik khong sansan phaengsapha" [Sansan Phaengsapha's "classic" postcards]. *Sarakkhadi* (December 1988): 145–151.

———. *Pramwan phap phrapiya maharat/Chulalongkorn the Great: Pictures of Thailand's Beloved King.* Bangkok: Saengdaet, B.E. 2532 (1989).

———. *Raek mi nai sayam* [First in Siam]. Vol. 1. Bangkok: Saengdaet, B.E. 2532 (1989).

———. *Singphim khlatsik* [Classic prints]. Bangkok: Matichon, B.E. 2537 (1994).

———. *Thairup muang thai samai raek* [Early photography in Thailand]. Bangkok: Saengdaet, B.E. 2533 (1990).

Anderson, Benedict. *Imagined Communities: Reflections on the Origins and Spread of Nationalism*. Rev. ed. London: Verso, 1991.

———. "Studies of the Thai State: The State of Thai Studies." In *The Study of Thailand*, ed. Elizier Ayal, 193–247. Southeast Asia series, no. 54. Athens: Ohio University Center for International Studies, 1978.

Apinan Poshyananda. "Modern Art in Thailand in the Nineteenth and Twentieth Centuries." Ph.D. diss., Cornell University, 1990.

———. *Modern Art in Thailand*. Singapore: Oxford University Press, 1992.

———. *Western-style Paintings in the Thai Royal Court*. 2 vols. Bangkok: Bureau of the Royal Household, 1993.

Appadurai, Arjun, ed. *The Social Life of Things*. Cambridge: Cambridge University Press, 1986.

Atthachak Sattayanurak. *Kanpliangplaeng lokathat khong chonchan phunam thai tangtae ratchakan thi 4-pho.so. 2475* [Transformation of the Thai elite's worldview from the Fourth Reign to 1932]. Bangkok: Chulalongkorn University, B.E. 2538 (1995).

Baker, Keith M. *Inventing the French Revolution: Essays on French Political Culture in the Eighteenth Century*. New York: Cambridge University Press, 1990.

Barmé, Scot. "Towards a Social History of Bangkok: Gender, Class, and Popular Culture in the Siamese Capital, 1905–1940." Ph.D. diss., Australian National University, 1997.

Battye, Alfred N. "The Military, Government and Society in Siam, 1868–1910: Politics and Military Reform during the Reign of King Chulalongkorn." Ph.D. diss., Cornell University, 1974.

Belk, Russell W. *Collecting in a Consumer Society*. London and New York: Routledge, 1995.

Bénézit, Emmanuel. *Dictionnaire des peintres, sculpteurs, dessinateurs et graveurs*. 5 vols. N.p.: Libraire Gründ, 1954–1959.

Bentmann, Richard, and Michael Müller. *The Villa as Hegemonic Architecture*, trans. Tim Spence and David Craven. New Jersey and London: Humanities Press, 1992.

Boorstin, Daniel. *The Image: Or, What Happened to the American Dream*. London: Weidenfeld and Nicolson, 1961.

Bourdieu, Pierre. *Distinction: A Social Critique of the Judgement of Taste*, trans. Richard Nice. Cambridge: Harvard University Press, 1984.

———. *The Field of Cultural Production: Essays on Art and Literature*, ed. and intr. Randal Johnson. New York: Columbia University Press, 1993.

Boyer, M. Christine. *The City of Collective Memory: Its Historical Imagery and Architectural Entertainments*. Cambridge, Mass.; and London: MIT Press, 1994.

Breazeale, Kennon. "A Transition in Historical Writing: The Work of Prince Damrong Rachanuphap." *Journal of the Siam Society* 59, 2 (1971): 25–49.

Breckenridge, Carol A. "The Aesthetics and Politics of Colonial Collecting: India at World Fairs." *Comparative Studies in Society and History* 31 (1989): 195–216.

Breckenridge, Carol A., and Peter van der Veer, eds. *Orientalism and the Post-Colonial Predicament: Perspectives on South Asia.* Philadelphia: University of Pennsylvania Press, 1993.

Brown, Ian. *The Creation of the Modern Ministry of Finance in Siam, 1885–1910.* London: Macmillan, 1992.

Burke, Peter. *The Fabrication of Louis XIV.* New Haven, Conn.; and London: Yale University Press, 1992.

Burton, Benedict, ed. *The Anthropology of World's Fairs.* Berkeley: University of California Press, 1983.

Campbell, Colin. *The Romantic Ethic and the Spirit of Modern Consumerism.* Oxford: Basil Blackwell, 1987.

Cannadine, David. "The Context, Performance and Meaning of Ritual: The British Monarchy and the 'Invention of Tradition,' c. 1820–1977." In *The Invention of Tradition*, ed. Eric Hobsbawm and Terence Ranger, 101–164. Cambridge: Cambridge University Press, 1983.

————. "Transformation of Civic Ritual in Modern Britain: The Colchester Oyster Feast." *Past and Present* 94 (1982): 107–130.

Çelik, Zeynep. *Displaying the Orient: Architecture of Islam at Nineteenth-Century World's Fairs.* Berkeley: University of California Press, 1992.

Centennial of Thai Postage Stamps. Bangkok: The Communication Authority of Thailand, 1983.

Chaiyan Rajchagool. *The Rise and Fall of the Thai Absolute Monarchy.* Bangkok: White Lotus, 1994.

Charnvit Kasetsiri. "Siam/Civilization–Thailand/Globalization: Things to Come." Paper presented at the conference of the International Association of Historians of Asia, Bangkok, May 1996.

Chatchai Pananon. "Siamese 'Slavery': The Institution and Its Abolition." Ph.D. diss., University of Michigan, 1982.

Chattip Nartsupha and Suthy Prasartset, eds. *The Political Economy of Siam, 1851–1910.* Bangkok: Social Sciences Association of Thailand, 1981.

————. *Socio-Economic Institutions and Cultural Change in Siam, 1851–1910.* Singapore: Institute of South-East Asian Studies, 1977.

Chaudhuri, K. N. *Asia before Europe: Economy and Civilisation of the Indian Ocean from the Rise of Islam to 1750.* New York: Cambridge University Press, 1990.

Child, Jacob. *Pearl of Asia.* Chicago: Donohue Hanneberry, 1892.

Chula Chakrabongse, Prince. *Lords of Life: A History of the Kings of Thailand.* New York: Taplinger, 1960.

————. *The Twain Have Met, Or, An Eastern Prince Came West.* London: G. T. Foulis, 1956.

Clark, John. "Yōga in Japan: Model or Exception? Modernity in Japanese Art, 1850s–1940s: An International Comparison." *Art History* 18, 2 (1995): 253–285.

Cœdès, George. *The Indianized States of Southeast Asia,* trans. Susan Brown Cowing. Honolulu: East-West Center Press, 1968 (orig. ed. Paris, 1964).

Cohn, Bernard S. "Representing Authority in Victorian India." In *The Invention of Tradition*, ed. Eric Hobsbawm and Terence Ranger, pp. 165–209. Cambridge: Cambridge University Press, 1983.

Colet, John, and Joshua Eliot. *Cambodia Handbook*. Bath: Footprint, 1997.

Conant, Ellen P. "Principles and Pragmatism: The *Yatoi* in the Field of Art." In *Foreign Employees in Nineteenth-Century Japan,* ed. E. R. Beauchamp and Akira Iriye, 137–170. Boulder, Colo.: Westview, 1990.

Cooper, Frederick, and Ann Laura Stoler, eds. *Tensions of Empire: Colonial Cultures in a Bourgeois World*. Berkeley: University of California Press, 1997.

Copeland, Matthew. "Contested Nationalism and the 1932 Overthrow of the Absolute Monarchy in Siam." Ph.D. diss., Australian National University, 1993.

Corbin, Alain. "Backstage." In *A History of Private Life,* gen. ed. Philippe Aries and Georges Duby. Vol. 4: *From the Fires of Revolution to the Great War,* ed. Michelle Perrot, trans. Arthur Goldhammer, 451–668. Cambridge: Belknap Press of Harvard University Press, 1990 (orig. ed. Paris, 1987).

Craick, Jennifer. *The Face of Fashion: Cultural Studies in Fashion*. London: Routledge, 1994.

Crinson, Mark. *Empire Building: Orientalism and Victorian Architecture*. London: Routledge, 1996.

Cushman, Jennifer W. *Fields from the Sea: Chinese Junk Trade with Siam during the Late Eighteenth and Early Nineteenth Centuries*. Ithaca, N.Y.: Southeast Asia Program, Cornell University, 1993.

———. "Siamese State Trade and the Chinese Go-between, 1767–1855." *Journal of Southeast Asian Studies* 12, 1 (1981): 46–61.

Dalmaso, F.; P. Gaglia, and F. Poli. *L'Accademia Albertina di Torino*. Turin: Istituto Bancario S. Paolo, 1982.

Damrong Rajanubhap, Prince. *Monuments of the Buddha in Siam,* trans. Sulak Sivaraksa and A. B. Griswold. Rev. ed. Bangkok: Siam Society, 1973.

Davis, Bonnie. *Postcards of Old Siam*. Singapore: Times Press, 1987.

———. *The Siam Society under Five Reigns.* Bangkok: Siam Society, 1989.

Deringil, Salim. "The Invention of Tradition as Public Image in the Late Ottoman Empire, 1808–1980." *Comparative Studies in Society and History* 35 (1993): 3–29.

Domosh, Mona. "A 'Feminine' Building? Relations between Gender Ideology and Aesthetic Ideology in Turn-of-the-Century America." *Ecumene* 3 (1996): 305–324.

Duindam, Jeroen. *Myths of Power: Norbert Elias and the Early Modern European Court*. Amsterdam: Amsterdam University Press, 1994.

Elias, Norbert. *The Civilizing Process: Sociogenetic and Psychogenetic Investigations,* trans. Edmund Jephcott, ed. Eric Dunning, Johan Goudsblom, and Stephen Mennel. Rev. ed. Oxford; and Cambridge, Mass.: Blackwell Publishers, 2000 (orig. ed. Basel, 1939).

———. *The Court Society,* trans. Edmund Jephcott. Oxford: Blackwell, 1983 (orig. ed. Neuwied, 1969).

Ferri de Lazara, Leopoldo, and Paolo Piazzardi. *Italians at the Court of Siam.* Bangkok: Amarin Press, 1996.

Finn, Dallas. *Meiji Revisited: The Sites of Victorian Japan.* New York: Weatherhill, 1995.

Friedman, Jonathan. "Global System, Globalization, and the Parameters of Modernity." Repr. in idem, *Cultural Identity and Global Process,* 195–232. London: Sage, 1994.

Fujitani, Takashi. *Splendid Monarchy: Power and Pageantry in Modern Japan.* Berkeley: University of California Press, 1996.

Geertz, Clifford. "Centers, Kings, and Charisma: Reflections on the Symbolics of Power." In *Rites of Power: Symbolism, Ritual, and Politics since the Middle Ages,* ed. Sean Wilentz, 13–37. Philadelphia: University of Pennsylvania Press, 1985.

———. *Negara: The Theater-State in Nineteenth-Century Bali.* Princeton, N.J.: Princeton University Press, 1980.

Girling, John L. S. *Thailand: Society and Politics.* Ithaca, N.Y.: Cornell University Press, 1981.

Gluck, Carol. *Japan's Modern Myths: Ideology in the Late Meiji Period.* Princeton, N.J.: Princeton University Press, 1985.

Greenhalgh, Paul. *Ephemeral Vistas: The Expositions Universelles, Great Exhibitions and World's Fairs, 1851–1939.* Manchester: Manchester University Press, 1988.

Halbwachs, Maurice. *The Collective Memory,* trans. Francis D. Ditter, Jr., and Vida Yadzi Ditter. New York: Harper Colophon, 1980.

———. *On Collective Memory,* trans. and ed. Lewis A. Coser. Chicago: University of Chicago Press, 1992.

Harris, Neil. "All the World's a Melting Pot? Japan at American Fairs, 1876–1904." In *Mutual Images: Essays in American-Japanese Relations,* ed. Akira Iriye, 24–54. Cambridge: Harvard University Press, 1975.

Heine-Geldern, Robert. *Conceptions of State and Kingship in Southeast Asia.* Data paper, no. 18. Ithaca, N.Y.: Southeast Asia Program, Cornell University, 1956.

Hewison, Kevin. "The Monarchy and Democratization." In *Politics in Thailand: Power, Oppositions, and Democratization,* ed. K. Hewison, 58–74. New York: Routledge, 1997.

Hobsbawm, Eric. *The Age of Capital, 1848–1875.* London: Weidenfeld and Nicolson, 1975.

———. "Introduction: Inventing Traditions." In *The Invention of Tradition,* ed. Eric Hobsbawm and Terence Ranger, 1–14. Cambridge: Cambridge University Press, 1983.

———. "Mass-Producing Traditions: Europe, 1870–1914." In *The Invention of Tradition,* ed. Eric Hobsbawm and Terence Ranger, 263–307. Cambridge: Cambridge University Press, 1983.

———. *Nations and Nationalism since 1780.* Cambridge: Cambridge University Press, 1990.

Hobsbawm, Eric, and Terence Ranger, eds. *The Invention of Tradition.* Cambridge: Cambridge University Press, 1983.

Hong, Lysa. "Warasan Setthasat Kanmuang: Critical Scholarship in Post-1976 Thailand." In *Thai Constructions of Knowledge,* ed. Andrew Turton and Manas Chitakasem, 99–118. London: School of Oriental and African Studies, University of London, 1991.

Hooker, Michael B. *A Concise Legal History of South-East Asia.* Oxford: Clarendon Press, 1978.

Horne, Donald. *The Great Museum: The Re-presentation of History.* London: Pluto Press, 1984.

Howland, Douglas R. *Borders of Chinese Civilization: Geography and History at Empire's End.* Durham, N.C.: Duke University Press, 1996.

Imponente, Anna. "Liberty e orientalismo nelle collezioni di corte in Siam." In *Aspetti del collezionismo in Italia,* 185–203. Trapani: Quaderni Museo Regionale Pepoli, 1993.

Ingram, James C. *Economic Change in Thailand, 1850–1970.* Stanford, Calif.: Stanford University Press, 1971.

Ishii, Yoneo. *Sangha, State, and Society: Thai Buddhism in History,* trans. Peter Hawkes. Honolulu: University of Hawaiʻi Press, 1986.

Jackson, Peter. "Royal Spirits, Chinese Gods, and Magic Monks: Thailand's Boom-Time Religions of Prosperity." *South-East Asia Research* 7, 3 (1999): 245–300.

Jansen, Pietro G. "Costruttori e artisti italiani nel Siam." *Le vie d'Italia e del mondo* 1, 10 (1933): 1279–1294.

Jay, Martin. "Scopic Regimes of Modernity." In *Modernity and Identity,* ed. Scott Lash and Jonathan Friedman, 178–195. Oxford: Blackwell, 1992.

Kamthon Kunchan and Songsan Nilakamhaeng. "Wiwatthanakan thangkai phap khong krung rattanakosin fang tawanook: tangtae kon remsang krung chonthung samai plianplaeng rabob kanpokkhrong" [The evolution of Bangkok's plan, from the initial settlement to 1932]. *Warasan mahawitthayalai sinlapakorn* 4–5 (B.E. 2523–2525 [1980–1982]): 221–244.

Kantorowicz, Ernst H. "Gods in Uniform." In idem, *Selected Studies.* Locust Valley, N.Y.: J. J. Augustin, 1965.

———. *The King's Two Bodies: A Study in Medieval Political Theology.* Princeton, N.J.: Princeton University Press, 1957.

Kaufmann, Thomas DaCosta. "From Treasury to Museum: The Collections of the Austrian Habsburg." In *The Cultures of Collecting,* ed. John Elsner and Roger Cardinal, 137–154. London: Reaktion Books, 1994.

Kenez, Peter. *The Birth of the Propaganda State: Soviet Methods of Mass-Mobilization, 1917–1929.* Cambridge: Cambridge University Press, 1985.

Keyes, Charles F. *Thailand: Buddhist Kingdom as Modern Nation-State.* Boulder, Colo.: Westview, 1987.

King, Anthony D. "Colonialism and the Development of the Modern Asian City: Some Theoretical Considerations." In *The City in South Asia: Pre-modern and Modern,* ed. Kenneth Ballhatchet and John Harrison, 1–19. London: Curzon, 1980.

Kirsch, Thomas A. "Modernizing Implications of Nineteenth-Century Reforms in the Thai Sangha." In *Religion and Legitimation of Power in Thailand,*

Laos, and Burma, ed. Bardwell L. Smith, 52–65. Chambersburg, Penn.: Anima Books, 1978.

Lalvani, Suren. *Photography, Vision, and the Production of Modern Bodies.* Albany: State University of New York Press, 1996.

Lamant, Pierre-Lucien. "La creation d'une capitale par le pouvoir colonial: Phnom Penh." In *Peninsule indochinoise. Études urbaines,* ed. P. B. Lafont, 59–102. Paris: L'Harmattan, 1991.

Lecoq, Anne-Marie. "La symbolique de l'État." In *Les lieux de mémoire,* ed. Pierre Nora. Vol. 2, pt. 2: *La Nation,* 145–192. Paris: Gallimard, 1986.

Le May, Reginald. *The Coinage of Siam.* Bangkok: Siam Society, 1932.

Leprun, Sylviane. *Les théâtre des colonies. Scénographique, acteurs et discours de l'imaginarie dans les expositions.* Paris: L'Harmattan, 1986.

Likhit Dhiravegin. *Siam and Colonialism, 1855–1909.* Bangkok: Thai Watthana Panich, 1975.

Lopez, Donald S., Jr. "Introduction." In *Curators of the Buddha,* ed. Donald S. Lopez, Jr., 1–29. Chicago: University of Chicago Press, 1995.

Ludden, David. "Orientalist Empiricism: Transformations of Colonial Knowledge." In *Orientalism and the Postcolonial Predicament,* ed. C. A. Breckenridge and Peter van der Veer, 250–278. Philadelphia: University of Pennsylvania Press, 1993.

MacCannel, Dean. "Staged Authenticity: Arrangements of Social Space in Tourist Settings." *American Journal of Sociology* 79, 3 (1973): 589–603.

MacKenzie, John. *Propaganda and Empire: The Manipulation of British Public Opinion, 1880–1960.* Manchester: Manchester University Press, 1984.

Manich Jumsai, M. L. *King Mongkut and Queen Victoria.* Bangkok: Chalermnit, 1972.

Mansel, Philip. "Monarchy, Uniform and the Rise of the *Frac,* 1760–1830." *Past and Present* 96 (1982): 103–132.

Marx, Karl. *Capital,* trans. Eden and Cedar Paul. New York: E. P. Dutton, 1951.

Marx, Karl, and Friedrich Engels. "The Communist Manifesto." In *The Marx-Engels Reader,* ed. Robert C. Tucker, 331–362. New York: Norton, 1972.

Maxwell, Robyn. *Textiles of Southeast Asia: Tradition, Trade, and Transformation.* Melbourne: Oxford University Press, 1990.

McCraken, Grant. *Culture and Consumption: New Approaches to the Symbolic Character of Consumer Goods and Activities.* Bloomington: Indiana University Press, 1988.

McCarthy, Terry. "Thailand: The King and Ire." *Time,* 6 December 1999.

McQuail, Lisa Taylor. " 'Articles of Peculiar Excellence': The Siam Exhibit at the U.S. Centennial Exposition (Philadelphia, 1876)." *Journal of the Siam Society* 79, 2 (1991): 13–23.

Metcalf, Thomas. *An Imperial Vision: Indian Architecture and Britain's Raj.* Berkeley: University of California Press, 1989.

Michaelsen, Helen. "State Building and Thai Painting and Sculpture in the 1930s and 1940s." In *Modernity in Asian Art,* ed. John Clark, 60–74. Sydney: Wild Peony Press, 1993.

Millar, Oliver. *The Queen's Pictures.* London: Weidenfeld and Nicolson, 1977.

Miller, Daniel. *Material Culture and Mass Consumption.* Oxford: Basil Blackwell, 1987.

Mitchell, Timothy. *Colonising Egypt*. Berkeley: University of California Press, 1991.

Moffat, Abbot Low. *Mongkut, the King of Siam*. Ithaca, N.Y.: Cornell University Press, 1961.

Mullen, Richard, and James Munson. *Victoria: Portrait of a Queen*. London: BBC Books, 1987.

Mumford, Lewis. *The Story of Utopias*. Repr. ed. Gloucester, Mass.: P. Smith, 1959.

Murashima, Eiji. "The Origin of Modern Official State Ideology in Thailand." *Journal of Southeast Asian Studies* 19, 1 (1988): 80–96.

Naengnoi Saksi, M. R. *Palaces of Bangkok: Royal Residences of the Chakri Dynasty*. Bangkok: River Books, 1996.

———. *Satthapatayakam phraborom maharatchawang* [The architecture of the Grand Palace]. Bangkok: Bureau of the Royal Household, B.E. 2531 (1988).

———, with Naphit Krittikakun and Daruni Keomuang. *Phraratchawang lae wang nai krungthep pho.so. 2325–2525* [Royal and princely palaces in Bangkok, 1782–1982]. Bangkok: Chulalongkorn University, B.E. 2525 (1982).

Nanthiya Sawangwutthitham. "Bothnam" [Introduction]. In *Chotmaihet kankosang lae somsaem phrathinang wimanmek, pho.so. 2443–2518* [Documents on the construction and restoration of Wimanmek palace, 1900–1975], 1–21. Bangkok: Bureau of the Royal Household, B.E. 2533 (1990).

Nidhi Aeusriwongse. *Latthi phiti sadet pho ro. 5* [The worship of Rama V]. 2d ed. Bangkok: Sinlapa Watthanatham, B.E. 2536 (1993).

———. *Kanmuang thai samai phrachao krung thonburi* [Thai politics in the Thonburi reign]. Bangkok: Sinlapa Watthanatham, B.E. 2529 (1986).

———. *Pakkai lae bairua* [Quill and sail]. Bangkok: Amarin, B.E. 2527 (1984).

———. "Songkhram anusaori kap rat thai" [The war of monuments and the Thai state]. Repr. in idem, *Chat thai muang thai baeprian lae anusaori* [Thai nation, "Thailand," textbooks, and monuments], 89–124. Bangkok: Matichon, B.E. 2538 (1995).

Nora, Pierre. "General Introduction: Between Memory and History." In *Realms of Memory: Rethinking the French Past,* gen. ed. Nora, English-language ed. and intr. Lawrence D. Kritzman, trans. Arthur Goldhammer, 1:1–23. New York: Columbia University Press, 1996.

O'Connor, Richard A. "Place, Power, and Discourse in the Thai Image of Bangkok." *Journal of the Siam Society* 78, 2 (1990): 61–73.

———. "Urbanism and Religion: Community, Hierarchy and Sanctity in Urban Thai Buddhist Temples." Ph.D. diss., Cornell University, 1978.

Panivong Norindr. *Phantasmatic Indochine: French Colonial Ideology in Architecture, Film, and Literature*. Durham, N.C.: Duke University Press, 1996.

Pearce, Susan M. *On Collecting: Investigation into Collecting in the European Tradition*. London and New York: Routledge, 1996.

Phisanu Chanwithan. "Wai khun to sewey ratchakan thi 5" [Wine on Rama V's table]. *Sinlapa watthanatham* 17, 1 (B.E. 2538 [1995]): 104–115.

Phra Rajavaramuni. *Thai Buddhism in the Buddhist World*. Bangkok: Amarin, 1984.

Phra Thammakit Sophana, ed. *Phraputtha chaoluang kap wat benchama bophit* [Rama V and Wat Benchama Bophit]. Bangkok: Wat Benchama Bophit, B.E. 2531 (1988).

Pin Malakun, M. L. *Dusit thani muang prachathipatai phrabat somdet phra mongkut-klaochaoyuhua* [Dusit thani, the democratic city of Rama VI]. Bangkok: National Library, B.E. 2513 (1970).

Piriya Krairikish, *Prawattisat sinlapa nai phrathet thai chabap khumu naksuksa* [History of art in Thailand: A student's textbook]. Bangkok: Amarin Press, B.E. 2528 (1985).

Pitipat Supamit. "The Evolution of the Thai Monarchy in the Constitutional Period, 1932–Present." M.A. thesis, American University, 1990.

Prayut Sitthipan, *Chomna prawattisat khut khunnang sayam* [Biographies of Siamese nobles]. Bangkok: Samnakphim Sayam, B.E. 2530 (1987).

Pye, Lucian W. *Asian Power and Politics: The Cultural Dimensions of Authority.* Cambridge, Mass.: Belknap Press of Harvard University Press, 1985.

Reid, Anthony. *Southeast Asia in the Age of Commerce, 1450–1680.* Vol. 1: *The Lands below the Winds.* New Haven, Conn.: Yale University Press, 1988.

Reynolds, Craig J. "Buddhist Cosmography in Thai History, with Special Reference to Nineteenth-Century Cultural Change." *Journal of Asian Studies* 35, 2 (1976): 203–220.

———. "The Buddhist Monkhood in Nineteenth-Century Thailand." Ph.D. diss., Cornell University, 1973.

———. "Globalisation and Cultural Nationalism in Modern Thailand." In *Southeast Asian Identities: Culture and the Politics of Representation in Indonesia, Malaysia, Singapore, and Thailand,* ed. Joel S. Kahn, 115–145. Singapore: Institute of Southeast Asian Studies, 1998.

———. "A Nineteenth-Century Thai Buddhist Defense of Polygamy and Some Remarks on the Social History of Women in Thailand." *Proceedings, Seventh International Association of the Historians of Asia Conference.* Bangkok: Chulalongkorn University, 1979.

———. "Thailand." In *Australia in Asia: Communities of Thought,* ed. Anthony Milner and Mary Quilty, 100–125. Melbourne: Oxford University Press, 1996.

———. "Tycoons and Warlords: Modern Thai Social Formations and Chinese Historical Romance." In *Sojourners and Settlers,* ed. Anthony Reid, pp. 115–147. St. Leonard: Asian Studies Association of Australia in association with Allen and Unwin, 1996.

Reynolds, Craig J., and Hong Lysa. "Marxism in Thai Historical Studies." *Journal of Asian Studies* 43, 1 (1983): 77–104.

Richards, Thomas. *The Commodity Culture of Victorian Britain: Advertising and Spectacle, 1851–1914.* Stanford, Calif.: Stanford University Press, 1990.

Riggs, Fred W. *Thailand: The Modernization of a Bureaucratic Polity.* Honolulu: East-West Center Press, 1966.

Rodio, Emilio E. "La perla di Bangkok." *Arte e Dossier* 19 (1987): 18–19.

Rydell, Robert W. *All the World's a Fair: Visions of Empire at American International Expositions, 1876–1916.* Chicago and London: University of Chicago Press, 1984.

Saengthian Satthathai. *Sam ratchani khu banlang ratchakan thi 5* [The three queens of Rama V]. Bangkok: Mahannop, B.E. 2539 (1996).

Said, Edward. *Orientalism.* New York: Pantheon, 1978.

Sakda Siriphan. *Kasattri lae klong* [Kings and cameras]. Bangkok: Dansuttha, B.E. 2532 (1992).

Sakerm Siriwong. *Thai Stamps 1983.* Bangkok: Siam Stamp Trading Company, 1983.

Samut phap ratchakan thi 5/A Pictorial Record of the Fifth Reign. Bangkok: River Books, 1992.

Sarasin Viraphol. *Tribute and Profit: Sino-Siamese Trade, 1652–1853.* Cambridge: Harvard University Press, 1977.

Schama, Simon. "The Domestication of Majesty: Royal Family Portraiture, 1500–1850." *Journal of Interdisciplinary History* 17 (1986): 155–183.

Scharf, Aaron. *Art and Photography.* Harmondsworth: Penguin, 1983.

Seksan Prasertakul. "The Transformation of the Thai State and Economic Change." Ph.D. diss., Cornell University, 1989.

Siffin, William J. *The Thai Bureaucracy: Institutional Change and Development.* Honolulu: East-West Center Press, 1966.

Silverman, Debora L. *Art Nouveau in Fin-de-Siècle France: Politics, Psychology, and Style.* Berkeley: University of California Press, 1989.

Sirichai Narumit. *Old Bridges of Bangkok.* Bangkok: Siam Society, 1977.

Skeat, William W., and Charles O. Bladgen. *Pagan Races of the Malay Peninsula.* 2 vols. London: Macmillan, 1906.

Skinner, George W. *Chinese Society in Thailand: An Analytical History.* Ithaca, N.Y.: Cornell University Press, 1957.

Smith, George V. *The Dutch in Seventeenth-Century Thailand.* Special report, no. 16. DeKalb: Center for Southeast Asian Studies, Northern Illinois University, 1977.

Smith, Malcolm. *A Physician at the Court of Siam.* Repr. ed. Kuala Lumpur: Oxford University Press, 1982.

Snodgrass, Judith. "The Representation of Japanese Buddhism at the World Parliament of Religions, Chicago 1893." Ph.D. diss., University of Sydney, 1994.

Somchart Chungsiriarak. "Satthapatayakam khong kharl duhring" [The architecture of Karl Döhring]. *Muang Boran* 19, 3 (B.E. 2536 [1993]): 66–101.

Somphop Phirom. *Phra meru rat phra meru lae meru samai krung rattanakosin* [Funeral pyres of state and royal cremations in the Bangkok period]. Bangkok: Cremation volume, B.E. 2528 (1985).

Songsan Nilkamhaeng and Phrani Sunthrayot. "Khrongkan burana prapprung phrathinang ananta samakhom raya raek pho.so. 2519–2522" [The original project and the first stage of restoration of the Ananta Samakhom Throne Hall, 1976–1979]. *Sinlapakorn* 21, 5 (B.E. 2522 [1979]): 1–34.

Sontag, Susan. *On Photography.* Harmondsworth: Penguin, 1979.

Sternstein, Larry. "Bangkok at the Turn of the Century: Mongkut and Chulalongkorn Entertain the West." *Journal of the Siam Society* 54, 1 (1966): 55–71.

———. "Krung Kao: The Old Capital of Ayutthaya." *Journal of the Siam Society* 53, 1 (1965): 83–121.

Stewart, Susan. *On Longing: Narratives of the Miniature, the Gigantic, the Souvenir, the Collection*. Baltimore: Johns Hopkins University Press, 1984.

Streckfuss, David. "Kings in the Age of Nations: The Paradox of Lèse-Majesté as Political Crime in Thailand." *Comparative Studies in Society and History* 37 (1995): 445–475.

Strong, Roy. *Splendour at Court: Renaissance Spectacle and Illusion*. London: Weidenfeld and Nicolson, 1973.

Suchrit Thawansuk. *Nangsu prakuat ruang phraprawat lae ngansilpa khong somdet prachao boromwongthe chaofa kromphraya naritsara nuwattiwong* [The life and work of Prince Naritsara Nuwattiwong]. Bangkok: Thai Watthana Phanich, B.E. 2509 (1966).

Sutcliffe, Anthony. "Introduction: The Debate on Nineteenth-Century Planning." In *The Rise of Modern Urban Plannng, 1800–1914*, ed. A. Sutcliffe, 1–10. London: Mansell, 1980.

Suwadi Tanaprasitpatana. "Thai Society Expectations of Women, 1851–1935." Ph.D. diss., University of Sydney, 1989.

Symonds, Richard. *Oxford and Empire: The Last Lost Cause?* Oxford: Clarendon Press, 1991.

Tambiah, Stanley J. *World Conqueror and World Renouncer: A Study of Buddhism and Polity in Thailand against a Historical Background*. Cambridge: Cambridge University Press, 1976.

Tarlo, Emma. *Clothing Matters: Dress and Identity in India*. Chicago: University of Chicago Press, 1996.

Tej Bunnang. *The Provincial Administration of Siam, 1892–1915*. Kuala Lumpur: Oxford University Press, 1976.

Terwiel, Baas. "Bondage and Slavery in Early Nineteenth-Century Siam." In *Slavery, Bondage and Dependency in Southeast Asia*, ed. Anthony Reid, 118–137. St. Lucia: University of Queensland Press, 1983.

Thak Chaloemntiarana. *Thailand: The Politics of Despotic Paternalism*. Bangkok: Social Sciences Association of Thailand and Thai Khadi Institute, Thammasat University, 1979.

Thongchai Winichakul. "The Changing Landscape of the Past: New Histories in Thailand since 1973." *Journal of Southeast Asian Studies* 26, 1 (1995): 99–120.

———. *Siam Mapped: A History of the Geo-body of a Nation*. Honolulu: University of Hawai'i Press, 1994.

Thongthong Chansangsu. *Khong suay khong di khrang phaendin phraputtha chaoluang* [Beautiful and precious objects of King Chulalongkorn's reign]. Bangkok: Akson Samphan, B.E. 2531 (1988).

———. *Phrathnang ananta samakhom* [The Ananta Samakhom Throne Hall]. Bangkok: Akson Samphan, B.E. 2530 (1987).

Tillotson, Giles H. R. *The Tradition of Indian Architecture: Continuity, Controversy, and Change since 1850*. New Haven, Conn.: Yale University Press, 1989.

Tobia, Bruno. *Una patria per gli italiani*. Bari and Rome: Laterza, 1991.

Van Esterik, Penelope. "Royal Style in Village Context." In *Contributions to Asian*

Studies. Vol. 15: *Royalty and Commoners*, ed. Constance M. Wilson, 102–117. Leiden: E. J. Brill, 1980.

Van Zanten, David. *Building Paris: Architectural Institutions and the Transformation of the French Capital.* New York: Cambridge University Press, 1994.

Vella, Walter F. *Chaiyo! King Vajiravudh and the Origins of Thai Nationalism.* Honolulu: University of Hawai'i Press, 1978.

———. "Thianwan of Siam: A Man Who Fought Giants." *Anuson Walter Vella,* ed. Ronald D. Renard, 78–91. Chiang Mai: W. F. Vella Fund, Payap University; and Honolulu: Center for Asian and Pacific Studies, University of Hawai'i at Manoa, 1986.

Vianello, Gianni. *Galileo Chini e il Liberty in Italia.* Florence: Sansoni, 1964.

Wales, Horace G. Quaritch. *Siamese State Ceremonies: Their Function and History.* London: Bernard Quaritch, 1931.

Ward, Charles A. *Moscow and Leningrad.* München and London: K. G. Saur, 1989.

Warren, William, and Luca Invernizzi Tettoni (photography). *Arts and Crafts of Thailand.* London: Thames and Hudson, 1994.

Weber, Eugene. *Peasants into Frenchmen: The Modernization of Rural France, 1870–1914.* Stanford, Calif.: Stanford University Press, 1976.

Williams, Rosalind H. *Dream Worlds: Mass Consumption in Late Nineteenth-Century France.* Berkeley: University of California Press, 1982.

Wolters, O. W. *History, Culture, and Region in Southeast Asian Perspectives.* Rev. ed. Ithaca, N.Y.: Southeast Asia Program Publications, Southeast Asia Program, Cornell University, 1999.

———. "Southeast Asia as a Southeast Asian Field of Study." *Indonesia* 58 (October 1994): 1–17.

Wortman, Richard S. *Scenarios of Power: Myth and Ceremony in Russian Monarchy.* Princeton, N.J.: Princeton University Press, 1995.

Wright, Gwendolyn. *The Politics of Design in French Colonial Urbanism.* Chicago: University of Chicago Press, 1991.

Wyatt, David K. *The Politics of Reform in Thailand: Education in the Reign of King Chulalongkorn.* New Haven, Conn.: Yale University Press, 1969.

———. *Studies in Thai History.* Chiang Mai: Silkworm Books, 1994.

———. *Thailand: A Short History.* New Haven, Conn.: Yale University Press, 1984.

Index

About the Author

Maurizio Peleggi is an assistant professor in the Department of History at the National University of Singapore, where he teaches courses on the history of art and on historical representation. He holds degrees from the University of Rome and the Australian National University and is the author of *The Politics of Ruins and the Business of Nostalgia* (Bangkok: White Lotus, 2002).